Dedicati

I would like to dedicate this book to:

Mammy, my first teacher. She taught me to be humble, to care for others, and to 'always try your best'. She lived an unselfish and generous life.

James, my next teacher. He believed in me when I didn't believe in myself. He nudged me towards my goals. He reassured me and praised me. I would not have the life I have now if it wasn't for his encouragement. He gave me confidence and was always in my corner.

'A friend is a loved one who awakens your life in order to free the wild possibilities within you'.

John O'Donohue

And finally, my sons and daughter, who I love and admire. I am proud of them every day. They each excel in their own unique way.

Acknowledgements

I would like to thank my brothers and sisters who have been quizzed and questioned over the past year as I tried to get the early memories down on paper.

A special word of thanks to the first reader of this book, Louise. Your advice, suggestions and approval were invaluable and uplifting.

Preface

'What made you decide to write a book?'

I have been asked this frequently over the past year.

It all started at the time when James got ill. When he got discharged from hospital the first time following his shock diagnosis, the house was full of his friends and work colleagues every night for weeks, reminiscing about the work and the craic they had in their early years.

Our family were very interested listening to old stories about James, learning about things that happened long before their time. Then, over the next few years, the idea of recording my life and our experiences for future generations kept popping into my head. I wanted future generations to know their roots and to know where James and I started. My hope is that they will appreciate the effort and the work it takes to become successful but also get inspired to keep going and never give up, even in the face of adversity.

I also believe that opening up and discussing how I handled the difficult times in my life might help others who may travel a similar road in their lifetime. We don't talk enough about how we feel. We are embarrassed to cry or show emotion but if we can talk about our feelings, we will discover they are very normal, and that other people have experienced similar emotions.

We also don't listen, then it's too late. I wish I had listened more to my mother when she rambled on about the 'days gone by'. My children and grandchildren will be no different; now they don't need to listen, they can read.

I hope within the pages of this book, the reader will be moved by the stories, motivated by the adventures and inspired by the love.

The Beginning: Curragh and Doon

My story begins in two small townlands near the town of Ballinascreen, Northern Ireland: Curragh and Doon.

My mother, Brigid Teresa McCullagh (née McNamee), was born on 2 January 1923. After leaving school at fourteen, Mammy left Curragh, a small townland near Cavanreagh in the Sixtowns, and headed to Straw to work her first job at Jim Joe Kelly's shop. She had no choice, as money was scarce, and she needed to earn a living for herself and to contribute to her household. I only vaguely remember my granny in Curragh as she died when I was three but by all accounts, from my older siblings, she was a kind, gentle, loving person. She lived on a very meagre income, which meant Mammy needed to get out as soon as she left school to make a living. She might not have earned much, but it was one less mouth for Granny to feed and Mammy got looked after well enough by her employer. While working there, she was sometimes sent across the road to work for an old lady called Mrs Cauley, whose house was opposite the shop (Coyle's shop now Toners). Mrs Cauley was a very strict lady and Mammy often recalled to me how she treated her unkindly and was very ungrateful for anything that was done for her. However, she did get on well with the Jim Joe Kellys, and although she may not have earned a lot of money, at least they were kind to her.

While working at the shop, Mammy met my father, Michael Gerard McCullagh, a man from Doon who was more than eleven years her senior, born on 22 November 1911. Daddy had recently returned from working in England for a few years, where he had been employed to do farm labouring on a big estate in Lincoln. Many young men went to England in those days as there was very little work in Ireland and no money. By the time she met him, he was ready to settle down.

My parents married on 23 October 1941 in Straw Chapel, outside Draperstown. Mammy was only eighteen and Daddy was thirty, so the night before their wedding, Mammy's mother cut her long, blonde wavy hair in an attempt to make her look like a more mature married woman. Daddy might otherwise have thought she looked too young beside him. Mammy often said that she wondered whether Daddy was annoyed, but he never said if he was. There was no honeymoon after their wedding, but they did go away for the day to Portstewart. Unfortunately, no photos were taken of the wedding.

After their wedding, they moved to live in Doon with Granny and Daddy's sister and brother for a short while. Mammy hated it. Can you imagine being eighteen and living in a household where all the duties were already assigned? She had no control of what she ate, when she ate, and she could not cook a meal for herself or her husband. Daddy went out to work and she was left there to cope on her own, and by all accounts the family were not overly welcoming. She felt very out of place.

However, Daddy soon rented a house on Bancran Road. Mammy referred to it as 'The Yankee's'. Most likely it belonged to someone who had been to America. This is where the first baby, Felly, was born. When Mammy was pregnant, she said she had no idea how this baby was going to be born. Obviously, there was no sex education in school, no antenatal classes, no books to read, and it was not a subject that was discussed with her mum. However, I remember her saying that when the baby was nearly due, her mammy arrived, having walked from Curragh to 'The Yankee's' to be there with her. She may not have had a scan to tell her the due date, but her Mammy had done the maths and knew when to show up. Mammy was very happy and relieved to see her. Felly would have been Granny's first grandchild. In fact, he was the first grandchild on both sides of the family. It was a long and difficult birth and Felly had to be revived with whisky because there was no other medication. So that's when he got the taste for a 'wee half one'! Mammy was quite weak after the birth and her mother stayed with her for a spell afterwards.

Before John was born, which was almost exactly one year later, Daddy had bought a 23-acre farm for £360 in Derrynoid. I know how much he paid because every time we took Mammy shopping in later years to buy her a new outfit for a wedding, she looked at herself in the mirror and then asked how much it was. When she heard the price, she would say, 'That's nearly as much as Daddy paid for the first farm.' I understood where she was coming from, but most of the time either me or Angela were paying anyway, and the price did not matter.

Uncle John helped when they moved from the rented house to Derrynoid. They carried the baby and all their belongings down Bancran Road and across the fields to the house. There was some furniture already in it, so it was liveable, consisting of a kitchen, a small pantry, one bedroom and a lower room. Although it was basic, Mammy was very happy to have her own corner. And it was in the lower bedroom where Mammy would give birth to all but two of her remaining children – eleven in total were born in that room – with only Brigid and Angela born in the hospital and for good reasons...

Mammy was expecting Brigid when she was sitting up with an old woman called Peggy who was dying and who lived over the lane past my brother Mickey's house. Mammy was nine months pregnant at that point, and when Doctor Mary called to visit Peggy, she thought Mammy did not look well. So, she took Mammy's blood pressure and found it to be so high that she immediately arranged for an ambulance – Mammy said she was seeing double. She delivered Brigid in hospital but was very upset that the old lady died when she was not there.

Then, when Angela was about to be born, Mammy was forty-two and had been having babies for twenty-three years, so the doctor again decided it was best for her to have the baby in hospital. Mammy retold the story many times about a doctor coming from Dungannon to deliver Angela, then she would add, 'And a man from Dungannon came and took her back up the road.'

We never noticed an age difference between my parents when we were children. Daddy was a handsome man and to me he always looked well, but especially when he dressed up. I remember him as being a bit stocky, broad and well-built, with large, strong hands, always well-worn by his work on the farm. His dark grey hair, always cut into a short stubble, was brushed with shoe polish to dye it black. He always wore overalls when he was working, best described as dungarees now, with a bib at the front that was fastened at his shoulders with suspender-like buckles. When he was dressed up in his 'good' clothes, he wore 'galluses' (as he called them), which were like braces that were pulled up over a crisp white shirt. He wore an old flat cap too, one for work and a good one for when he was dressed up. I can still visualise him taking his flat cap off when he came inside, and how he always blessed himself with the sign of the cross before he ate his meals, no matter how busy he was. He was very courteous and never wore the cap in the house. He also respected the tradition in the chapel whereby it was deemed disrespectful at the time for men to wear caps or hats. This has always stayed with me – to this day, I find it irritating when I see men and boys eating their meals with caps on. I hope my grandsons will always adhere to this tradition in the chapel in the future.

Before my time, Daddy grew flax, which got sold on to make linen. I recall hearing Mammy recount stories about Daddy leaving the house after dark, barefoot, to go and tramp the flax in the dam. After the harvesting, the flax was put in the dam to allow the woody bark and core of the plant to separate – a process known as retting – which dissolved the pectin that binds the different parts of the plant together. Daddy would tramp it down without shoes so as to prevent destroying or breaking the stems. Unfortunately, retting did not remove all the unwanted material from the plant, so, after the retted flax had dried, it was beaten, scutched, and combed; a labour-intensive and back-breaking process.

When I was growing up, however, Daddy's main work was looking after cows, ploughing, working in the hayfield and cornfield, and cutting and footing turf. He also maintained the farm, which was what he was doing the day he died.

Mammy was about five foot, three inches tall with just about enough padding on her bones to make her hugs very comforting. She had naturally wavy hair that was always kept fairly short, and she was quite fussy about getting the wave of her hair just right – she kept it in place by crunching it with her hand and using hairspray to hold it. As the years went on, her hair lightened but she would never give in to getting it coloured and so kept her hair natural, aside from using some coloured mousse to dampen the greys.

She never wore earrings and didn't like her ears being seen, so her hair always had to cover them. She also never wore makeup when we were young, although she did in later years when I was getting her ready for a wedding, perhaps putting on some makeup and lipstick. I thought it suited her and made her look even more lovely, but she would proceed to the bathroom and use a towel to wipe most of it away. She did, however, sometimes use a powder compact, but it was barely visible on her face. She was very modest and never courted the limelight.

When we were young and she was still a busy housewife, she always wore a dress with a cardigan or a skirt with a wrap-over apron that had wee flowers printed all over it and two pockets on the front. She had a black one and a blue one with pink flowers on it. That was her outfit from morning to night when we were children and she never wore trousers, not even on the coldest day. Her apron was even on when she was walking around the farm in her wellies. She almost always had a soother in one of the front apron pockets, and safety pins were pinned to the lapel of the apron – she was always ready for an emergency. Sometimes, she would take clover rock sweets out of her pockets with the paper stuck to them.

Another lasting memory is of how her hands always smelt of meal, which she fed to the pigs. She would mix the meal with her hands and the smell lingered. This scent, along with turf, never fails to bring me back to my childhood days.

It's funny because when I think of Mammy, she never grew old in my eyes; staying the same to me from childhood to the day she died.

As you will hear, Mammy was always on the go, bringing in water (we didn't have running water), feeding or tending to the pigs and chickens, cooking, carrying out all household chores, and always with her hands full when looking after all of us children.

Dreaming of America

My connection with America began the day I was born.

Daddy's sister, my Aunt Etta, who emigrated to America when she was eighteen, returned from America for a rare visit and became my godmother. This was in the 1960s, when babies were christened the same day they were born, and it was not unusual for the godparents to walk to the chapel with the baby without the parents. However, on this occasion, maybe because Aunt Etta was now considered a yankee on a return visit to Ireland, Daddy wanted to treat her well, so he ordered a taxi and accompanied us to the chapel, along with our neighbour, Charlie Kelly (Andy), who was my godfather.

They arrived at Moneyneana Chapel, our local church, but there was no priest available, so they went to Straw Church instead at the other end of the parish. After the christening, they all went to my granny's house in Doon to introduce her to me. Mammy said she got worried that something had happened to us as we were gone a long time. No wonder Mammy was worried; imagine giving birth to a baby, watching the baby being taken away almost immediately to be christened, and then waiting for hours with no news. Once back at home, to Mammy's relief, there were lots of nice treats for tea, something which I've been told was again due to Aunt Etta being around.

Having Etta as my godmother brought me many benefits. From age one until I was twelve, I received American dollars every year for my birthday. I loved getting her card in an envelope addressed to me, with the money enclosed. I enjoyed buying new shoes or something else I needed with the money. My best memory about this was that Daddy would sit me down and make me write a thank you letter to Etta. He'd get the writing paper and pencil out and tell me what to write and how to spell the words. He would then also write a letter to her and put my letter into the envelope. It was very thoughtful of him to do that. It made me feel a wee bit special getting his undivided attention, even if it was only for a few minutes.

We loved going to the parish missions, usually held in May. Although, we loved them not for the prayers but for the stalls outside. A mission was a week set aside by the parish to devote to prayer. It started with a dawn Mass every morning, and every evening there were devotions and a homily by the missionary. Depending on the order of the missionary, some of these homilies were all fire and brimstone and we were going to burn in hell if we didn't repent and mend our ways. As a child I didn't listen but was more interested in getting out to the stalls, which sold holy beads, holy pictures and prayer books, but also some fashion rings and bracelets. One Sunday, there was a parish mission on, and Daddy bought me a ring with a big emerald stone in it and said, 'Come on in now and write that letter to Etta.' It was a bribe, but I welcomed it. From the research I have done in writing this book, I have come to the conclusion that Daddy had a very close relationship with his sisters, especially Etta.

As a child, I dreamt of going to America and meeting my godmother for the first time. In the darkness of my bedroom, and when I had trouble sleeping, I escaped to sunny America. I would visualise a warm welcome in a rich and affluent home, imagining the large buildings, the wide streets, and the shops and parks I'd visit. In my child's mind, it was a far-off and mysterious place that I would probably never see. It was incredulous to believe that America would have a significant influence on my business and family life fifty years later…

Six and Seven

This book couldn't go without an introduction to my siblings.

There were thirteen living children in my family. Sadly, though, one of my brothers died around 1955 or 1956, born a still birth. This means I have always been counted as number twelve even though I was the thirteenth born, and Angela was then the thirteenth living child but fourteenth born.

I don't remember us all living together at home because all of my brothers and five of my sisters are older than me, so some of them had left home before I can remember.

My oldest brother, Felix, aka Felly, was born on 12 August 1942. He is twenty years older than me. I always thought he was a bit of a worrier. He is always looking out for people, but he does it in a quiet way without making a big fuss. Maybe that's what happens when you are the oldest of a large family. He is not very comfortable in stressful situations, but always shows up when needed, even if it's difficult for him to be there. He knows his place and would never do anything to annoy anyone. He avoids conflicts as much as possible. He is very traditional and likes things done the 'aul' way, although he will admit now that times have changed. He attends all our family gatherings and always loved to dance at the weddings. He was very close to Mammy, probably because he was first born, and she was only nineteen at the time. Mammy remembered all the milestones about Felly and John as they grew up, but not so much for us, so we used to tease her and say the rest of us just faded into a blur. In her later years, Felly would frequently drive up and around her yard, check she was up and moving about, then leave without going in. He just wanted to know she was alive and well but didn't take the time to go in. He did, however, visit her at other times.

Unlike all his five brothers, Felly has no interest in farming or livestock and would be content living in a town or city. He celebrated his eightieth birthday last year and still works, maintaining and repairing houses. He has always worked in the building trade. Felly is married to Anna and lives in the same house he moved into after their wedding.

John came along a year after Felly, on 6 August 1943. He has a quiet, caring nature and is very aware. He generally keeps himself to himself. He was known to be very intelligent at school and is still sharp-witted.

Before he married Madge, he spent some time in Coventry building roads and a college when working for McAlpine. As is evident from the letters he sent back home to Mammy, he did not like it and was just there to earn some money. His love is farming. Even in his eightieth year he is still very active around the farm and still has a well-cared for flock of sheep.

In more recent times, he has become more reclusive and rarely attends social or family events. When we do see him, however, he can chat all day and I enjoy listening to him tell stories about the past. I did talk to him about writing this book, and I have realised that I did not get to know John as an adult as he was the first in the house to get married when I was so young. As children, though, we loved having another house to visit, and we would go down the fields and over the bourne (a small stream) to visit him and Madge. Daddy was alive when John bought that farm, and we called his place 'Joe McKenna's' as this was the name of the former owner. John has since added to his acreage many times by buying more farms.

Mary was the next to be born, on 7 May 1945. She was at home a lot while we were growing up, as she never left home until she got married, there was a big age gap between us as she was twenty when I was three. She worked in John Burns's shirt factory in Draperstown after leaving school, travelling there on her bicycle like all the girls at that time. The shirt factory, like so many across the country, was a major employer especially of women. Because Mary was earning, she bought the young ones new clothes and shoes – especially for the Fheis, which took place every summer in the town. She went on to marry Jamie Kelly who was a neighbour in Derrynoid (who she always called her 'hubby'!), and now lives in Drumderg. Jamie passed away in December 2018. More on Mary later…

Next came Paddy, born on 23 October 1946. He was always clean and tidy, keeping the house in order. He swept the street at least once per week, which was a large concrete area. My most vivid memory of Paddy when we were young was his annual ritual of snowceming the outside walls of the house and whitewashing the byre walls. He wore glasses and they were always sparked with whitewash as he flapped the big brush across the walls. Everything always looked neat and clean when he was finished. He also always drove a good car, and the most memorable of his cars for me were his Volkswagen Beetles. He had a bright green one and a bright yellow one with the eight-track tape player. We would sit out in his car on the front street and listen to the music, as he loved country music and loved to dance. He also loved to dress well, and the most remarkable outfit he had was a red three-piece suit, which he wore when Aelish got married in Jersey. I loved it. We called him 'Big Tom' (Big Tom was a very popular Irish country singer at the time). Rumour has it that his wife Teresa was not as taken with the red suit as Paddy was and it disappeared from sight.

After Daddy died, Paddy took on the father figure role. He certainly kept us on our toes, and you will hear more about that later. He was strict but kind, for example taking me and Angela to Devlin's shop in Draperstown and buying us two new watches shortly after Daddy died. It was my first watch and I still have it. He lived at home longer than the others and remained a bachelor at thirty, which, incredulously, was considered old at the time. However, he did eventually marry Teresa when he was about thirty. Paddy is the only one of my siblings to have passed away in 2016. It was very sad to lose the first of the thirteen.

Lizzie, born on 23 March 1948, trained to be a nurse at Whiteabbey Hospital in Belfast. I don't remember her living at home, as she is fourteen years older than me, but she has told me how she remembers being the first to feed me when I was born. Lizzie was a really hard worker and always cleaned the house when she was home from nursing, grouting and scrubbing the tiles around the big stove which heated our water. She was always full of energy, extremely lively, good fun, and a great help to Mammy when she had her days off. When I was about fifteen, she was selling AMC cookware, and I used to babysit for her so she could go out in the evening to do cooking demonstrations with the cookware. I accompanied her to a sales meeting in a hotel in Belfast where she was awarded for being the best salesperson of the month. I admired her confidence and her energy. Nothing seemed too much for her. I used to wonder when she did her housework and gardening as she was rarely home when you called to see her, but the garden and the house were always sitting perfectly tidy.

Later in life she became a salesperson for Britannica Encyclopaedia and was very successful at this. She married Francis Kelly, brother of Jamie, and now lives in Lisnamuck.

Mickey (named Michael after my father) was born on 30 April 1950. Mickey was a big part of our lives when we were growing up, and as you will learn he worked with my father and took over the farm after Daddy died. Hence, Mammy and Mickey had a close relationship after Daddy's death. She always supported him in whatever he was trying to do to develop and grow the farm. Shortly after Daddy died, I remember a farm (Hagen's), which marched our land, coming up for sale. It was a farm which Daddy probably planned on buying one day and was being sold by private auction. One of our neighbours was also bidding on it and whilst Mickey was keen to get it, he was also aware of the financial burden of buying more land. So, he returned from the auction and told Mammy that he bid so far but that it got too expensive and then he stopped. She said, 'Why didn't you keep going when you went so far?' That's when he clapped his hands and cheered with delight as he had already bought it. He had first wanted to test Mammy's opinion on the price he paid for it before telling her. She was very happy he got it, even at an inflated price. Although, she was not too happy with the neighbour who bid it up! I admired her courage and her encouragement. Mickey is a real home person and has never really left home or travelled much. He has visited Aelish a few times in England, Jersey and Spain but only out of loyalty to Aelish and not out of love for travelling.

He married Anne the year I passed my eleven-plus exam and I still remember how Anne bought me a lovely pencil case for passing my exams. They now live in Derrynoid.

Aelish, the middle child, was born on 29 August 1952, though she discovered she had celebrated her birthday on the wrong day for years. Aelish is a nurse, who also trained at Whiteabbey Hospital, and one day she was called to the matron's office where she was told she had the wrong date of birth. She had always thought she was born on 6 August! One of my earliest memories of Aelish is of her coming home from Belfast, on her day off, wearing navy and white hotpants and a long jacket over them. I was about seven or eight and I thought she looked so grown up and cool. She always hitch-hiked from Belfast, which made her even cooler in my eyes, but displeased Mammy as she felt it was unsafe. Due to 'The Troubles' in Northern Ireland she was very anxious about Aelish hitch-hiking.

When Aelish qualified as a nurse she got itchy feet and wanted to travel. She went to work in Jersey, which started off as a six-month period, but then she fell in love with Jersey and a man who she married there. Paddy went out to give her away, and after her honeymoon, she came back home, and we prepared a lavish wedding reception for her at our house. One memorable occurrence from that evening was when John (the quiet one) got up and made a speech congratulating the happy couple. After her first marriage ended, she met Terry and has been married to him for over thirty years. Her wanderlust didn't end when she first married, and she has moved many times over her lifetime in Spain, England and Ireland. I would like to think she is now settled but the travel bug could be alive and well yet. I once wrote a poem about my siblings and one line about Aelish said, 'She's lived in more houses than we have all put together'. At the time of writing this book, she lives in Portstewart with her husband, Terry Nye.

Geraldine came next, born on 6 June 1954 – The Marian Year. This was a holy year that Pope Pius XII proclaimed 'that the faith of the people may be increased and their devotion to the Virgin Mary'.

Geraldine was always one who stood out, as she had exceptionally long, blond, thick hair, which she kept off her face by always wearing a soft hair band. Even today people will say, 'Is that the one who had the long blonde hair?' Geraldine was very exact about her hair. When she would get it cut, she would get upset if she thought the hairdresser did not cut it straight and she would fix the mirrors in the bedroom so she could examine the back of it closely. I admired her hair as mine was short and black – the total opposite to hers. My earliest memory of Geraldine is her going to the tech school in Magherafelt with her green blazer, a white blouse and striped tie. There she studied commerce, which included shorthand and typing – a course designed for those wishing to become a secretary. Geraldine was very meticulous about her shorthand. She had numerous wire-bound jotters and pencils sharpened very finely, which could not be borrowed or touched by anyone else. She kept them in the top small drawer of the high chest of drawers in the girls' room. I was eight years her junior and fascinated by the well-kept tidy books with no dog ears and sharp pencils, but we were forbidden to use them. If she found out we had used them and a pencil lead was broken, there would be 'wigs on the green'. This was a popular phrase of Mammy's and one we tried to avoid if possible.

In the end, the shorthand and typing were replaced by anatomy and physiology, as she, like her two sisters, pursued a career in nursing. Geraldine trained in the Massereene Hospital in Antrim. She had a spell in Accident and Emergency, which she loved, and later worked in Holywell Psychiatry Hospital.

Today, Geraldine and I have a close relationship. She has been there for me many times. I looked to her for advice when I was a teenager. And I stayed with her and Sean when I was on placement in Antrim. She even helped me choose my graduation outfit and helped me choose my career path in occupational therapy. We have been through a lot together and shared similar experiences. Sometimes the roles are reversed, and I take on the older sister role – it just depends on the day and how we are feeling. She is very lucky to be married to Sean McKeever, who is a gentleman and looks after her very well. I enjoy meeting up with her in Donegal when we are staying in the holiday home, but we don't do it often enough.

Joseph (Joe) was born on 11 October 1957. He is incredibly religious – he's done Lough Derg umpteen times (St Patrick's purgatory – an ancient pilgrimage site on Station Island in Lough Derg, County Donegal, Ireland). I've done it four times myself, and I can tell you it's not easy. It was always said if you did Lough Derg three times you got to heaven, so I should! I'm not sure it works like that but it's a good story. Pilgrims on Lough Derg stay for three days, walking barefoot from day one, staying up a full twenty-four hours to pray, with only one meal per day of black tea and toast. Joe is so good. I couldn't say one bad word about him. That's not to say he doesn't have a defiant streak in him though, and he is certainly not someone to be easily pushed over. Teachers have been known to run and hide in cupboards to get out of his way! Growing up, Joe loved to go to the pictures in Draperstown to see the cowboy films. He would take home the programme for the month ahead and study it to decide which film he would go to see the next week. I loved going through the programme with him, and that's when I was first introduced to Lee Van Cleef, John Wayne and Clint Eastwood. For years he kept a daily diary and there's a possibility he still has those old programmes from the Draperstown picture house. He also collected football cards and we would go through them at night, as we had no television to entertain us. I learned all the names of the English Premier League teams from that experience. When Joe left school, he went to Loughry Agricultural College in Cookstown. He really enjoyed his time there and made good friends. He loved learning and always kept his books neat and tidy. Even though he was interested in farming, he went to work with Felly in the building trade and has had several jobs over the years. However, like his brothers, farming is his love, and he still keeps cows and calves and when he was recovering from the stroke a few years ago the livestock was a great diversion, giving him something to do when he got up in the morning.

Before I met James, Joe would take me to Ardboe Dance Hall and we had a great time, as you will learn more about. Over time, he developed a great interest in vintage machinery and for years he has been collecting instruments, tools and machines. He has held vintage rallies and raised money for good causes. Kathleen has been by his side for over forty years. She is a constant support and advocate for Joe, and I am extremely grateful that Joe has been so blessed to have a wife so loyal to him.

On 25 March 1959, Brigid Rose, called so after Mammy, came along. Like Joe, Brigid has great faith in prayer. She has a special prayer for every member of her family and for every occasion. She spends time in the chapel and she, along with Patsy, would rarely miss Sunday Mass. She is very traditional in her views and carries on many of the Catholic traditions, which are sadly fading away in Ireland today. She is three years older than me, so she was doing homework before I went to school, and I remember Mammy helping her to spell and read the clock when she was little. Looking back, I am amazed by the amount of time Mammy spent helping her and all of us with homework when she already had such a busy life. She was determined to help each and every one of us succeed in whatever we wanted to do, and she was there to give us a helping hand when needed.

Brigid has a very kind nature. She never arrives in anyone's house without a gift, flowers, cakes or sweets. She always buys birthday and Christmas presents and acknowledges the birth of all the new babies including all my grandchildren.

After James's passing, I found Brigid to be very supportive and one person I could be myself with. I think that because she is older than me, I was not afraid to cry and let her know how I was feeling, whereas with Angela, although I know she has seen me cry too, I was always aware that I was upsetting her and so I tried to be brave. I think Brigid is not aware how valuable she has been to me in the past and I hope I can always be there for her if she needs me. She is happily married to Patsy and lives in Donegal.

Brendan, my righthand man, was born on 19 August 1960. There is one year and nine months between us, and we are really close. Brendan is incredibly caring, emotional, compassionate, and soft-natured, but he was the big tough guy when he was young. He never wanted to do homework and hadn't time to play with us girls as he had work to do, out with Daddy and Mickey as soon as he got home from school. The school bag was pitched under the sofa not to be seen again until the next day. He had no time for fun or playing except to climb high trees and have me standing at the bottom, pleading with him to come down.

As he got older his great sense of humour and love for life and fun has become evident. He loves to dance, enjoys a party and a bit of craic. He is a farmer through and through and although for a very brief time he thought he wanted to go to further education, the notion didn't last long. When we were younger, he took me to the dances with his friends and if a scrimmage broke out in the dance hall or outside you would be sure he was there in the middle of it, but mostly just as an onlooker. I was always concerned he would end up in the fight, so I stood close by to make sure he was ok.

Hugging wasn't really a common thing when we were younger, and although Mammy was very caring, hugs and kisses were not so common. This changed as we grew up and we were less afraid of displaying outward signs of affection. I'm happy to say that as we got older, some of our brothers, including Brendan, are no longer reserved about giving hugs. It's always good to see Brendan coming as he will lift the mood, but I am also aware of how sensitive he is to the plight of others, and he takes the loss of friends and family very much to heart.

He never left Derrynoid and, fortunately, he has a very considerate wife in Geraldine who has always gelled well into our family. They looked after Mammy so well in her later years, making sure she had everything she needed. She went to them regularly for dinner and always on Christmas Day.

I came along after Brendan, on 23 May 1962, followed by my only younger sibling, Angela, who was born on 9 May 1965.

From my earliest memory I felt I was always looking out for Angela. Later in this book I refer to the difficult period after Daddy's death, not only for Angela but for everyone who lived at home during that time. However, that time, although it had a lasting imprint on Angela's life, does not define everything about her childhood. Contrary to what you might expect from the youngest child of thirteen, she was not a spoiled child. She was a hard worker.

Angela became an auntie at three, and when Mickey and Anne's children came along when she was ten, she became the main babysitter. She didn't just look after the children, she bathed them, cleaned the house and made dinner. She also babysat for the other sisters and brothers too, especially when a new baby was due or had just arrived. It is unimaginable now that a ten or twelve-year-old would be given the responsibility of looking after babies and toddlers without adult supervision. She often recalls the time she was with Mary helping her after the birth of one of her children. At night they would go to bed and Angela was left in complete darkness in the bedroom across the landing. She was not used to sleeping alone. She was terrified. Hence, even when we are sharing a room now in any hotel across the world, Angela must be sure there is at least a glimmer of light in the room before she sleeps.

Unless I have suppressed this memory, I can never recall quarrelling with Angela when we were young. I will wait and see if she ever reads this book and corrects me if I've made a mistake! Certainly, as adults we have rarely disagreed, and it will always be my fervent desire that we remain good friends all of our lives. I know that is what Mammy would want, but it is also what feels right for me.

Since James's passing, Angela has been very supportive. She was always very attentive and vigilant towards me and had compassion for what I was going through, and although I still wanted to shield her from my grief, I don't think I was entirely successful at that. She had lost a friend too, and I was conscious she was also grieving. One day a short time after James's passing, we were at a health farm on a brisk walk, chatting as we walked. After months of mindless eating, I was trying to get into shape for Martin's wedding. I asserted that 'I need to try to learn to do things on my own', and then I noticed Angela had fallen behind me on the walk. I looked back to see why she had slowed down. Then I saw her tears. There and then I made a conscious decision that I needed to pluck up.

We have travelled many miles together both physically and metaphorically and I hope we are there for each other in all the joys and tribulations to come.

Limbo

My stillborn brother was never really talked about when I was young, and the date of his death is uncertain as stillbirths were not registered. What we do know is that my mother carried the baby full-term, but a few days before she delivered him, she fell down a ditch. The umbilical cord had been around the baby's neck and sadly he was already dead when she gave birth to him.

When we were growing up, death wasn't spoken about much, but we asked Mammy about it when we got older. She told us how a day had never gone by that she didn't think of him, and how she'd cried about his death for years. Mammy hadn't even got to hold him, and he was never given a name. In the 1950s, the Catholic Church in Ireland had strict rules: if a baby wasn't baptised, he or she couldn't be buried in a consecrated graveyard. It meant that my father had to take our baby brother to be buried in un-consecrated ground, with no priests or prayers said at home. My brother John, who was twelve years old at the time, still remembers looking at the baby in a small, white coffin, and seeing the baby's fingers. He said they looked perfect.

In modern times, Mammy would have had counselling and the chance of being part of support groups. There also would have been a naming ceremony for the baby and a resting place to visit. Instead, Mammy said that Daddy never mentioned the baby after the burial. I suppose he didn't want to upset her. But it must have been very difficult because she didn't even have anywhere to go and mourn him. It was as if he never existed. More so, Mammy had been brought up to believe that babies who died before being baptised went to a place called Limbo – meaning they never got to heaven or saw the face of God. This haunted her for many years. Fortunately, one day Mammy asked a priest about it, and he told her that the baby had had 'the Baptism of Desire'. This counted just the same. Now, whether this was accurate or not, or whether he just told her this to help her through the grieving, it worked. She most definitely felt better about it. I feel this priest showed some compassion for a grieving mother and knew what to say to ease her burden.

It wasn't until the 1990s that the Catholic Church recognised all the babies that were buried without baptism. A monument was erected for them in Straw Graveyard in 2003, where all the burials had taken place. At last, two years before she died, Mammy had some closure.

My Early Years

Our house consisted of three bedrooms, which we called 'The Women's Room', 'The Lads' Room' and 'Daddy's Room'.

Daddy and Mammy's room was very small and had a door directly in to the living room. It was warmer than the others as the chimney brace was in the room and the fire was rarely out. There were two double beds in the other rooms, so we always had to share a bed. There was a fireplace in both the rooms, but we didn't light them much as they smoked a lot due to a very poor draft in the chimney. These two rooms were damp and cold, and built on to the original house in about 1957 or 1959 by Paul McCormick and Jim Kelly (Brine). Felly had left school at this time and was working for these two men.

When the older ones in the family lived there, they slept in the loft, and I've been told that their mattresses were bags of hay – that was before my time! At least we had the luxury of a sprung mattress. Though, when the mattress got old, you could feel the springs coming through, so we put an extra blanket on top of the mattress until Mammy could afford a new one.

With no heating, the bedrooms were cold in the morning, so Mammy got up early before everyone else to light the fire, so we were not cold going out to school. Sometimes, the top blanket would be a bit damp if the weather was frosty, and

I can remember even seeing our breath in the air. But when we came down to the living room – what we called 'The House' – there would be a good fire on, and our clothes would be warmed by the fire.

We also had a small scullery and a 'good' room, which we called the 'Lower Room'. We never used the Lower Room much, except at Christmas, when we had visitors, or at one time when my 'Granny in Doon' as we called her – Daddy's mother – came to live with us. She stayed for a short time before returning to her home in Doon. Looking back, I don't know how Mammy coped with all of us and Granny, even it was only for a few weeks. I remember her sitting in the Lower Room with coal in a gold-coloured bucket. A rare sight in our house. We never burned coal. But she needed to be kept warm.

Until I was about thirteen, we had no indoor bathroom, running water or electricity. The living room was heated by a stove using turf we cut in the 'moss', a place called Finneglen. The stove was also used to cook on and boil the kettle, but it only heated one room. Later we got a gas cooker too, which was great as we could cook easily on it. The lights in the house came via a gas light on the ceiling. There was a special and very delicate mantle on the gas light which needed replacing very often, and when the mantle was done and in need of replacement, it gave a very poor-quality yellow light. The yellow light was dull and gloomy, and I remember having a feeling of anxiety when the light was dull. If there was a hole in the mantle, a blue flame would gush out making a whooshing sound. And when a new mantle was put in, the fresh smell from it lasted for about thirty minutes and the house light was bright and cheerful. I always liked to see the new mantle going in. It lifted my spirits.

There were times when cushions or other objects were flung at each other as we played or maybe quarrelled with each other, but with the mantle being such an important part of our home, Mammy used to caution us not to throw things across 'The House' in case we 'broke the mantle'.

Our household was by no means affluent, as you may have gathered. It wasn't easy to hear the adults having concerns about money. I remember worrying we wouldn't have enough to get by – we were certainly stretched financially, and nothing was to be taken for granted. Still, we were never hungry as children and we always had 'good' clothes for school and chapel, which we'd take off the minute we got home. Our good clothes were saved, kept well, and usually handed down to the next person. It is obvious from the family photos, usually taken after Sunday Mass, how well turned out we were for the occasion.

There were very few treats like biscuits or sweets when I was growing up. If we were having a visitor to the house, for example, Mammy would get nice food in, but we weren't allowed to eat it. It was only when the visitors left that we could eat the leftovers. We were never in short supply, though, and Mammy was always making bread and scones, given the breadman only came twice a week. Because of this, she always had dough and flour encrusted around her fingernails, and always had a large bag of Morton's Early Riser flour in the pantry – a staple in most homes at that time. This flour was packed into 50lb bags that became almost as famous as the flour itself. I remember washing these bags and reusing them as pillowcases! We soaked the bag first to get the label off and then washed it several times to make sure the flour was all out of it. Nothing was wasted.

Mammy made us pancakes for special treats, and when she burnt her griddle scones, she gave them to us, saying, 'Now watch the butter doesn't run off!' so that we wouldn't turn them over and realise they were burnt on the bottom. She always made sure that we got a good breakfast before we went to school, too, with homemade bread, fried with hard cheddar cheese on top. It was delicious. I don't remember having cereal when we were very young, but we had cornflakes when I was in secondary school.

Even milk was a luxury, and we certainly didn't buy milk until I was about eleven or twelve. Instead, we had a cow that Daddy milked every day, which Mickey would have milked after Daddy died, but because there were so many of us in the house, the milk was in limited supply. So, we were never allowed to drink the milk, with it being strictly for our tea or cereal. In fact, the phrase 'Don't drink the milk' stayed with me into adulthood. I had to tell myself later in life that a jar of milk was only 99 pence, and it was ok to let the weins drink it!

With the house and all of us children to look after, my memories of Mammy from my earlier years are of her always running around, busy making sure everything and everyone was looked after. Since there was no electricity in our house, there was no washing machine, and we also didn't have running hot water. So, Mammy would light a big boiler out in a little house called 'The Milkhouse'. I still remember how she'd fill the top of the boiler with cold water and then light a fire underneath to heat it. She also washed all the clothes by hand, and we helped put the sheets and blankets through a mangle to start drying them. The clothes were then hung outside if the weather was good and then taken in and put on a line across the ceiling above the fireplace to dry. It went without saying that everyone helped around the house with whatever jobs needed done. We were just brought up that way.

Mammy had about six sow pigs spread over four pig houses and the sows were kept in a pig crate so the young piglets could feed from her. We used to help Mammy feed the pigs and carry water to them and I would also sit with Mammy when the 'sow was pigging'. The pig shed would be very warm and the sow pig was in a crate surrounded by bales of straw and a tilly lamp to keep the little piglets warm. The smell was rather suffocating when I went into the pig crew, but I got used to it after being in there a while. Mammy would sit up with the pigs all night if necessary to make sure they were born safe and sound, as she depended on the pigs as a vital part of her income. Once the piglets were weaned off their mother's milk, a man came along and bought them for around £4 per piglet.

We also had quite a lot of hens because Mammy sold the eggs. We children would help by collecting and using a dry sandpaper brush to lightly clean them. We had to be incredibly careful as a broken egg cost us money.

We were self-sufficient with our own eggs, milk, potatoes and homemade bread. And Daddy grew vegetables up in the 'Three Fields', including beetroot, carrots, scallions and parsley, which I loved to chew on. Mammy boiled the beetroot whole and when it was cooked, she gave it to us wrapped in newspaper as it was still very hot. We put salt on its thick skin and ate it like an apple. It was delicious. Daddy also made nettle soup and he killed rabbits and cooked them, though I hated the smell of the rabbit boiling – it turned my stomach and I most definitely never tasted rabbit meat.

As you can see, the food was all very healthy. Certainly, none of us were overweight as we didn't have many sugary foods. Daddy, however, did like pouring the gravy from the frying pan over his potatoes. It was pure lard from frying bacon. It was probably very tasty, but also very good at clogging arteries…

We all helped out in the moss footing turf, which was an important job given that the turf fire was our only form of heating. Getting the turf dried and into the shed was, therefore, a priority. If there was a very wet summer, it would be very late before we got the turf home, and I would worry when the turf shed got empty in case we would run out. Thankfully, though, we never ran out, but sometimes the turf came home very wet. Getting the turf home was a worrying time for Mammy. I recall standing out in the middle of our road looking upwards towards the mountain at the end of a long summer day when it was nearing dusk, waiting on the men to come home from the moss. They were taking home turf with a tractor and trailer with no lights and probably not very well equipped for the job at hand. Mammy and I would stand out, waiting and waiting, listening for the familiar sound of the jiggly tractor coming rumbling round the horseshoe bend. I dreaded that horseshoe bend each time we travelled home by tractor. I had a fear the tractor would topple over the edge, there was nothing to stop it. There was palpable relief for both Mammy and me when we could hear the rattle of the tractor coming closer and closer. She worried so much; it rubbed off on me.

As you'll read later, we also harvested potatoes in later years – another back-breaking job.

This reminds me of another abiding memory I have of Mammy. She used to make tea for the men working in the fields or the moss. She did not have a thermos flask, so she put the tea in a glass bottle, secured the top with paper, and put a sock over it to keep it warm. With the added milk and sugar, the tea was hot and sweet and very tasty. I still remember how, when carrying the tea out, we were given strict instructions to hold the bottle straight so the tea would not spill out.

We got most of our groceries from a mobile grocery van on Saturdays, which Pat McCormick ran. When he retired, his shop was sold to the Joe Peter Roes – now Mulligans Bar – though their right name was McCullagh, but no relation. Anyhow, Peggy Peter Roe came with the groceries packed into large boxes in the back of her hatchback car, and I would sit in the front seat of the car with her while she wrote down the shopping list and counted the money. One purchase that dominated my memory from those days was the little blue sachets of Supersoft shampoo which we bought each Saturday. We divided one sachet between two of us. Mary would place a basin of warm water on a chair in the middle of the floor and proceeded to scrub our hair with the warm water and shampoo. Hot water was very scarce as we had to heat it in a boiler at the side of the stove. She then used clean water to rinse our hair, throwing it over our heads. It scared the life out of me. I was terrified waiting for the water to splash over my head, into my eyes and ears. We were warned to 'hold steady' as she didn't want the clean water wasted.

Bread was bought from one of the two breadmen: Brooster came on a Tuesday and Matt Taylor came on a Friday. They would reverse up our street to the front door and pull out large drawers from the back of the van to reveal a spread of fresh bread, scones, buns and loaves. Sometimes we would even get a treat of Paris buns, which were not quite a scone, not quite a cake, but more of a sweet, bread-like cake. On Fridays, Matt Taylor would also bring the newspapers and we'd get the Northern Constitution from him, a paper

Daddy liked to read (as a child, I thought it was very boring!).

From feeding us, to the little details like making sure we always had a good anorak with a hood to wear as we walked to school, Mammy worked hard to make sure we had what we needed. I even remember Mammy showing me how to tie the knot in the hood before I left for school. We had good shoes for school, which we tried to save. And we wore wellies around the house in winter, but never to school. Incidentally, the wellies would leave a track on my leg which was sore if I didn't pull my socks up far enough. In the summertime, I loved getting new white socks and plastic sandals to wear with our new summer dresses. But we did not get to the shop to choose new shoes whenever we needed them. Mammy would place our feet on a piece of cardboard and draw around our feet, then cut out the image of our foot to get our size before taking them into Burns's shop to get our new shoes.

Summer Days, Flowers and Joe Nan's House

We had an innocent and happy childhood, spending most of our summer days outside as young children.

The summer seemed to last forever.

Brigid, Angela and I would go up the 'cuts' to gather primroses in the summer. We played along the small stream that ran through the trees and would be away for what seemed like hours, with no one coming to look for us. There was never any worry that anything would happen to us as it was a safe place to play. We just went home when we got hungry.

During the summer we spent time in the hay fields when the hay was being dried. This was always a time of fun as there was no work involved in this for the children.

We also had hours of fun in Joe Nan's old house. Joe was an elderly man who lived alone, just over the ditch from ours. His wee cottage consisted of one room and an outshut. He slept in the outshut with a curtain as a screen, which he pulled over when asleep. The door of his house was split in two. The top half was always left open, but the lower half was closed to keep the hens out. There were always roses growing outside his door and over the roof. When he left the house, he would leave a sign written with chalk on a slate which said:

'If I'm not in I must be out,

If you need me badly just hang about.'

It was a great Ceili house and attracted men from all over the townland and further afield to play cards. Any visitor who came in was invited to 'Pull up a chair' and they would join in with the craic or the storytelling.

I'm sure it wasn't all truths and facts, there would have been a few yarns spun too!

As children, we visited him and sat by a big open fire. The main reason for our visit was the biscuits he kept on a high, small shelf. Our eyes were firmly fixed on the shelf, and he knew it. But we waited patiently for him to offer us one, as Mammy had told us not to ask. It could be ages before he succumbed and gave us one, but he knew that was why we were there.

When he got old, he started to 'dote' (we would say he had dementia now, but 'doting' was the common way to describe an old person who was forgetful back then). At this point, Mary was charged with looking after his sleeping pills, which were kept at our house as he used to take too many of them. He always wanted more than was prescribed, so Mary would empty the capsules and fill them with flour!

He would come to our house in the morning before we left for school with his bacon to get Mammy to cook it for him. Angela was about two or three at the time and she would look at his plate of bacon and say, 'Can I have a bit of baccy Joe?' We still remind her about that yet.

Joe Nan died on 4 February 1968, and the house and the fields were left to Daddy. The house was never lived in again after he died, so we used it to play in. We had a play shop in there, where Brigid, Angela and I would gather up empty tins, bottles and packages, and put up shelves to make a shop, taking it in turns with my siblings at being shopkeeper.

The furniture was still in there, with a table and chairs, and we also enjoyed lighting the fire. Really, it was a life-size playhouse where we had hours of fun; keeping it tidy, brushing the floor, and cleaning the one small window. We put flowering corn which grew along the hedges in jam jars and displayed them on the window. It was a great shelter in the wintertime when we couldn't play outside.

Mammy also used the house to dry clothes on the line she had put up in there, as well as on the outside line on Joe Nan's street.

I recall taking it upon myself to look after Angela one summer. I set out her clean clothes every morning and washed the clothes from the previous day and put them on the line on Joe Nan's street to dry. I remember washing her hair and looking at her wee hands, which were all dry and hard before I rubbed cream on them. I was the big sister, after all.

Another enduring memory from childhood days is of how, every May, we made a May altar with a statue of Mary (Our Lady) and put wildflowers on it. This altar was a devotion to Mary during the month of May. As we didn't have fancy vases, we used small glass jars which we saved throughout the year to hold the flowers. We gathered primroses and flowers called Mary Needles in Felly McCloskey's field to keep the altar fresh and we said our prayers at the altar every morning. When I look back now, I think how innocent and simple our life was then.

During lent we went 'off sweets', but it wasn't as hard as it would be for children now as we didn't have access to sweets every day anyway. Nevertheless, it was a 'sin' as we thought to eat sweets during lent. I used to wonder why Patsy Cassidy still sold them if it was a sin to eat them…

When I went to the convent school, the practice remained but I realised that not everyone followed the same strict traditions we did.

We were steeped in Catholicism and tradition, but it was never forced on us. It was just something we accepted as the right thing to do. I know other parents who were much stricter about religion, but Mammy always had a moderate approach to it. On a Sunday there was half ten Mass in Moneyneana, which we never missed. It was a sin to miss Mass as the third commandment said, 'Remember thou keep holy the Sabbath day'. That, to us, translated into faithfully attending Mass every Sunday. Mammy would get us all ready and dressed and send us 'out and down the road', walking to mass. She would then get herself ready to go on her bicycle. She often recalled that many a time she would hear the 'five minute' bell ringing at the chapel as she stepped on her bike to cycle to Mass. I can remember her passing us on her bike as we walked up McShane's Brae leading to the chapel.

As well as the weekly Mass we had a 'Holy Hour' or Benediction on a Sunday evening during lent and at other special times in the church calendar. I did not like the holy hours as it was just prayer after prayer with very little singing. The priest came out and kneeled for one hour at the altar rails and rhymed off a litany of prayers. It was very monotonous. Angela, who was about six, used to fall asleep. The Benediction was more interesting, however, usually held at evening devotion, and included the singing of certain hymns and litanies before the Blessed Sacrament, which was exposed on the altar in the monstrance and surrounded with lights. At the end, the priest, his shoulders draped in a gold veil, would take the monstrance into his hands and make the sign of the cross in silence over us as we kneeled. There was always a strong smell of incense and wax candles, and the altar would be illuminated with two rows of candles. The choir would then sing 'Tantum ergo' as the priest blessed us all. The lights, the candles, the music combined with the gold robes made it less dreary than a holy hour and it was much shorter.

For my First Holy Communion, when I was six years old, Mammy and I walked to Moneyneana Chapel where Fr. McGlinchey was the curate at the time. Daddy did not go to these events, however, as fathers were not expected to attend. Afterwards, the parochial house tables were put outside, and we all got a welcome treat of juice and buns. It was a sunny day and as Mammy and I walked back home, she said, 'You were the nicest girl there today.' It was a compliment I never forgot, and which made me feel special. I still remember the exact spot on the road where she said it.

Mammy was very restrained in her praise for us, especially in public. It was not the practice for Mammy to brag about us to outsiders, and she rarely spoke about our achievements to anyone. My aunt, on the other hand, was always boasting about her children. One day, I said to Mammy, 'Why do you never boast or say nice things about us to outsiders?' She said, 'You will show yourselves – you don't need me bragging about you's.' Even so, she *was* proud of us, I know that for sure.

We never had holidays as children, except when we visited our sister Lizzies' house in Antrim or when we all piled excitedly into the back of Felly's big van on occasions when he took us to Portstewart for a day out during the summer. That was always a fun day out. When we got to 'The Port', Mammy would buy us a beach ball to play with and wee windmills which twirled round as we ran along the promenade. We always got an ice cream cone and a stick of rock before we left, too. It was the highlight of our summer and the only real holiday we had. It was also a real treat to go to Lizzie's house during summer holidays. She lived in Antrim before buying the house and farm in Lisnamuck, and we found it very exciting because she had electricity, a bath, carpets and a coin-operated television with a box attached to the back, and stairs. From her house, we could also easily walk out to the park where we played on the swings and slides and walk to the shops or get on a train to go to Belfast.

Of course, throughout my childhood we also had all my siblings' weddings. In fact, it felt as though we were constantly going to the next wedding, which meant getting new outfits – this was such a treat. Since we did not have a school uniform in primary school, we were then allowed to wear our nice clothes to school the day after the weddings, and I remember my friends being jealous because most were the eldest in their families and so had never even been to a wedding.

I was five when John got married in 1967, so I wasn't there. He had a very small wedding and the wedding breakfast, as it was called then, was held in Madge's home.

The next to get married was Lizzie in 1968, I was a flower girl at Lizzie's wedding when I was six, and I got to wear the same dress I wore for First Communion earlier that year. I felt very special on her wedding day.

At Felly's wedding, in 1969, I was seven and Angela was four. We got matching red checked dresses with white collars and cuffs and white crocheted caps to match. These were bought from McConway's van as he travelled around the countryside on a Monday with his van packed with new clothes. He had a shop in Magherafelt, but he had regular customers in the countryside and Mammy was one of them. Since she did not drive, she took advantage of the convenience of having the clothes brought to her door. We have a family photo at Felly's wedding with Angela and I in the front row holding hands, and with Angela's face glued to my arm. We looked inseparable.

In 1970, when I was eight, Mary got married and this time it was Angela's turn to be flower girl and I got to wear a navy and white dress which I loved. It had a chain that went across the front which threaded through loops in a zigzag pattern. The next day, at school, I must have played with the chain all day, distracting the others, because the teacher called me up, took the chain off me, and placed it on the desk, saying, 'You can get that when you go home.'

Mickey's wedding took place when I was eleven, but, sadly, it was tinted with sadness as it was the first wedding without Daddy. Mammy was still in mourning and heart-broken, so she was not looking forward to it – understandably, it was hard for her to celebrate at a time like that. She looked a bit sad in the photos. I remember being excited the day before the wedding as I had just passed my eleven-plus and our class went on our P7 school trip to Portrush. During the trip, I was boasting that I was coming back the next day for my brother's wedding. It was the icing on my cake.

When Geraldine married in 1975, we were renovating our house and getting our first bathroom. I remember her being quite stressed the night before her wedding, as she had an extremely long veil, and she was worried it would get creased. Mammy fixed a hook to the ceiling in the bedroom so it could hang at the full length without getting crushed. This settled the nerves.

Christmas

We were very lucky to have wonderful Christmases as children.

Mary worked in Burns's factory. She always had some money, so she bought the Santa presents, and my favourite toys I remember were a doll with a yellow raincoat and hat, and a small grand piano on three legs. We got colouring books and crayons, too. I particularly remember getting gloves and a hat to match my coat and thinking how clever Santa was because he matched them perfectly.

Mickey always went into the forest to cut a real tree down in the run up to Christmas, but it always seemed like we were asking him for ages and ages before he actually went to get one. Obviously, as children, we were much more excited about Christmas than he was, but he never let us down and he would arrive with a large tree rousing great excitement. We put it in a big bucket with stones, to hold it steady, and enjoyed decorating it. Since we had no electricity, we had no lights on our tree, but I remember Mary once bought chocolate foil covered tree decorations in the form of Santas and snowmen. There were also brightly coloured decorative balls on the tree as well as tinsel. As Christmas Day drew near, the chocolate decorations gradually disappeared because the novelty of chocolate was too great a temptation to resist.

We adorned the house with paper decorations which draped from one corner of the ceiling to the other and met in the centre where a large paper bell was suspended. We then placed a paper bell at each corner of the ceiling, too, which was made of wooden boards, so it was easy to push small pins into it.

In my mind, it was a very joyful and fun-filled time, and the house was cheerful.

On Christmas Morning, we got up early to see our presents and hoping we would see the Christmas star. I still remember how dark it was when we were opening our presents. We then went to Mass, clad in our new coats, gloves, hats or scarves, or in whatever we were lucky enough to get that year.

The Neighbours

The neighbours would frequently call on their 'ceili' to our house without warning, while on their way home from the shop or just to pop in for a chat. This included the McKillops, Mrs Toner and Charlie O'Connor (known to us as Charlie Conyer). The McKillops (proper name Kelly) were three bachelors who lived up the road: John, Joe and Frank. They were uncles of Brigid's husband, Patsy Kelly. Their father, Mickey, was well into his eighties when I was very young, but still an energetic man. I remember him coming in one cold day while on his way to collect his pension at the post office in Moneyneana. He had a cap on, but Mammy thought it was very cold for him, so she got a scarf and wrapped it around his ears and neck, securing it with one of those safety pins she kept pinned to her overall. And off he skipped across the street.

Charlie Conyer was a regular visitor. He was a good friend of Daddy's but a few years younger, and he took Daddy's death very sorely. After which, he continued to visit, usually after Sunday Mass. For some reason he took a shine to me and every day he came up, he gave me Embassy Regal vouchers. These were vouchers that came in the cigarette packets. You could save them up and once you had enough you could flick through the Embassy Blue catalogue and use the vouchers to buy whatever you wanted. I loved to see him coming, hoping that he had smoked the twenty packets of cigarettes during the week, and not the ten – as there was a smaller voucher in the ten pack and I had my heart set on a typewriter which had caught my eye in the catalogue. The catalogue contained many useful items, which might have been needed in the house, but Mammy paid no attention to it and allowed me to dream about my typewriter. After months of collecting these vouchers, my blue typewriter arrived in its little case addressed to me. I was overjoyed. I felt very important typing away, scrolling the paper, replacing the ink ribbon and clicking away at the keys. I aspired to become a secretary then, but my focus shifted after a few years at the convent where no commercial subjects were studied. I still have the typewriter.

This reminds me also about how Mammy collected 'Green Shield stamps' when she did her shopping in the co-op. The more she bought, the more stamps she was rewarded with. It was the early version of the Clubcard, with those stamps being stuck into books that could be used to select things from a catalogue. It was often new towels, sheets, cups, and other useful items for the house that she exchanged the stamps for. She kept the stamps in a wooden box with a small hole on the lid which was made by one of the boys at woodwork class. She referred to it as the 'Green Shield box' and it sat for years in our hot press in the same spot.

As a point of interest, Green Shield was rebranded to Argos in 1973 and has become one of the most recognisable brands on the high street.

Charlie was a kind man who ended up living alone. His brother Joe, who was blind, had lived with him until he got older and could no longer manage independently. Joe had been blind all his life but could manage to walk to the shop and take care of himself. No matter who he met on the road, he could say their name even though he had no sight because he could identify people by their step and their voice. I also remember visiting Charlie's mother, Martha, a few times as a child when I was returning home from school and delivering the Sacred Heart Messenger, but she was a fearsome character and put the fear of God in me.

Throughout my life, I always had a soft spot for Charlie, who called me 'Teen'. When James started coming up our road to visit me, he would often come across Charlie walking home; he never drove a car and was fond of a drink or two. So, James would drive him to his house and when he was getting out of the car, he would say in his soft, slurred voice, 'Be good to Teen'.

I invited him to our wedding, but he didn't come, and he passed away when I was expecting Ryan. It was the end of another era, but I have fond memories of him.

St Mary's Primary School, 1966

My older siblings attended Bancran School, where all the local country children went. It had very few amenities, though at least all pupils were in the same boat. Geraldine was the last of our siblings to attend Bancran School because, when Joe was ready for school in 1962, Mammy decided to send the 'five young ones', as we were collectively known (Joe, Brigid, Brendan, Angela and me), to St Mary's Primary School in Draperstown. That school had opened the year I was born. One of the benefits of going to St Mary's Primary School was that we could walk to the 'foot of the road' and get on the bus, which was a luxury compared to my older siblings who had to walk across the fields to their school in Bancran.

The process of changing our school hadn't been an easy feat, however. Mammy had to go to Father Collins to get his permission. He was not in favour of the move as it meant a decline in the number of pupils attending the country school, which he wanted to keep open and ensure the teacher's job was secured. Andy O'Neill was still the principal, as he retired in 1967. However, Mammy said that there was a bus going to the town, a new primary school had opened, and that she did not want her weins 'crossing ditches anymore'.

'They will cross many ditches in their life,' he retorted.

But she was not to be deterred. She told him they were her children and she had decided they were not going to Bancran School. So, in 1962 Joe was the first to attend the new town school, and in 1966, I started at St Mary's Primary School.

Mammy was a courteous and respectful person, but she was also strong-willed and when she knew something was right, she stood her ground. In fact, a common instruction of hers was: 'Stand your ground'.

This was 1962. Mammy was almost forty years old and the mother of twelve children. She had gained a lot of experience in the previous twenty years since her first-born, and maybe one thing she learned was to challenge authority and put her children first.

My memories of primary school were generally good, and I had a few close friends, one of whom I remain in touch with.

Though, I always felt we were poorer than others in our school as all of them were townies; there were no other pupils from the country areas, as there were still four country schools in the parish. The townies had all the mod-cons in their homes, the latest games and toys, televisions, and money to go to Patsy Cassidy's sweet shop, which was open every day, and where pupils were allowed to go during their lunch break. I rarely had money for sweets, but sometimes, when we were walking across the street to go to school, Daddy would give me a thrupenny bit or, if he was flush, a sixpence piece which was worth twice as much. I can still see him taking the coins out of his pocket, mixed with straw dust. These were the days when I couldn't wait for lunch to get spending it in Patsy's, showing off that I had money too. It didn't happen often, but that's what makes it memorable. Many of the children also got weekly comics, with the girls getting Mandy and the boys buying Beano, but again, it was not a luxury we could afford.

On those occasions I went to Patsy's, I bought a Betta bar (puffed rice covered in a sweet syrupy coating like rice cakes), and I always tried to keep some for Mammy. But the temptation I got from getting off the bus until I reached home was usually too great and there was very little of the bar left when I reached home. Another favourite sweet from Patsy's was Spangles – a boiled sweet sold in a paper packet and individually wrapped. And then, when we were allowed to accompany Mammy to Molly McGuigan's shop in the town, she always bought a quarter pound of clover rock. Molly weighed them out and put them in a small white paper bag. We often found clover rock sweets in Mammy's coat pocket with the paper stuck to them!

It wasn't all bad having fellow pupils that were more affluent than me. One girl at school, an only child, nearly always had money and she shared her sweets with me. It was also eye-opening. One boy in the class had parents who owned a shop in town, and one day he had a five-pound note in class, which was a huge amount of money at the time. He had also been on an aeroplane and described the experience to us in class as being like sailing through large balls of cotton wool. I recalled this memory many times when I was flying in later years. It's funny the details that stick in your mind all these years later.

When I got older, I understood that many of the children in the town school lived in council houses, which provided them with all the mod cons, whereas electricity had still not reached the rural parts. There were plenty of jobs around Draperstown, and many of their parents had jobs in Burns's factory, Taylor's yard, Sperrin Metal or with Heron Brothers, so they had a steady and reliable income. There were some affluent children in the school as well, whose families owned pubs and businesses in the town.

Incidentally, thinking back to school days has reminded me of Brendan in the mornings… Brendan never liked school, so it was a coaxing session by Mammy to get him out of bed in the morning to go. When he eventually got up, he would sit with one leg on either side of the fire she had lit a few hours earlier. Mammy would then bring his breakfast in and place it on the mantlepiece in the hope it would entice him to go. Brigid, Angela and I would leave on time to walk to the bottom of the road to catch the bus and we were often about to board the bus when I could see Brendan running down the road, blazer flapping and his schoolbag swinging. I regularly had to ask the bus driver to wait for him. It was just as well he was a fast runner, or he would have missed many more days at school.

*

The headmaster, Master Alfie Kelly (Alphie), was quite a character and depending on who you talked to, you could get very different views on him. He filled me with fear as he was very tall and used to slither round the school with a long black strap up his sleeve, which we called a liquorice. He never spoke when we met him in the corridor, and we would move to the side and slip past him, glad that the liquorice did not appear. But we weren't all so lucky. There was a very small boy who always seemed to be getting into trouble. Master Kelly used to lift him up and put him over his shoulder to transport him to class. Fortunately, he never did anything bad to me. I also think he mellowed over the years. Certainly, he wasn't as bad as used to be – I heard that many years before he had been a teacher at Bancran School alongside the dreaded and cruel Master O'Neill, the principal there at that time, and Master Kelly had been very ferocious back then. It was a well-known story in our home that he ran after John over the fields to catch him and give him a beating. John had to scramble over the barbed wire fence to get away!

Corporal punishment was legal in schools then, only being banned in 1987. Typically, teachers made use of a rattan cane, with which male and female pupils were struck across their bare hands, clothed legs or clothed buttocks. Sometimes, at Bancran School, the pupils were even sent out to get a rod from the ditch for the teacher to administer punishment on them, whereas other teachers used a slipper. At St Mary's Primary School, however, I was only slapped once. And that was Mrs McGuigan using a ruler across my hands for talking in class when I was in Primary 5. I felt very aggrieved as I was only asking my classmate for a rubber. Though, many others suffered a worse fate at the hands of the teachers. James, for example, was beaten regularly by his teachers at Dungiven School.

One day, Master Kelly came in to Primary 7 class and called out the names of a few pupils to go to his office. One of them was me. Given that his reputation was vividly emblazoned in my mind, I was filled with trepidation and nervousness. I thought I had done something wrong. Thankfully, it transpired I had nothing to fear, except for having to do a test I wasn't prepared for. Much later, I discovered it was an intelligence test, and he reported back that I had done very well in it. I think it was something the Department of Education needed done and he randomly selected pupils to sit it without warning. It is very regrettable that nothing was explained to children back then. We were just told to obey without any explanation.

We did not wear a uniform at primary school, but we were told we had to wear shorts for P.E. As I didn't have any shorts, Mammy made me a pair one night, using material she had in the cupboard – she was always buying remnants and saving them for when she needed to make something. She had a manual Singer sewing machine with the treadle and two small drawers on the left-hand side for storing spools and needles. The sewing machine, which she used a lot, sat at the front window most of the time. As it folded down, I loved using it as a desk to do my homework on.

Mammy made curtains, new clothes for us, and mended old clothes, especially the men's trousers. This work was usually done at night when everyone was asleep. It was the only time she had peace to sit down and sew. I remember one time she was sewing a patch on a pair of trousers, and she nodded off to sleep in the middle of the sewing. On waking up she found she had sewn the trousers to her skirt! It just shows how tired she was at the end of the day.

When she got a bit older, I had to thread the needle for her as her eyesight was not as good (I've now joined that club!). When she made my shorts, she used a navy-blue material with fish printed on it, swimming about. When I sat on the school stage the next day lined up with the other pupils, I was the only one with bespoke shorts. Everyone else was wearing navy, and I felt very conspicuous and ill at ease. I'm not sure if anyone else even noticed, and if they did, they never said anything.

The most memorable garment that Mammy made me was a beautiful red checked pinafore. She made one for me and one for Brigid for the Religious Examination (R.E.) when the priest came into the school and grilled us on our catechism. It was usually a priest we didn't know from another parish, and we'd spend a lot of time revising before the big day. Everyone wore their Sunday best clothes for the occasion, and I wore my red checked pinafore with a red jumper underneath it. I loved it.

*

In 1971, decimal currency came in, and our old money of pounds, shillings and pence was replaced with fifty pence, ten pence and five pence pieces. I was in Mrs McGuigan's class then, in Primary 5, and I loved learning about the new money and its value. Master Kelly would then come into class and test us on what we had learned. Following which, he said I was the only one he could trust with his money at Patsy Cassidy's.

Daddy

Sadly, 1971 brought some very hard times for my family.

My memories of Daddy are quite limited, although I distinctly remember him helping me with my reading before he went to our neighbour Felly McCloskey's house on his ceili. Felly McCloskey had a small eighteen-inch black and white television, which was run off a car battery, and Daddy went there most evenings to watch the news. It was a treat to get to watch TV. When he came home one night in 1970, he told us he saw Dana win the Eurovision Song Contest. Dana, only sixteen, was from Derry. This was during The Troubles, so it was very uplifting for everyone when a local person won such a coveted prize.

I also remember him coming home from the town on a fair day, with sausages from the butchers wrapped in brown paper and tied with a string, which Mammy then cooked. It was the tradition to go for a drink in the pub on a fair day, so he was in a happy mood. On the occasions he had a few drinks, Daddy would take me on his knee, which I was quite shy about because this was unusual.

Sometimes, Daddy brought Mammy home new shoes, which reminds me of his saying, 'If you have good shoes on your feet, you are dressed.'

Daddy liked to sing, too, especially when he had a few drinks, with the song 'Lovely Leitrim' being his favourite. In fact, there was always music at home after Mary bought a record player in Leo Kelly's shop in Draperstown, from the money she earned at the factory. She brought home a new record every Friday night, usually American and Irish Country Music. This is where I gained my love for country music and when I went to The Grand Ole Opry in Nashville, many years later, it was Mary I had to thank for knowing the words to all the old country songs. It brought back fond memories. Mary wrote out songs for Daddy to sing and played the record over and over until she got all the words written down.

Another lasting memory of Daddy is from when he had a mishap with some eggs. Mammy usually collected the eggs, but Daddy sometimes collected them when he was out and about. On those occasions, he put them into his flat cap to carry them to the kitchen. One day, when Angela and I were around six and nine, we saw the eggs breaking in his cap and we giggled as he scrubbed the raw egg off his cap. It was only in later years, when looking back, that I felt guilty about having laughed. This has always been imprinted on my mind, as it was the first time I remember feeling guilty.

Daddy always looked out for us, and when it was his turn to look after us, he always put us first. For example, it was customary for the men to get fed before us when they came in from a hard day's work. Men first, then the children. In later years, however, when my sisters were having babies and Mammy went to stay with them, Daddy looked after us younger ones and would give us the priority instead. This always makes me smile. Also, Mammy usually prioritised giving any spare eggs to the men, but Daddy kept the eggs for us on the occasions he was in charge of us. This has remained ingrained in my mind, along with his refusal to use fairy liquid to wash the dishes. Apparently, the soap left a taste on the plates. He wouldn't dry anything, either, simply scalding the dishes and cutlery with boiling water before leaving them to dry… These are the sorts of fond memories I reflect upon when thinking of him.

*

On 18 November 1971, when I was nine years old, Daddy died very suddenly from a heart attack while fixing an iron gate over at Peggy's, an old house and farm he bought across the lane at Mickey's house.

That day, he was working there alone and Mickey, who worked on the farm, was picking potatoes in the shed at our home. Daddy walked as far as our front gate before calling for Mickey. He was blue in colour, so Mickey helped him into the house and got him on the sofa. Obviously, there were no phones to call for help, and none of our neighbours had phones either, so Mickey had to get in the car and drive to the nearest public phone to call for an ambulance and to get the priest. When the ambulance arrived, it was too late. He had already died.

Mickey was only in his early twenties at the time. The whole experience was very tough for him and has stayed with him throughout his life. I find it very emotional to think about what he went through that day.

At the time, Aelish was nursing in Belfast, Lizzie was married and living in Antrim, and Mary was married and had just had her first baby about three weeks earlier. As Geraldine was working in the factory in Draperstown at the time, while waiting to get into nursing, she was the closest to home that day. So, she was the one called to come home to console Mammy. By the time she arrived at home, Daddy was lying on the sofa, already dead. She implored the medics to do something for him. She could not accept he was gone. It was very distressing for Geraldine. Father Collins was very stern with her and told her she needed to be strong to support Mammy. She was only seventeen, and I imagine this must have had a lasting impact on her.

As it was two o'clock on a Thursday afternoon when this happened, and the 'young weins' were due in from school, including me, the priest asked the ambulance paramedics to take Daddy to the hospital. Normally, if the person is dead, it's the undertaker who is called, but the priest did not want us seeing Daddy lying on the sofa, so the ambulance men agreed to take him.

I always remember meeting the ambulance on Sarah's brae just at 'Kanes Lonan' when we were walking home from school. It was driving very slowly with Mickey and Fr. Collins in the car behind it. When he saw us, Mickey got out of the car and told us Daddy was sick. We walked on home and when we got to the house Mrs Toner, our neighbour, was there with Mammy who was crying. All I remember then was being taken to Mrs Toner's house with Angela and Brigid.

It must have been a 'wild handlin' trying to get the news out to the other family members and to get them all gathered up, as there was no easy form of communication. The older boys in the house, Felly, John and Paddy, were all away on building sites in Antrim or Belfast.

Later, we found out that Daddy's sister in Belfast only learned of his death when she got the Irish News the next morning. It was not a great way to find out, and Daddy's brother Felly in 'Doon' really should have let her know. Everyone else was in too much shock to think about that.

Daddy's death had a very profound effect on everyone. He was a strong, young man of fifty-nine, with lots of plans for the future. Like the song says, 'We thought he'd live forever, he seemed so big and strong'.

But it was all over so fast.

It was a lot to process.

I particularly remember being shocked that my old, big brothers were crying. I couldn't understand it. They had always been the strong ones in my eyes. It was only later when I got older that I thought back to how Felly, John, Paddy and Mickey must have felt, realising how young they were when Daddy died. They had seemed old to me as a nine-year-old.

Daddy's funeral was on a Saturday. It snowed and was very cold. When I was going back to school on the following

Monday, I remember asking Mammy if I was allowed to play at school. The atmosphere around our home was so sad and mournful that I thought it was wrong to have fun. When I grew up, I often thought that this must have been a very sad thing for Mammy to hear me ask.

Adjusting to Life Without Daddy

After Daddy died, each of us siblings were impacted in a different way. Paddy, for example, took a more paternal role, as Felly and John were married, and Mickey got married a year and a half later. Paddy was the main adult at home. He was very caring but strict, wanting to make sure we behaved and didn't upset Mammy.

Mickey, on the other hand, took over the farm and absorbed a lot of Daddy's responsibilities, staying at home, farming, buying more land and working long hours.

Before Daddy died, big plans were made to reclaim land, take out ditches and make the fields bigger and more productive. Money had to be borrowed from the bank to fund the work, and I still remember a well-dressed man, in a suit, from the bank coming up to our house. He was there to see what work was going to be undertaken and how the borrowed money would be spent. The well-dressed bank man put on a pair of wellingtons and walked around the farm, and upon seeing that Mickey was a hard worker with a good plan, they lent him the money. Bank business has lost the personal touch since those days.

None of us could have prepared for him dying so young and so suddenly. Death was not something that was ever contemplated. Daddy hadn't even considered making a will, so Mammy signed everything over to Mickey when Daddy died. He consequently inherited all the money worries as well as the hard work, but at least this meant Mammy was able to claim the widow's pension, enabling her to raise us 'weins'. The problem had been that the farm didn't have a regular, steady income, so it wouldn't be enough to raise us. But even so, if Mammy had kept the capital against her name, she wouldn't have been able to claim her pension. So, all things considered, this was a good move.

For a period of time following Daddy's death, Mammy moved up to the girls' room where there were two double beds. Brigid and I were in one bed and Mammy and Angela were in the other. We needed her and she probably needed our company too. Brendan was eleven at this point, and when we were all ready for bed he would come in from his own room and lie across the bottom of Mammy's bed on top of the clothes. I remember looking at him one night, and Mammy must have thought I was going to tell him to get out, so she shook her head silently at me, indicating that he was to be left alone. As far as I remember, he would go back to his own bed during the night. I have often wondered if he remembers that. He was so close to Daddy and the shock of losing him so quickly and without warning was overwhelming for him.

For me, the lasting memory of that time was Mammy having no interest in herself. She cried a lot, especially in the chapel. She wore the same brown mourning coat everywhere she went. Then, one day, when I was getting off the bus in Draperstown after coming from school, I saw her standing at Burns's Corner waiting for me. She was dressed in a white and navy coat. I remember thinking to myself, 'She must be getting better.' I must have been at least eleven at that stage, as I was coming from the convent school. So, it took her at least two years to come to terms with his death. This memory came flooding back to me years later when I was faced with loss myself.

After Daddy died, I found myself taking care of Angela a lot. The suddenness of his death left an indelible mark on her. She was only six years old and there was no such thing as counselling or talking to the children about how they felt at the time. She refused to go to school and cried every morning. If we got her coaxed out and down the road, Paddy Toner, our neighbour, gave us a lift in his car to the bus, as he went to work in Taylor's yard as a mechanic. Sometimes she would not get out of his car, and many times she went back home. If I got her to school, she would not go into her class until the teacher was in, so we both sat out in the cloakroom when all the other pupils were in their class. I would then go to my class, but later I would often get word from Angela's teacher that she had run out of the school and gone down to Taylor's yard to Paddy Toner. That happened many times.

Every evening she promised she would go to school the next day and I really believe she meant it, but the same thing happened when morning came. One day, Mammy and Aunt Katie were on the school bus as they were going to visit Lizzie in Antrim, and when they got to Draperstown, Angela would not get off the bus to go to school. So, she got a day away with them. Katie bought her a beautiful wee case for her books to take to school the next day, but it did not help. Everyone bought her nice clothes for school, too, as we did not wear a uniform in primary school, but that did not help either. I was never envious of the attention Angela got because, although I was only nine, I just wanted her to stop crying. She eventually did, but I cannot remember how long it took. It seemed like a long time. Looking back as an adult, I realised that what was wrong with her was that she was afraid Mammy would disappear just like Daddy did, and no one really understood that or knew how to deal with it. These days there would be child psychologists assigned to talk to children, or trauma therapists, but back in 1971, children's feelings were not considered a priority. Children were just supposed to get over it and get on with their life.

Eleven-Plus Exam

I think they were renovating the school, perhaps when I was in Primary 5, when they merged the classes. That meant that I was in the same class as Brendan and Brigid for a while.

I always did my homework as I liked school – there was also the fact I was afraid not to do it because I didn't want to get into trouble. But getting into trouble didn't bother us all, and certainly not Brendan. He would come home from school and throw his school bag under the sofa and – when Daddy had been alive – he headed out to help Daddy with the sheep or whatever work was going on. When he came in at night, he then copied down my homework. He took no notice in class of what homework he had to do as he knew that I was writing it all down.

As I mentioned, Mammy did her best to help us with our homework when we were struggling. And one day, Brigid was asked to spell 'together' in class, and she was very proud to be able to do it as Mammy had taught her an easy way to remember: 'to get her'. It stuck with me every time I saw that word.

In Primary 6 and Primary 7, we had two lovely teachers, Mrs Regan and Mrs McKernan. Mrs Regan had a piano in her room, on which she played music and got us to dance round the room singing 'Frère Jacques'.

During the summer of 1972, I was thinking about the eleven-plus exam as I was due to sit it when I returned to school in September. I must have really wanted to pass it because I remember asking Mammy if I could send away for a verbal reasoning book the teacher had recommended. She agreed, of course, and so we went to town and got a postal order to send off; there were no cheque books or online payments in 1972. I loved verbal reasoning so much that I waited patiently on the postman every day. It wasn't often that I received mail addressed to me. When it finally arrived, with its green and white chequered cover, I was very proud of it. I would do the tests every day during the summer holidays, but I was very careful not to write on the book's pages, as I knew it might be useful for others after me.

The work paid off as I passed the eleven-plus.

When the letter arrived with the results, I was expecting it to say 'Pass' or 'Fail' or give me a grade. The letter was very complicated to read but it stated that I was selected as one of the scholarship holders, which meant the school fees were paid. It took me a few times reading it before I realised, I had passed the eleven-plus.

*

Looking back, if you were to ask my older brothers and sisters, they would say we – 'the younger ones' – got it easy. Not only did we have a bus to take us to primary school, when they had to walk across the fields, but they would also say that their Bancran Primary School was very selective about who did the eleven-plus and who didn't. It was most definitely not on academic merit. It was also the practice at that time for the parish priest to select the teachers for the schools, and because the Catholic Church financed and managed the schools and exerted their authority and considerable influence, the selection of teachers was usually from a wealthy or prominent family in the parish. Therefore, the appointed teachers used the same criteria of wealth or prominence to select pupils for the exams. Poorer families did not always get equal chances.

By the time I got to St Mary's Primary School in Draperstown, this practice did not appear to be common, and I never felt any disadvantage from the teachers. I also feel that the town school was less parochial and children were treated on their merit. So, Mammy's determination to move the 'five weins' from Bancran School to the town school certainly gave us an advantage.

I now feel incredibly lucky to have had the opportunity to get into a grammar school education. It set me on a path which, in the end, influenced not only my own career but that of my family.

The Convent

After primary school, I went to the convent school in Magherafelt, now known as St Mary's Grammar School (SMG).

Back then, children did not travel far and Magherafelt felt extremely far away. Everyone else in the family was at school in Draperstown except me. I did not get home from school until five o'clock every evening, which was a long day for an eleven-year-old. I always walked home up the road by myself after getting off the bus, and sometimes, especially in the winter when it was dark, Angela would come down to meet me as it was about three-quarters of a mile away.

One dark evening, the bus did not stop to let me off at the end of the road and took me instead over to Charlie Andy's house. When I reached the bottom of Derrynoid Lane, I could hear someone crying and it turned out to be Angela! I do not know if she was crying because she thought I had got lost or was afraid of walking back up the dark road on her own, but either way it was a lovely gesture of my eight-year-old little sister to come and meet me off the bus.

I perceived the convent to be a strict, elitist school run by nuns and I felt very out of place for the first few years. Initially, I was not happy there – I thought everyone else was rich and clever. I did not fit in.

The principal was Sister Marie Thérèse (nicknamed Tess), who remained in the role until 1977. She was followed by Sister Immaculata (Maccy). The day I arrived, Tess, who was quite small in stature, came strutting into the assembly hall, where about ninety children sat on their first day at the convent. She then declared she had broken a mirror and that it meant seven years of bad luck. Just the length of time I was due to be there... A great start for an anxious, fearful child who already felt overwhelmed.

Thankfully, I became close with three girls at the convent. I already knew Una O'Neill (née Donnelly) from primary school, who happened to be in the same class as me at the convent. We then met Caroline McCloskey (née McCormick) and Frances Gormley (née Flanagan) in our first year. We all remained good friends throughout school and socialised at the weekends together when we were teenagers, until they settled down with boyfriends. We keep in touch and meet up about twice per year to catch up on the families and have a bit of craic.

St Colms Secondary School in Draperstown, where the rest of the family attended, was completely free. Books were free, travel was free and there were no fees for the parents to pay. At the convent, on the other hand, we had to buy everything: textbooks, exercise books and jotters. We also had to go to the convent school once per year to buy our uniform. The nuns wanted to make sure we were all in the exact same uniform and I think they got commission from the supplier when we bought from there. So, we could not buy a cheaper option anywhere else.

At that time there were stalls in Cookstown on a Saturday selling blue cardigans, almost the same colour as our uniform but at half the price. The problem was that if you bought one of the cheaper cardigans, the nuns would bring you up on the stage during the morning assembly and make you parade across to demonstrate you were not wearing the correct uniform. For the first few years, I only wore the accredited uniform as I was too embarrassed to be paraded on stage in front of everyone. But after I got some confidence and realised the extra cost to my mother, I just wore the cheaper cardigan.

We also paid capitation fees every year to the school. Again, the other members of my family did not have to pay these fees, and I always felt bad asking Mammy for the money as I knew she was struggling to pay for everything. She got a widow's pension and that was to keep five children. I was almost always last in my class to pay as I kept putting off asking Mammy for it. Nevertheless, we always paid in the end, and I felt relief for another year.

Our school uniform consisted of a school beret, school blazer for the summer, a gaberdine for the winter, black laced leather shoes for outdoors, black strapped leather shoes for indoors and plimsoles for P.E. We could only wear the plimsoles to P.E. and were forbidden to wear them indoors in class because Sister Marie Thérèse said they caused a sweaty smell. After the first mid-term break, blazers were no longer allowed to be worn, and we had to change into the gaberdine – you were singled out at assembly or confronted in the school corridor by the nuns if you were still wearing a blazer in the winter term. I always tried to fit in and obey the rules, but by the fourth and fifth year I didn't care so much about fitting in. I was starting to realise that we were mostly all in the same boat, and there were not too many of my friends who were rich.

The blazer I wore in the first year carried me through the seven years at the convent. It was bought too big so it would fit me for a long time and when I outgrew it, I just pushed the sleeves up and carried on. It was then given to my niece Annette, as she was the only one who went to the same school. I think she wore it for most of her time there too. I was also very careful with the black strapped leather indoor shoes, which were never worn by me outdoors and were kept in the school all year. I wore those same shoes for the seven years I was at the school. In the end, when they got too small my big toe peeped out but again, I didn't care, they were worn only for a few hours inside every school day, and I made them do. I got new outdoor shoes at least once per year.

This was all to save money for my mother, as I felt I was already costing her more than the other children. I was always conscious of that, and even though she never made me feel guilty or complained about it, I just knew money was tight. I never felt any annoyance toward my mother about the lack of money; I always felt she was doing her best and she was a very caring mother to us all. She had extraordinarily little for herself.

In about my third year at the convent, I remember our class going on a skiing trip. I didn't even mention it at home because I knew I would not be going. Later in life, when my own children got the chance to go on school trips, I was very keen to allow and encourage them to go. Deep down inside I dreamt what it would be like to go on a trip, and I wanted my children to have the opportunities I didn't have. However, I realised many years later that you don't need to be seen to have or do things to feel confident. Confidence comes from deep inside, not from material things. Treating children with respect, spending time with them, and reminding them that they can do anything will build self-confidence more than giving them lots of material things.

As you have read, I really didn't like the first few years at the convent and I would have preferred to be with the others at Draperstown, so I planned, in my head, to move school at the end of each term. However, I never had the courage to discuss it with Mammy as I thought I would be letting her down, and so I persevered. I'm now very glad that I did, as the school prepared me for taking the next step to university. Sometimes, it is the challenging situation that gives the greatest reward.

Overcoming Anxiety and Growing in Confidence

Despite the loss of my father at a young age, memories of my childhood are generally very happy. Even so, as far back as I can remember, I was always a bit anxious. The feeling of anxiety came and went throughout my life, and although at times it was worse than others, I learned to control it. When I was about thirteen or fourteen years old, however, I started having panic attacks. Daddy was dead by this time and Mammy would take me to her side and talk to me. She was always able to calm me down and talk me out of the anxiety.

In my early years at the convent, I was also very shy. I had a few friends but was never the popular one or part of the 'special group'. In every class there is always the class favourite, and everyone wants to be like them and be with them. That was not me. At P.E. the teacher picked two captains (always the same pupils) for team activities and then she asked each captain to choose their own team. I stood mortified as I was nearly always last to get picked, maybe because I was not keen on sports but mostly because I was quiet and didn't really get to know the class very well. I lacked confidence. Writing this now brings back those horrible feelings, but I have grown so much over the years. I never feel the need now to be part of a group, preferring a few close friends or family instead.

Another challenge for me at school was that I had trouble reading out loud in class. It was customary during English and R.E. (Religious Education) for the teacher to go around the class and ask each pupil to read a paragraph. When I told my English teacher, Mrs Clayton, that I was afraid to read out loud, she was very nice, reassuring me that it was not something I would ever have to do if I didn't want to. But I did want to. I just couldn't do it. So, although she was very nice and did not put me under pressure, she did not resolve my problem. Even though it was never addressed publicly, the other girls in the class became aware of my problem and when the girl on my left finished reading, the girl on my right would start and leave me out. They were very kind, but even so, each time I felt awful. Even though there was no pressure on me to read out loud, I put pressure on myself. I hated that I could not do it. So, after some months thinking about it and not mentioning anything to anyone else, I decided that I would read one day. When the girl on my left finished, I started with a bolt and read the paragraph. I had it done before I even realised I was reading! My heart was pounding, my pulse was racing, my palms were sweaty, but I did it. The best part of this story is one girl in the class congratulated me after and said, 'Well done.' I felt she cared about me, which surprised me, but it felt good. This was a momentous moment for me which probably no one else even noticed. It was a turning point and the start of me building my confidence.

At this point, I was in my third year and my confidence grew. I began to enjoy my time at school and became more outgoing, and as a result I was more involved in the class and my academic work also improved.

One Friday afternoon I was approached by Sister Anne who asked me if I would like to go and spend a weekend with the nuns. She said I was a 'nice wee girl' and I should consider becoming a nun. She didn't know I had plans to go to a disco at the weekend, and although I might have been quiet at school in the first few years, I had NO intention of joining them at the convent!

Dancing Days and Teenage Years

Outside of school, aged about fourteen, I began going to discos, often with Una, Frances and Caroline.

Mammy was lenient with me when it came to getting out at the weekend, but it hadn't been so easy for the older sisters… As I mentioned, the older ones in my family say we younger ones were spoiled, having luxuries they didn't have, and this extended to us being able to go out more freely. Mammy had been overly protective, especially of Mary and Lizzie as they were the first to start socialising. On the occasions when they were allowed out, if they returned home with a boy, they weren't allowed to sit very long in the car outside the house. There were no lights on the street and Mammy would sit up and wait for them to come in. If the car they came home in stopped on the street and sat for too long, Mammy lit a sugar bag and threw it out in front of the car. It burned long and bright. My sisters knew that was the signal telling them they needed to get inside the house before the sugar bag burned out. There was to be no hanky panky! This image has always made me smile.

Fortunately, by the time I became a teenager, Mammy had relaxed. When I asked to go to the dance at thirteen, there was no question about it. I barely had to ask, only saying, 'The disco is on this Friday night.' Mammy would reply, 'Oh, ok.'

At first, I was allowed to go to the 'Hib' hall up in Tonagh Hill in Draperstown, where they held a disco once a month on a Friday night. This was the highlight of my month, and the constant topic of our conversations at school in the week leading up to it: Would we be allowed to go? What would we wear? Who would be there? Coming from a convent school, the chance to see and socialise with boys was a great thrill. Every now and again, there was also a disco at Moneyneana Old School, as a new school had been built in Moneyneana and the old building was kept for social gatherings, and sometimes there were discos in St Colm's School. And, of course, they were all safe, alcohol-free places.

Now and then, when Mammy gave in to buy me something new to wear to the disco, we headed to the factory shop run by Mrs McGuigan on Tonagh Hill. Mickey's Anne would drive me in. I loved getting in there, but it was a haphazard place with everything piled on top of each other everywhere, usually in plastic bags and boxes, with only a few rails stuffed with clothes. Mrs McGuigan was very helpful. She would pull out clothes for us to try on and I always came away happy with my purchase and excited about getting out to wear them. I was easy to fit then, and the clothes were worn and re-worn month after month. My favourite purchase was a pair of white jeans matched with a red and white jumper.

When I was older, I was then allowed to go to The Castle in Dungiven, The Loup Dance Hall, Ardboe Dance Hall and Clady Dance Hall. These halls attracted big country bands. The weekend wasn't complete unless we got to at least one dance. We jived and waltzed and had a great night without any alcohol being consumed.

Brigid and I didn't go to the dances together very often because by the time I was old enough for going out she was working away from home. When Brigid was school leaving age Mammy spoke to a teacher at St Colm's School and found out there was a job going in St MacNissi's College at Garron Tower, which was five miles from Carnlough on the North Antrim coast. It was a boy's boarding school at the time and although it was situated in a beautiful location with rolling green hills and extensive gardens, it was always very sad leaving Brigid there when she was returning after a weekend at home. I remember Paddy driving her down on a Sunday morning and Mammy, Angela and I would go to see her off. Initially I was enamoured that she had her own room with a small sink in it and she didn't have to share it with anyone. To me this was a luxury as we never had our own room at home or a little private place just for our own things. But the novelty of this was less appealing when I thought of Brigid being there alone. There were other girls working there in the same boat as her, and she did get to dances in Ballymena now and then with her work colleagues, but I always felt sad and heart broken when we were leaving. Mammy didn't like it either, but she did want Brigid to have a job, a career and independence. This turned out to be the start of Brigid's career in the catering business.

I was still at the Convent school when Brigid was in Garron Tower, and I remember how Mammy would buy the Mid Ulster Observer (our local paper) every week and ask me to look to see if there were any job vacancies closer to home which would be suitable for Brigid. This was in the late 1970s and jobs were scarce. When a suitable vacancy arose in Mid Ulster Hospital, Mammy asked me to send for the application and complete it on Brigid's behalf as she was still away working in Carnlough. The interview was arranged for Brigid to attend, and she got the job. Her experience in Garron Tower helped her get the job closer to home. We were all delighted that she was no longer so far away.

When Brigid was in Garron Tower, Mammy had also insisted that she learn to drive. She took lessons on her days off in Ballymena and passed her test. Mammy had foresight for all her children; she knew that being able to drive would give Brigid freedom and independence in the future. It was well used because Brigid became a very skilled driver and delivered and collected kitchen doors and other products for Patsy up and down to Dublin and across Ireland when they were growing their business.

Although we didn't go out so much together, there was one occasion when Paddy drove Brigid and me to The Castle in Dungiven. But the evening didn't quite end the way I had hoped… As I mentioned earlier, Paddy was very kind, and I will never forget what he did for us before he got married. He was always there to take us places in his car and help Mammy out. Even so, he could be strict with us too, more than Mammy. After he dropped us off at The Castle carpark, Brigid and I had a good night dancing, and the music was good. Then a boy asked me to dance, and I liked him, so we walked outside after the dance was over. It was fairly common practice to go out for a kiss if you met someone you liked. It was innocent fun. The timing was rather unfortunate, however, as it was precisely the same time as when Paddy drove back to pick us up. He was furious with me. When Brigid came out, she got in the back of the car, so it was me that had to sit in the front and listen to him scowling me the whole way home as we bumped along the Birren Road. The minute we got home, I jumped out of the car and went inside to wake Mammy up. I knew I needed to be the first one to tell her about what had happened. She was sleeping in the girls' room with the two beds to keep Angela company when we both were out, and when I got to her, I said, 'Paddy saw me outside The Castle with a boy and he scolded me the whole way home. He's really, really cross.'

'Oh, never worry,' Mammy said, to my surprise, 'Get into bed, you'll be alright.'

That was a relief. After all, she had been through it all before.

Brendan also took me to dances with his two friends, which was great fun, especially as I was the only girl going along in the car with them. Angela, on the other hand, was three years younger and so I didn't socialise much with her when I was a teenager. When she did start coming out, James and I took her out to Cookstown where she met her husband-to-be, Francis. Subsequently, every time she went out, she went out with him.

Joe used to take me to Ardboe Hall, but it wasn't a completely selfless act, however, as he had another good reason to go there every Saturday night. He had fallen for the lovely 'Kitty' who lived in Ballinderry, which was enroute to Ardboe Hall. After he left Kathleen at her house and got his tea, Joe would put on his car stereo, and we would sing all the way home. Don Williams was his favourite singer back then and because of Joe I still remember the words of all his songs.

Aside from dancing, I didn't partake in many other activities outside of school because it was hard to organise transport. We were busy at home, anyway. We did occasionally go to a youth club, aged thirteen or fourteen (which Mammy wasn't so keen on), but otherwise we had quite a simple life at home, helping Mammy. I was also studying to keep up with my schoolwork.

Potatoes

There was a lot of money to be made with potatoes in the 1970s and early 1980s, so Mickey spent a lot of time putting in acres of them. This meant a lot of work. He first had to plough the field, after which we sometimes gathered the stones in the fields, and then he would rotavate the soil to prepare it for the potatoes. We would help to drop them into the drills, using what we called a 'pratie dropper' – a machine with a long blade that turned over the soil. There were two seats, one on either side of the blade, and a long tube where you threw the potatoes down. Each time you heard the bell, we were supposed to drop a potato down the tube. This would give an even flow of potatoes into the drill below. It was very monotonous. Sitting there with our hands freezing, we alternated hands and dropped the potatoes down this tube. Sometimes, my mind would wander, and sometimes, the tube would block because a large potato or stone was stuck at the bottom. The next thing you knew, the tube was full of potatoes up to the top. We were supposed to be alert to this and keep checking, especially as whenever this happened, Mickey would have to get off the tractor, clear the tube, and walk back down the drill to plant the potatoes. I hated when this happened. I never liked when I got something wrong. He never said anything, though. And it was a defect that kept reoccurring.

At the end of September and beginning of October it was time to gather the potatoes and all the neighbours came to help.

When I was between the ages of thirteen and fifteen, we were also employed to help, but unlike our neighbours, we didn't get paid. Being a teenager, I thought it would have been nice to have some extra money to buy things like clothes and makeup, as we had always been unable to afford those luxuries. I'd protest to Mammy, saying, 'But we're not getting paid!'

'Well, you're not sitting in the house while the neighbours are working there.'

To appease us, we were promised money by Mickey, but it never came because Mammy wouldn't allow it. As long as there was enough money for the neighbours, she was happy. 'Hadn't we a roof over our head and clothes on our back?' she would say.

In fairness to Mammy, when we did earn our own money, she never asked any of us to contribute to household costs, unlike many of my friends' parents at that time.

Potato gathering was also a bit of fun. After the day's work was over, we would go back to Mickey's house with all the gatherers, where Anne would have a big dinner ready for us. The craic was good as we chilled out for the evening. However, we were quickly reminded the next morning of the work at hand when we could hardly get out of bed with a stiff back and sore legs.

Then there was the writing of the labels for the potato bags. Another monotonous job. When the potatoes were picked and bagged and ready to be collected by the merchant, each bag needed to have a label attached with Mickey's name and address. I always got this job along with Angela because we were 'good writers'. We had to write hundreds of the same thing over and over again. I was never cut out for a repetitive job.

My potato gathering days were limited, however, as when I started doing my O-Levels in 1978, Mammy was very keen that I focus on my studies instead.

I surprised myself and probably others too when I achieved eight O-Levels of B grade. Not much to write home about these days, but an achievement for me. It meant I could stay on and do my A-Levels, which lead me to third level education.

Meeting James

As a teenager, I did meet some boys and wanted to see some more than others, but it was all very innocent. And I didn't really have any significant loves or boyfriends before James.

In 1979, when I was seventeen, I had spent the summer in Jersey, Channel Islands looking after Aelish, Julie and her new baby Lisa. Aelish was pregnant with her second baby when she had to undergo open heart surgery. She was living in Jersey but had to travel to Southampton to have the surgery, and Lisa was born there on 26 June 1979. When Aelish and Lisa were ready for discharge, Mammy, Brigid, Angela, Michelle, and I went to Jersey to be there to help her. After two weeks, Mammy, Brigid and Angela went home, and Michelle and I stayed for another four weeks. Every day we helped Aelish, looked after Julie, did the washing, cleaning, cooking and shopping. In the evening, when Colin came home, Michelle and I went to the beach to swim in the sea and jump over the waves. It was invigorating after a day of work, so we looked forward to our playtime every evening. I was glad to be there to help Aelish but missed the craic at dances in Dungiven and Ardboe. I kept in touch with my friends by letter, though, and they all wrote to me to fill me in on the news. I have kept the letters to this day.

When Michelle and I were leaving Jersey, we got fog bound and sat at the airport all day. Eventually, we boarded a plane which was to take us direct to Belfast, where Mammy and

Lizzie were waiting for us. However, we were diverted to London and put up in a grand hotel. This was my first ever stay at a hotel.

I had never been in a hotel before, let alone one with an en-suite bathroom and shower (we only had a bath at home). We even had a television and room service. We loved it. Meanwhile, Mammy and Lizzie were very worried about us, but we rang them from our room to reassure them and let them know we were having a good time.

When I got back home, I was starting my last year at the convent and in my A-Level year. It was customary for the sixth-year students to have a 'Social' before Christmas – the Nuns' version of school formal, except it was held in the school. Some girls had a plus one to take, but I didn't.

A few weeks before, however, I had met a handsome man called James on a Sunday night at The Castle in Dungiven, who had asked me to dance but hadn't asked me out. I met him again another Sunday night and the same thing had happened. I told Mammy about him when I went home and said I was going to ask him to the Social, but I didn't pluck up the courage, so I went alone (James later told me he would have said yes had I asked!).

After having met twice, I wondered why James hadn't asked me out yet. It was only later that he explained why. It transpired that the group of friends he had been with on those occasions were into pranks at the time, and he didn't want me being subjected to a practical joke. He waited for a time when he would be on his own at the dance as he said first impressions were very important. He was very serious about me from the start.

The next time I saw him he did ask me out, but I was with my friend, Frances, and didn't want to leave her, so I said, 'Not tonight, maybe another night.' He was happy with that as he knew it wasn't a brush off, but I really wanted to say yes! Then, at Ardboe Hall on the following Saturday night, on 28 December 1979, I saw him come in the side door and walk across the top of the hall past the stage. My heart did a flip. He was wearing tan corduroy jeans with a checked shirt and a leather belt. He was tall and slim and very handsome with his wavy hair brushed back and cut neatly around the ears. I was hoping he would see me as there was a huge crowd on the first Saturday after Christmas. He was on a mission. He came straight towards me and asked me to dance. I was certainly going to say yes tonight.

At this time, I was already in the middle of A-Levels and had applied for Occupational Therapy. I was captivated by him, and thought he was very attractive. James was easily the tallest person I had ever met, and I must admit I even wondered whether he might be too tall for me!

Until I met him, I had not heard of the Tierney family or even anyone with that name, so he was a complete stranger to me. But it turned out that he had relatives who lived close to us, so he knew more about me than I did him. He was very familiar with my hometown and townland, too, as he took cattle to the Draperstown market on a Friday and took his uncle Mick to the pub in Moneyneana on a regular basis. He already knew where I lived as he had sussed it out before we had even gone out together.

The day after we went out for the first time, he arrived on our street, knocked on the door and walked into the house undaunted by the crowd that had gathered. It was a Sunday evening just after Christmas, so the house was full of family and children. He walked in and lifted the baby, who was sitting on the floor, and held the baby on his knee. I suppose it was a way to divert the attention. The baby was my first godchild, Paul McKeever, Geraldine and Sean's son, who was eleven months old at the time. Paul and James bonded then and continued to have a mutual respect and admiration for each other's ability and work ethics in the years to come.

I enjoyed getting to know James very much. He had left school at sixteen to attend a training centre where he was learning to become a joiner. He was a real craftsman and perfectionist when it came to his joinery work, and with his skill and creativity, he could make anything. I liked how independent he was, with his own car, and found his ambitious character attractive. He had so many ideas of how he wanted to make money, determined to become more financially comfortable in life. For this reason, although he was a very good joiner, he soon realised that this work wouldn't be enough to give him the sort of prosperity he aspired towards. He always had a solid belief in himself, so when he was eighteen, he took on his first big contract when Whitehill Park Limavady was just being built. He had been initially employed on the job on a weekly wage but was frustrated because no matter how hard he worked, he still got the same money at the end of the week. So, along with his friend Seamus Healy, he agreed a price per roof with the main contractor. This was his first experience of 'the harder you worked the more you earned'. He worked long hours and weekends and at eighteen he was delighted with the reward. This taste of success meant that he never again worked for a wage. He then went on to employ more workers so he could leverage in time and increase the productivity.

At the beginning of our relationship, I only saw him once a week, on a Friday night, as I was busy studying for my A-Levels. I would really look forward to him collecting me to bring me to a dance in The Loup, and I was always touched when he paid the five-pound entrance fee. I was quite curious, too, as to how he had such a big wad of money when he took it out of his pockets at the entrance to the dance. It was only in later years that he explained himself, 'Martina,' he said, 'I got paid on a Friday and was just showing off, trying to impress you!'

We had great times together, and I enjoyed the new experiences that came with courting, such as going out for meals, which was something I had never done before. My first meal out was in a lovely hotel called the Montague on the promenade in Portstewart. There, James asked me if I wanted an Irish coffee. 'Why not?' I thought, not wanting to admit that I didn't know what it was. After the meal, I walked into the fresh air with my head spinning. I asked him, 'What was in that coffee?'

'That was whisky.'

I had never had alcohol, so it was quite a new experience for me.

James and Angela always had a very good rapport. He called her 'wee Angela' at times, and she could do no wrong. I think the feeling was mutual. We were also both with her the night she met Francis when she had come with us to The Clubland in Cookstown. I was very protective of her as I had no idea who this boy that she was dancing with was. He was a stranger, but Angela seemed taken with him, so I asked James to check him out. After the dance set was over, James and I manoeuvred towards them, and James and Francis started to converse. The conversation lasted longer than either Angela or I wished as the music was playing, and the night was passing. I, for one, wanted to dance, so I nudged James to get back on the dance floor, and when we finally resumed dancing, James reassured me that Angela was in safe hands. James was always a supporter to Angela and Francis and their family.

The more I got to know James, the more I liked him.

He came from a large family. His only older sibling was Monica, who was four years older than him, and then he had Anne Marie, Dympna and Eugene (all who came in quite regular, two-year gaps after him), and finally Sean who was ten years younger than James. Although Monica was older, James was almost treated as the eldest child as he was the first boy. He did a lot of work around the house, including helping his father with the farm work.

Quite early on in our relationship, James took me to meet his parents. I remember driving down a very long lane before approaching a grand, two-storey house, feeling a little nervous. Inside the house, I was impressed to see the lovely carpets on the stairs – it was all very well furnished, with an old grandfather clock in the living room alongside a beautiful dresser, and another cupboard beside the large range decorated with fine chinaware and dinnerware. This house was very different from mine. It certainly looked more affluent than the McCullagh residence. And his parents were courteous and well-spoken.

Though, when I got to know James better, I realised that we both had similar upbringings. Although he had a few more luxuries than I did when growing up, they still worked hard and had similar financial struggles to cope with.

*

Life got much happier for me after meeting James. There was a lightness and a joy that I had never felt before. After going out with him for the second time, I knew he was different and that I wanted to be with him. From a very early stage in our relationship, he became my main encourager and supporter. He developed my confidence and had a belief in my ability that I did not have. He admired my ambition and was proud of what I was trying to achieve.

This was so important to me. I trusted him and valued his opinion.

Sometimes, I think, in a large family you can get lost as everyone is trying to get on with their own life and survive. There's so much happening around you. But when James came along, I felt special to someone. There was always someone in my corner, someone who put me first and thought about me, someone to talk to when I had fears or worries, and someone to share my dreams with, who didn't judge me.

It makes me smile to remember how years later, I said to him, 'Wasn't I very lucky to get you?'

'You didn't get me,' he said, 'I found you.'

That is what he believed.

Stepping into Adulthood

My last day at the convent school was also my eighteenth birthday. It was the last day we would all be together as a class because we were about to sit our A-Levels. As was customary, we had no structured classes that day and from my memory, we were just going about the school having a bit of fun and letting our hair down. It was the one and only day in the seven years there that we had any freedom in the school to just have fun. We just went from class to class and met up with friends and chatted.

I was sitting in the classroom when the secretary came in to tell me there was a phone call for me. Now, I feel I need to put this in perspective: no one ever rang the school. I had never had a call to the school and neither had any of my classmates. The whole group of friends accompanied me to the public phone box in the corridor, which I had never used before, as no one I knew had a phone. To my sheer surprise, it was James ringing to wish me happy birthday! It was a Friday, and I was seeing him that evening, but he just wanted to do something special and memorable. The girls got very excited about this as only my closest friends had known I even had a boyfriend. The wider circle still saw me as a shy girl and were very surprised.

That evening, James came over and took me to The Golden Grill in Letterkenny, where I had never been before. He gave me my first present too, which was a gold watch. We had only been going out for five months, but he had already made his mind up that I was for keeps.

We had many great adventures even in those early years of being together.

In the summer of 1981, we went on our first holiday to Jersey at a time when going on holiday with your boyfriend before you were married was seen as unacceptable behaviour by those who adhered to a stringent upbringing. Thankfully, Mammy was much more relaxed about this, perhaps because of the combination of her thirty-eight years of experience as a mother, her trust in me, and most definitely her trust in James. Right from the start, she knew James's only intention was to love and protect me, and that nothing improper would take place, which it didn't. However, my brother Paddy had adopted the father role after Daddy died and he was less lenient… He was disapproving of the holiday and made his objection very clear to Mammy. Even so, she never said anything to me and so I was blissfully unaware of this until I reached Jersey. Aelish told me when I arrived, but I was away with Mammy's blessing, and I was going to make the most of it.

We were away for almost three weeks. We spent a week in Jersey, then we took a terrifying flight in a small aircraft to Cherbourg in France. After a few days there, we had arranged to meet up with a coach of people coming from Ireland who were travelling to Lourdes, where they were going to spend a week volunteering. It was my first trip to Lourdes, but James had been there many times. I spent the week taking the wheelchair bound pilgrims to the Grotto and religious ceremonies, and James spent the week repairing the houses and doing maintenance work in the buildings we were staying in. He had much more freedom than I did, though. At night, I was not allowed to leave the facility. It was run by an Irish Priest who had strict rules about socialising at night. Unsurprisingly, James did not abide by the rules, and he found a way for us to get out and about in the evening to have some freedom.

I was looking forward to getting back on the road again with James when the week was over and the bus left Lourdes to return to Ireland. We hitched a lift with them but got off at a train station in Paris, as we were resuming our holiday in Jersey. Unfortunately, the train station we chose was only a freight station with no passenger trains leaving from there. It was the middle of the night in Paris, everything was very quiet and still, and we were having difficulty communicating in French. But even though we had no idea where we were, I was content. I had full confidence that James would sort it out. We walked until we eventually reached a taxi rank, and in the early hours of the morning, we then got a train back to Cherbourg.

As James was working at the time and I was a student, he was constantly paying for everything while we were courting. So, before we had left for this holiday, I had decided that we should both take the same amount of money with us. I wanted this holiday to be equal, with me paying my way. James had agreed to this, but about three days before we were due home, my money was getting very scanty, and I knew James had been spending an equal amount. When I told him how much I had left and told him I was concerned that we'd run out, he put his hand in his zipped pocket and showed me the extra money he had taken… 'Just in case,' he said.

It was typical of him to always be prepared and to never get caught off guard.

The Poly, 1980

From the moment I had passed the eleven-plus, there were times I felt like I was put on a conveyor belt from which I could not get off – leading me on a different path to my other family members, which sometimes felt lonely. I was studying when they were playing, and worrying about exams when they were gathering potatoes. I sat up at night revising for exams with my feet in the gas oven to keep me warm, slept for a few hours, and then set the clock to wake me up again. I then sat up in bed revising in the wee small hours of the morning, looking at my other sisters sleeping peacefully and wondering how I got into such a situation. Again, my mother never put pressure on me, and when I got stressed, she'd say, 'There's a factory in the town, it was good enough for other girls, its good enough for you too.' But just like the situation with reading out loud in class, her words did not resolve my problem. I didn't want to go to the factory in the town to work. I felt I needed to do something more. Something different.

Looking back at this from where I sit now, I feel this was all meant to be. And at my age, I'm doing what Steve Jobs talked about, 'I'm connecting the dots'.

After I had looked up Occupational Therapy in The Polytechnic prospectus and was considering it as an option for further study, it was Geraldine who told me more about it. She had been working on the wards and had some contact with the occupational therapists, and felt they had a 'cushy wee number'.

'They have a nice wee easy job and don't need to work as hard as nurses,' she told me. That was her view then and it appealed to me at seventeen as I had heard so many stories from my three sisters about authoritarian matrons, bedpans and bed baths and long working hours on the wards as nurses. Doing that felt like going back to the convent with the nuns, so I decided I did not want to follow in my three sisters' footsteps, but a career in the caring profession was something that I was attracted to.

I felt I could get the grades required, so I applied for 'The Poly' – now the Ulster University – to do Occupational Therapy. As part of the entrance criteria for the occupational therapy course, I had to write about the role of the occupational therapist. It was Geraldine's knowledge that got me through, but I left out the part about the 'nice cushy wee job'.

I got a grant to go to university because Mammy was a widow and I was determined not to ask her for any money, so I made sure the grant money lasted me through the full academic year. I was now financially independent. In fact, with my first grant money, I bought Mammy a brand-new suite of furniture for the 'Good Room', or the 'Lower Room', as she called it. It was the first brand new suite she had ever got. Prior to that, she always bought a second-hand suite. It felt good to give something back to her. And all through my adult life I tried to give her as much as I could to repay her for all the sacrifices she made for me.

I was living in Block H9 in halls of residence. Some things you never forget. Like with school, it took me some time to settle into being so far from home when I first started at The Poly. Belfast was far away in my eyes and not getting home every night was difficult to get used to. Like when I was at the convent, I considered leaving, but giving up is not something I do easily… I know now that I will stick with something even when the going gets tough.

In the back of my mind, I always wanted to make Mammy proud of me. I felt she had given me so much opportunity while denying herself of any sort of luxury.

She worried about me and wrote me letters every week at first so even though I left home on Monday, I got her letter on Wednesday and was home on Friday! There were no mobile phones at the time and Mammy didn't have a phone back then – she only got one when I got married, as I put one in her house so we could stay in touch. So, when I arrived at The Poly on Monday morning, I headed straight for the phone box on the mall to ring Mickey's house. Anne would be waiting on the call to tell Mammy I had arrived safe.

This period was a very worrying time for everyone as The Troubles were raging and the Hunger Strike of 1981 caused severe unrest and anxiety for the whole community. In Mammy's letters she was warning me not to get involved in politics and to 'say my prayers and do my lessons'. She warned me not to go out at night as I would get enough 'outings' at the weekend. I can understand how it was worrying for her, as bombs were going off regularly in Belfast. There was a lot of security getting in and out of The Poly campus, too, as there was always the threat of a bomb. In 1983, a bomb exploded in a lecture theatre killing two people and injuring thirty-three.

James's Support

If it had not been for James, I don't think I could have got through university. He was always there to encourage me; he was very proud of what I was trying to achieve and was fully behind me.

In my first term at Jordanstown, in October 1980, he got a job in Carrickfergus, just down the road from Jordanstown, with Seamus Healy working for Tommy O'Connell in Dungiven. He would call at the halls of residence and we would go for food. Sometimes I made him dinner, which I really enjoyed, but it was fish fingers and beans as there was a limit to the cooking appliances in the halls. Despite the basic meals, I spent more on one dinner for him than I spent on myself all week!

We enjoyed going out dancing on Fridays and Saturdays, but I didn't always go out on a Sunday as I had classes on Monday mornings. If and when we did go out on a Sunday, though, we went to a place called Clady where they had various dance bands playing. There were a few discos we went to in The Arches Hotel, too, along with other places.

On 8 December 1981, James and I spent our first night together in my room at the halls of residence. This may not seem like a big thing now, but back then it was massive. Firstly, boys were not allowed to stay in the student accommodation and secondly, and most importantly, I was not allowed to spend a night with James before we were married. Before this story goes any further, I need to add that I insisted he remained fully dressed for the entire night! So, James slept on a single bed, fully dressed, while I lay on the floor. And the reason James stayed with me in the first place was because I was extremely upset about a woman who died very prematurely at home, who was the mother of a young family whose father was already dead. I had taken the day off to go to the funeral and I missed a very important first anatomy exam.

This death devastated me, and the stress of exams was more than I could take. I was about to give up the whole idea of university and if it had not been for James, I think I would have gone home that day and not done the exam. James stayed with me, calmed me down, and helped me revise. I got the exam done the next day. No one ever knew James spent the night, and it was the one and only time he did, but it was worth it for me.

During my time studying occupational therapy, I got the opportunity to go on placements at various hospitals. My first big placements, at the beginning of my second year in October 1981, were in Bath and Bristol in England. This was another step for me. I had never been to England before and I was really going to miss James more than anyone else. I had been seeing him every weekend and sometimes during the week, so it wasn't easy going away for two months. It was also quite a trip for me; the only time I had been on an aeroplane had been when I went to Jersey to see Aelish, and even then, I had always been in the company of Mammy, Angela or Brigid. This time I was on my own. But again, even though I dreaded going and hated leaving James and home, it was something I knew I wanted to do.

Many months later, James said that he thought that was the end of us. He thought I would grow away from our relationship when I saw more of what the world had to offer. But my focus was always on graduating. I wanted to learn as much as I could, get as much experience as I could, and qualify.

I had no interest in anything else at that time and James was my rock.

After being in England for a few weeks, I was sitting in my lodgings looking out the window while waiting for Elsa Davidson, my fellow student, to return home from work, as we always made dinner together in the evenings. I could see her walking in the distance, but this particular evening she was accompanied by a man. I thought, 'Who is she taking home?'

When they got closer, I realised it was James. He had been working in Belfast with his Uncle John and had told him he would like to visit me for the weekend. His uncle arranged for him to get across to England with a lorry driver he knew, whom he travelled with from Stranraer to Bristol before making his way to my lodgings. I was truly delighted to see him. It also made me feel I was not that far from home.

He stayed for the weekend and for the first time since arriving in Bath, I went out to a disco and actually had a small alcoholic drink. I only did this because I knew I was safe with James, but I never drank again unless I was with him.

When he left, I was sad, but I found a wee note he left me and that helped. It is hard now for young people to understand that we did not have phones so there were no calls, no WhatsApp, no texts. He had no landline phone either, so if we wanted to talk by phone, he would have to go to a public phone box and ring the public phone in the nursing home I was staying in, and we would have to arrange the time by letter. It seems so odd and old fashioned even to write this now.

When he returned home from his surprise visit, he went to see Mammy and told her he had been to visit me. She was delighted to hear I was well and was very pleased James took the time to go and see her. They always got on very well, which was great for me as it made my life very easy. He never complained about the time or money I spent on Mammy either and she was always on his side no matter what. So, as you will read in later chapters, when her end of life came, and I thought she should come and live with us, James had absolutely no problem with it at all.

I gained a lot of experience on that placement in England which made me grow as a person as well as an occupational therapist. Little did I know back then that years later I would travel to England two or three times a month to do training and promote my own business as an independent occupational therapist.

Australia, 1982

Australia has played a major part in my life and in our family over the years, all starting because James had the courage to go there when he was twenty to get a good start in life.

James had always wanted to go to Australia and in March 1982 he left with Mickey McKenna (the Laddie) from Maghera. Not many people from our area were travelling to Australia back then, so this was a big deal for James, me and his family. Being the oldest boy in his family, James was very relied upon by his parents and his siblings, so his emigration had a huge impact on everyone.

To start with, I was very upset when James told me he was going. Even if I had been allowed to go, I wouldn't have been able to leave without dropping out of my university course. So, as you can imagine, it wasn't easy to digest his news. I thought he should have been content at home with me and his work. James listened to my worries and tried to help, suggesting he would send me money so I could visit him in the summer, and that we would get engaged when I went out there.

This helped me to feel more secure and hard as it was, I knew I needed to accept that James had always had the idea of going. He had, after all, always said that meeting me delayed his plans, but it was still something he really wanted to do. In the end, I adjusted myself to the idea that he would not be around to help and support me. I am now very grateful that he went at that time as it cemented our relationship.

It was very brave of him to leave at such a young age.

One characteristic of James was that he always knew what he wanted, and he quietly persevered until he achieved his goal. He was never very aggressive about his goals, but he was very persuasive. He did consider how others felt, but he knew what was right for him and that mattered to him. He gently brought me and others round to his way of thinking. I think this is a good lesson for everyone: it may seem selfish at the time but looking after yourself is not selfish. James sent a lot of money home from Australia and many people benefited from him going away, including himself.

The day James left, his father, mother, and grandmother all went to the airport to see him off and called at my house to collect me too. It was a very sad day; everyone was upset, and I cried most of the day.

When I returned from the airport, I went straight to my room and started to revise for the exams I had coming up that next week. I was at the end of the second year of my three-year course, which was quite intensive, and these exams were very important. I remember my brother Paddy coming to visit that day and he asked me how I was, which was quite touching at the time. I always knew my brothers cared for me, but they were never very good at expressing it. So, the fact that he even recognised that I would be upset meant a lot to me.

I think my family thought that James was gone for good, and that it was possible that he would settle in Australia. I knew this was not the case, however, despite feeling sad and upset. I knew he had not left me – we even had plans on getting engaged. He just wanted to fulfil a dream he had held for a long time.

With no phones, emails or text messages to keep in touch, we relied on a weekly letter and a monthly phone call. James loved receiving my letters, as I did his. He was very organised when he knew he was moving jobs, which he did frequently, and I got plenty of notice of his change of address. It wasn't always easy, but our love and commitment to each other grew stronger than ever. Our relationship had passed an important test.

I was very lonely without him but kept myself busy with studies and a clinical placement in the Royal Victoria Hospital in Belfast, which I hated. I also decided to get a part-time job after James left as I did not intend to socialise at the weekend when he was not there. Previously, James and I went to 'The Loup' Dance Hall on a Friday, Ardboe Dance Hall on a Saturday and The Castle in Dungiven on a Sunday or Clady (we did not go to all three every week, it just depended on what bands were playing). After he left, I had no interest in going to dances (or discos as they were called in the 1980s). I also wanted to save money for my trip to Australia – though, as it happened, I didn't need it in the end, as James ended up sending the price of the flight anyway, and he paid for everything when I got there. Still, I applied for a job at The Arches Hotel. At the interview, the owner, Patsy O'Kane, asked me what I was studying at university. I had been asked this question many times before and when I answered occupational therapy, no one ever knew what it was. So, for the first time ever, I said, 'I suppose you don't know what that is?' and she replied 'Yes, I do. I'm an occupational therapist myself. I work in Altnagelvin Hospital.' I was very surprised and a little taken aback.

It worked well for me, as I got the job as a waitress. However, on my first shift the receptionist did not turn up for work and Patsy asked me to stand in for her. It was 'a cushy number'; I answered the phones, took bookings, made up the clients' bills and looked after the till. I never had to waitress after that. Later, I paid the wages of the casual staff too.

Angela also worked there, so we always tried to get the same shifts so that we could travel to work together.

I got the grand sum of £1 per hour for my work. It may not sound like much, but I was not the lowest paid. Some casual workers were getting 75 pence per hour – Angela being one of them. One day, I urged her to ask for a raise, and told her I would do so if it was me. But Patsy was not the easiest person to approach… That day, the brave Angela did ask her for a raise, and she got it. She was very pleased with herself and so was I. On the way home, I admitted that I would probably not have asked!

I enjoyed earning my own money, as I had never had a job outside the house or a paid job until that point. Growing up, I had often asked if I could get a job in Draperstown, in a shop, but I was never allowed. I had wanted my own money, as my older sisters had all worked away from home from a young age. They went to Portstewart, a thriving seaside tourist place in the 1960s, to work in guest houses. This had all finished by the time I was old enough to go. I know it wasn't all fun for them though, and it was hard for them leaving home, but I sometimes think I missed out on an adventure when I hear their stories now. But maybe it was felt Mammy needed the help at home.

Still, my time came and aged nineteen, I finally had my own job and was glad to be working at The Arches Hotel. It also helped keep my weekends busy; it made being without James easier. Sadly, this was another lesson I had to learn later in life. Keeping busy was the only way I could get through a difficult time.

James was very successful in Australia. He was only there a few months when he had a quad of men old and young working for him before his twenty-first birthday, which he celebrated alone there while undertaking huge jobs.

James became very friendly with an Irish man called Jim O'Keefe. Jim was in his forties and along with his wife Rita, they had three young sons. Jim had been in Australia for about twenty years when James met him, and they got on very well, taking on large contracts together shuttering. They also did a huge job at Muswellbrook Dam in NSW. Jim always said James got him started into bigger money, as he'd never liked taking the risk of starting out on his own until he met James. At twenty, James was fearless, daring and ambitious. He wanted to make the most of the time he had in Australia and worked hard… Often, he was working in the bush seven days per week, and he only went into town now and again. He always said he went to Australia to earn money and not spend it, so there was no need to take a day off. He did not drink alcohol or socialise very much.

Sometimes James stayed at Jim's home, and it was there that I sent many of my letters, especially if James was moving around from job to job. He always knew they would be private there and would receive them every week. The address stuck with me all my life: Sandy Creek Road, McCullys Gap, Muswellbrook. I also received phone calls from James about every month or so. But as I had no phone at home, he arranged to ring Mickey's house on a Sunday morning. Usually, I knew when he was calling, so I would go down to Mickey's house and sit on the last step of his stairs to wait for the phone to ring. Sometimes, though, he rang spontaneously or maybe he just got the chance of being near a phone box. As you can see, it was very different back then, and in our modern day it's hard to believe that even public phone boxes were not readily available everywhere.

On the occasions James rang spontaneously, Mickey came up to our home and shouted, 'Sydney James is on the phone!' I would leap out of bed at maybe eight in the morning and run down the road. One Sunday morning, as I was running to the phone, I fell flat on my face on the road and cut both my knees. The blood was pouring out of them, but I never told James. He was on the phone for such a short time I did not want to waste the time complaining. It was a coin box, after all, and the money did not last long.

He also rang the hotel in Dungiven some Sunday nights, when Monica was working there, to catch up on the news from home, as his mother and father did not have a home phone at that time.

I was very happy that he asked me to visit him in Australia during the summer of 1982 – the thought of getting out to see him had kept me going for the previous six months. It was especially exciting knowing we would be getting engaged while I was there. We had managed to keep it a secret from everyone else all that time, so it would remain a surprise.

*

In 1982, Joe and Kathleen had announced their wedding date. It was 21 August 1982 and while I was so eager to get to Australia to see James, I also knew I did not want to miss their wedding. I could have been away in June as I was finished at The Poly but I'm glad I stayed.

Monica and I went to Australia for six weeks a few days after the wedding. It turned out to be the first of many trips to Australia for my family and me.

I was very excited at the thought of getting to Australia, although I was very anxious about the long-haul flight. I had only ever been on an aeroplane for one hour when I went to Jersey and then to my placement in England, and the thought of thirty-six hours closed in a capsule filled me with dread. But as the quote says, 'If the dream is big enough, the facts don't count.' I certainly had a big enough dream to see James again.

Monica and I flew with Air India as it was the most economical. We flew from Belfast to London, then we stopped in Geneva, Delhi, Bombay, Singapore, Perth and eventually arrived in Sydney thirty-six hours after leaving London. It was certainly not a pleasant journey, and I was extremely sick on the flight. The smell of curry nauseated me for years. I was so unwell that the cabin crew brought me up to the pilot's resting area and looked after me. They gave me a lemon to suck to settle my stomach, which worked surprisingly well, but I only ate bread and drank water for the entire flight, and I was given a small bed to lie on. Monica, on the other hand, slept most of the way and did not even miss me when I was taken to the sick bay!

When I reached Perth, I was beginning to feel a little better as I foolishly thought the journey was over. After all, we were in Australia. The flight took off and to my dismay another five hours passed before I got my feet on terra firma. I had no idea how big Australia was and was totally disorientated with the time changes and the long journey.

I have travelled to Australia many times since then and have never flown with Air India. I also made certain there was only one stop between London and Sydney. It most definitely helps with the jetlag…

The sickness and the jetlag were soon forgotten when I reached Sydney for the first time in 1982. It was replaced with excitement and anticipation to see James. But there was something that caused me a slight niggle of unease… Would James have changed since he left? Would I have changed? Maybe things would be different.

I need not have worried because as soon as I saw him, I knew that everything was fine. I was not disappointed; he was thrilled and overwhelmed to see us and was waiting in the arrivals hall as soon as we entered. He had been looking forward to it as much as me. In fact, in later years, he told me how he'd been lonely in Australia at times, but that work and his determination to succeed had helped him to deal with the loneliness.

I didn't know if Monica knew of our plan to get engaged, but it transpired James had indeed told her and even arranged for her to spend the day with his friends to give us some time to be on our own. In those days, however, proposals were not huge events as they are today, and he already asked me before he left. Still, we had a beautiful day together, going to a jewellery shop where he asked me to choose a ring. I was afraid I would pick one that cost too much, as I knew how hard he had been working, but James reassured me that I was not to worry about the money. In fact, he insisted on spending 995 Australian dollars on the ring. That was expensive then, but he said he would have it earned the week after I left, and he wanted to do it right. That's just how he was; he worked hard but was never tight fisted or penurious. He never squandered money but was generous to those he cared for, and he never put money before people.

Aged twenty I was engaged. This was the beginning of a very exciting part of our lives.

I was delighted when our engagement was official and felt as if I was walking on the clouds. I couldn't stop looking at my ring, too, marvelling at how beautiful it was. It was certainly the best possible start to our trip. That night, I dressed up and we went to Pizza Hut to celebrate. We had never eaten a pizza before, so the excitement continued…

James enjoyed showing us everywhere he had been working, and then we travelled thousands of kilometres in his Ford Holden car from Sydney along the Gold Coast to Brisbane. We left at the end of August and travelled until the end of September. We were mesmerised by the stunning scenery as we drove along and enjoyed stopping off at various locations along the way.

The first night or two, when we set off for the big tour, we stayed in hotels. We then hired a towing caravan, and the adventures began. It was exciting for all of us, including James, as he had waited for our arrival to travel around the country and see the sights. He was also happy to have a few weeks off work.

One day, we pulled down to a place where we could use public toilets and I took my ring off to wash my hands. We were back in the truck and travelling down the road when James said, 'What do you think your Mum will think when you go home with that ring?'

I opened my mouth to say something but, to my horror, I realised didn't have my ring.

'Stop!' I called out, 'I left my ring on the sink in the toilets!'

'No,' James replied, 'you wouldn't do that, would you?'

I went into meltdown.

'I did. Please stop!' I begged.

But James had known all along. He had gone to the same bathroom after me, saw the ring, and picked it up for me. He had only asked me that question to see my reaction.

The positive from that experience was that the incident scared me so much that I have looked after the ring with great care ever since.

The six weeks I spent there were one of the most memorable and enjoyable times of my life. I was on an adventure. I was on the other side of the world. I was with

James. The weather was beautiful. I thought about nothing or no one except him. I was in love with James and Australia.

Music always brings you back to a date and time. According to scientists, a song triggers an emotion that matches the emotion felt at the time the event happened. The memorable song for me at that time was Leo Sayer's 'I Love You More Than I Can Say', which was released in 1980. James sang it all the time when we were together in Australia. It became our song, and it brings back fond memories every time I hear it.

Sometimes now it can bring a tear to my eye.

I never once thought about the return journey – I put it out of my head – as I didn't want to think about leaving again. But the day arrived when I had to leave Australia and James.

I was about to start my third year of university, so staying in Australia was out of the question. I really did want to qualify as an occupational therapist. So, instead, we talked about returning to Australia after I finished my course.

If the time in Australia was one of the most memorable and enjoyable, then leaving was one of the saddest. I thought I would never stop crying on the way home. If I wasn't asleep on the aeroplane I was in tears. I couldn't even say James's name without crying. When I got home and Mammy asked me how James was, I started crying again.

Once the sadness of leaving Australia eased, I was very euphoric when I returned. My head was full of dreams about getting a job after I qualified, planning to get married and looking forward to James's return to set up home together. The adventure of going to Australia also helped me to overcome some fears and doubts I had about travelling and being away from home. I was a much more confident person.

When I was in Australia, I was so captivated by James and the country and being reunited with him that I never once considered that Mammy was at home worrying about me. When I returned, she told me how much she had fretted about me. I suppose I was the first one to travel so far from home and with no real means of regular communication it must have been a worrisome time for her. When I became a mother of four wanderers who like to do their share of travelling, I had to frequently remind myself of that time in Australia when I was carefree and did not give much thought to my mother's anxieties. I tried to remind myself not to worry and that they were very likely having the time of their life and not giving me a thought.

Completing My Studies

Back at The Poly, I had other clinical placements as well, but the most enjoyable was at Galway, Ireland from October 1982 to December 1982. This time I didn't have James to come and visit me, as he was still in Australia. But I was engaged and a much more confident and outgoing person, so it was a fun experience and the people I met were really easy going.

During the Galway placement, I worked in Clarinbridge in a learning disability hospital for adults run by The Brothers of Charity. I stayed with a couple called Anne and Sean Lynch in their home called 'Tara' near the world-famous Moran's Oyster Pub on The Weir, Kilcolgan. They also owned a pub and restaurant and had a bed and breakfast house.

In the evenings and weekends, I helped Anne in the pub, though my student colleague had no interest in it, so she did not. Having worked in The Arches, I was familiar and experienced around the hospitality scene. There were always social functions on, so I enjoyed working there. It was also easy work, given my previous experience.

Anne was very fun-loving and good craic, and I got on very well with them both. We became friends, and when James returned from Australia, we visited them several times and stayed with them. We invited them to our wedding, but they had never been to the North due to 'The Troubles' and were too afraid to cross the border. They gave us a wedding present of a Tara China vase which was made in Galway. The vase still holds great memories for me every time I glance at it. I have lost touch with them now, but I would like to rekindle that relationship at some point in the near future.

Each time I hear 'Come On Eileen' by Dexys Midnight Runners, which was a very current song when I worked with the patients in The Brothers of Charity in 1982, I recall that time with fond emotions.

One of our patients, Eileen, had a learning disability and had been in an institution since her birth. We had to teach her how to climb stairs as she had never seen a staircase before coming to this facility. We would take her for walks around the gardens to build up her stamina, but she always sat down on the grass and would not move. Then we would all sing 'Come on Eileen, Too-ra-loo-ra Too-ra-loo-rye-ay'. That eventually got her going. We had great fun on this placement, and I gained great experience on how to handle this group of patients.

When the placement in Galway finished, I went back to university, still living in Belfast and going home for the weekends to see Mammy. I continued working in The Arches, too, which was fun as they hosted many events, including weddings, so I enjoyed meeting lots of people.

Then, James returned from Australia in March 1983, in time for Brigid and Patsy's wedding and my graduation. I was bridesmaid for Brigid, and I was delighted to have James there as my fiancé.

I had worked very hard to get qualified and I was proud to be graduating. It was my reward for all the worry and sleepless nights. As Theodore Roosevelt said:

'Nothing worth having was ever achieved without effort.'

Angela, James and Mammy were my guests at the graduation ceremony. It was Mammy's first graduation ceremony, and I bought her a new suit for the occasion – she deserved it after all she did for me. She wore this suit to my wedding the following year.

And James bought me an engraved gold bracelet to mark the event.

A New Start, 1984

After graduating, I moved back home full-time, living with Mammy and Angela, having a special few months with them. I also got my first job at Magherafelt Hospital, as a qualified basic grade occupational therapist. I soon learned that I trained for three years to become an occupational therapist at a time when occupational therapy wasn't really a profession people respected or knew so much about. So, I spent a lot of my early career explaining what an occupational therapist was; even at work, it was a bit of a struggle to be part of the team and to get people to see what value an occupational therapist could bring to patients. I persevered with my work, however, and it very much felt like a new beginning in many ways. I was also still working in The Arches at the weekend, so I enjoyed having a better income.

When I got my first job, I purchased a brand-new Ford Fiesta from Sean McKeever. Having a car allowed me the freedom to take Mammy on many expeditions without borrowing a car.

As I was working in the community, the Health Board gave me a loan to buy the car at very low interest, which I paid back from my salary every month. However, they only gave me two thirds of the money needed, so I needed to raise the remainder myself. I asked Mammy how to go about it, and she told me to ask Mickey. I was anxious about asking and when I did, Mickey told me to go to the Ulster Bank where he was on good terms with the bank manager, Mr Ward. Mickey said if the bank did not loan me the money, he would help. So, I entered into what would become the first of many negotiations at a bank.

Mr Ward first asked me who my family were, then he asked me about my work, and within thirty minutes, he had agreed to give me the money. There was no formal application, I just signed to confirm I received it and agreed the terms of repayment. I was walking on air when I came out of the bank, feeling very adult and grown up.

Initially, I had been disappointed Mickey did not lend me the money, but I later realised he gave me more than money could have given me. The experience of going to the bank gave me confidence to be independent, self-reliant and to face my fears. Sitting in front of a bank manager asking for money was an uncomfortable position for me, although Mr Ward probably would have given me the loan confident that Mickey was there as a guarantor if I didn't pay it back. There was no need for that, though, as I repaid the bank within one year with the money I got at The Arches. I wanted it paid off before I got married.

On many occasions since then and throughout our lives, James and I have sat in front of a bank manager with business proposals and were successful as a team. I got more confident as the years went past, and the bank manager became less intimidating. I also never, at any stage of my life, felt discriminated against as a woman in business. When I eventually started my own business in the year 2000, as you will read about later, I approached the bank on my own with my proposal and got a very affirmative response.

*

With James back home, it was finally time to think of our own wedding, and, over time, James and I decided on our wedding date. It was to be on Saturday 25 August 1984. The Arches was a popular venue for weddings at the time, and Saturdays in August were always the first to get booked up. So, while I was still working there on the weekends, I put our wedding date into The Arches' event calendar to keep it free.

During this time, I also applied for a post in Coleraine Hospital, because even though I enjoyed my first job in Magherafelt, I wanted a job closer to Limavady after I got married.

Mammy came with me to Coleraine Hospital when I went for the interview. This is where I met Mrs Anne Campbell for the first time, and she made a lifelong impression on me. When the interview was over, I told Mrs Campbell my mother was waiting in the car. She came out and spoke to Mammy and was very courteous towards her. I knew before I left that I had been successful.

After my interview, Mammy and I went shopping and we bought my wedding dress. I had not actually told Mammy we had settled on a date, but she knew that it was imminent, so, although she was surprised to be ushered into a bridal shop that day, I don't think she was shocked. The dress cost £300, which was more than the average at that time but a lot less than nowadays. In the 1980s, the average cost of a wedding dress was just £125. More so, many brides either wore a dress that their sister or friend had worn, or a dress they hired. My sister Mary, for example, wore her sister-in-law's dress (Felly's wife, Anna). They altered it themselves to make it fit.

I loved my dress and still do. It had to be decent, as Mammy would not approve of a low neckline, and I wouldn't be comfortable in it anyway. It was ballroom style with a large, hooped skirt which swished when I twirled around, with lace across the top and lace sleeves. I also wore a short veil and a tiara given to me by Kathleen.

Following the interview and the dress purchase, Mammy and I travelled via Limavady and stopped in at St Pat's Hall where James was working on repairing the roof with Seamus Healy. I told him I had bought the wedding dress and that it was in the boot of the car. It was quite different back then; we didn't have a number of dress fittings, an entourage of guests to preview the dress before buying it, and we didn't have to order the dress first before getting fittings done. Buying a dress in 1984 was much simpler. I never even altered it. I put it on, and it fitted.

Everything was coming together.

After my successful interview at Coleraine Hospital, the date was set for me to start my new job, and I got promoted to

Senior 2 Occupational Therapist within six months of qualifying. This was not unusual then, as there was a shortage of occupational therapists, which made finding a permanent job achievable. The only downside now was that I was moving out of home again to be closer to work.

I never lived at home in Derrynoid full-time after that.

I was also yet to tell my current manager Pat Harris in Magherafelt that I was leaving. Not knowing how to approach it, I kept putting it off. After all, I had only been there six months and I was loving the experience and getting on with the job very well. Pat had an austere outward appearance, with her military walk with her shoulders back and her short hair brushed away from her forehead. She was a formidable force. In fact, I found out later she was a part-time soldier, something that would have been kept very confidential at this time in Northern Ireland. This made it very daunting for me to communicate with her, especially as I was still very inexperienced in dealing with people in authority. Every evening for about a week, Mammy asked me if I had told her I was leaving.

I finally braced myself and asked to speak to her, only to learn she had known all along. Of course, head occupational therapists communicate with each other! I quickly learned that the occupational therapist world was very small and that when someone applies for a job, the first thing the new manager will do is to find out about the applicant before they even arrive for interview. It demonstrated how naïve I was. It transpired that my fear of Pat was more to do with my lack in confidence, and not Pat's demeanour. We stayed in touch, and Pat and her husband even came to my wedding. Throughout my career, especially when I set up my own occupational therapy business, Pat was always an enthusiastic supporter of me.

I began the second post of my occupational therapy career in January 1984 in Coleraine. It seems bizarre looking back that I didn't travel to Coleraine from home every day to work. But Mammy thought it would be too far, so she got in touch with a lady she knew called Mrs Duffy, who kept a bed and breakfast house in Coleraine. The large three storey house on 44 Upper Captain Street was where I stayed from Monday evening to Friday morning. It was another joyful chapter in my life. While I was there, Mrs Duffy still had her husband, son and daughter living with her, and I became part of the family. The Duffy family were a large family and full of fun. Mrs Duffy's big golden labrador, Major Duffy, also can't go without a mention. He'd lay passively on a mat in front of a small stove, which Mrs Duffy kept lit all day for cooking and heating water. If you needed to pass Major, you just stepped over him as he rarely moved!

Mrs Duffy was a gracious, kind, soft spoken, fun, loving woman who devoted herself to her family and to me when I was there. She had long grey hair which she kept neatly tied in a roll around her head, and always looked the same – always happy looking. Every morning, Mrs Duffy made my breakfast and packed a lunch. The sandwich was always brown bread, cheese and Branston pickle. She also had a hot meal for me every evening. I enjoyed staying there very much, and every week, I went out to the The Bulls Eye, a local pub, with the family and their friends and we danced and sang and had great craic. Sometimes James would come down and join us too. Again, the music from those times always reawakens those memories, especially 'Wake Me Up Before You Go Go' by Wham, which was played over and over in that pub.

It was a hot, beautiful summer. I was in a great family home. The job was perfect. My work colleagues were cordial and polite. And I was getting married and enjoying all the arrangements. Life was very good.

I stayed with Mrs Duffy right up until the week before I got married.

Mrs Duffy was delighted when I invited her to the wedding. I felt it was my duty to ensure everyone invited had a means of transport, so when Mrs Campbell – always the lady again – suggested that Mrs Duffy could travel with her and Shaun to the wedding, that was a perfect arrangement. Mrs Duffy loved the wedding and even met an old friend, Mrs Toner, my neighbour from Derrynoid, whom she had known from her time living in England. Mrs Toner was from Galway, but she met her husband Matt Toner in England, and they came back to Derrynoid after they got married. Mrs Duffy and her husband had lived near them in Manchester. It was a great reunion for the ladies, both of whom I had a great fondness for.

I kept in touch with Mrs Duffy for many years after. I called from time to time, too, and she was always pleased to see me. One of her sons emigrated to Australia after I left, and she travelled unaccompanied to Australia twice to see him when she was in her late eighties. She was a lady of steel. Unfortunately, when she died, I was not informed, which is a regret I still hold.

On the job front, I learned a lot from Anne Campbell, my new manager in Coleraine, especially about etiquette. Anne always knew when to do the right thing. She was always full of gratitude and valued everyone. She came from a middle-class background but never looked down on anyone who was less well off than she was, and she treated everyone with respect. I built a lasting friendship with Anne and invited her to my wedding, too. The week following the wedding, Anne wrote a beautiful letter to Mammy thanking her for the invitation and congratulating her on the success of the day and her beautiful family. It was a very rare thing to get a letter of thanks after a wedding, but it was something that stuck with me, and I've tried to emulate this on occasions throughout my life. Thanking and appreciating people not only makes the person feel important, but it also helps the person who is giving the thanks. As the below quotes say:

'No duty is more urgent than giving thanks.'

'I would maintain that thanks are the highest form of thought; and that gratitude is happiness doubled.'

Anyhow, I have jumped ahead here a little. Back to the wedding preparations…

The hotel was booked.

The dress was bought.

I had a new job in Coleraine.

But now we needed to decide where we would live after we were married.

James had a few ideas of places where he would like to build a house, and one of them was Terrydremont. This land belonged to Bernard Tierney (James's uncle) and James approached him about buying it. This was not to be, as all Bernard's brothers and sisters had to agree to the sale and there was no consensus. James was disappointed, but then his father offered him a site at the 'Two Trees', on the lane leading into Ballyquin house. So, James applied for planning permission and got plans drawn up for a house.

Before we got married, we purchased a mobile home and placed it near the site. It had become quite common during the 1980s to live in a mobile home, especially if you were planning to build a house. Brendan and Angela also did this in the two subsequent years.

Our mobile home was situated on the back street behind James's homeplace. We got it rigged up and I was very happy to have my own wee corner where James and I could just be ourselves. I always enjoyed looking after James and making his meals and his lunch every morning before he went to work. Now we had our own abode, and I was excited to share it with James.

Wedding Bells

During 1984, I saved most of the money I earned as an occupational therapist for the wedding and lived on the money I got in The Arches at the weekend. I bought my 'Going Away Outfit' in a very expensive shop in Magherafelt during my lunchbreak one day because, as per the age-old tradition, the couple changed from their formal bridal attire into another outfit that they wore as they departed from the reception to embark on their honeymoon. The shop I went to was very posh and all the dresses were covered with a dress bag as they were considered very expensive. My dress was blue and white, and it cost £125, which was more than I or anyone I knew ever spent on a dress at that time. It stayed in the shop, and I paid it off each month.

The weeks leading up to the wedding were very relaxed. I was off work the week before and the weather was beautiful. Mammy and I had an excursion planned for every day to finalise the plans for the wedding, sorting out the flowers, the cake, shoes for Mammy, as well as shopping to keep the cupboards stocked up for all the impending visitors. We also had guests to entertain, such as our guests from Jersey, Elise and Marcel Toudic (Aelish's parents in law). We took them to Portrush for an outing and over to meet James's parents at their house. I still remember Mrs Toudic insisting on the tea being served outdoors at Ballyquin, an unusual practice for us Irish as we had no grand outdoor seating. The only time we ate outdoors was in the hay field, when gathering potatoes, or working in the moss. Mrs Tierney was gracious but uncomfortable with the arrangements.

Prior to the wedding day, many of the neighbours and the invited guests called at the house with wedding gifts. I always tried to be there to greet them. The gifts were displayed on a table in the 'Good Room' and when a new visitor arrived, we talked through all the gifts and revealed who bought each gift.

I don't remember being stressed in any way. It was all pleasant and heart-warming.

I have many affectionate memories of our wedding day, which happened to be on a very hot and sunny day. In the morning, I didn't get my make up done as it wasn't the practice then. But I did go to the hairdresser, as did my bridesmaids and flower girls. I then got my dress on early for the photographer coming to capture a few moments before I left home.

It was the tradition for all the family and the neighbours, regardless of whether or not they were guests at the wedding, to assemble at the house to see the bride off on the morning of the wedding. Since the sun was shining that morning, everyone was outside for the occasion, the children were playing, and a neighbour even fired shots from his shotgun! Another tradition.

I came down to the living room where large flames from the fire were roaring up the chimney – Mammy had a big coal fire lit to heat the water through the back boiler, as we had no oil burner or immersion heater. As I spun around on the floor to show off the wedding dress, Mammy saw the tail end of the dress skimming the flames. Thankfully she had quick reactions, grabbed me and pulled me down to the floor. No damage was done; a disaster was averted. I was unaware of how close I had been until Mammy retold the story with horror on her face a few months later.

James asked his brother Eugene to be best man, but he was sixteen years old and very quiet, so he wasn't keen on carrying out the duties involved. So, James decided that his friend and ally at the time, Seamus Healy, would be best man instead. Eugene became groomsman, which carried less duties. Angela and Michelle were my bridesmaids, my flower girls were Aelish and Claire McCullagh, and our page boy was my one and only godson, Paul McKeever.

One story that can't go without a mention is how James was late for the ceremony – a privilege usually afforded to the bride.

James's timekeeping was always questionable, so the night before the wedding, he had promised he would be on time. The wedding was planned for 11 am, but it didn't start until 11.30 am! When the phone call came through to Mickey's House from Anne Marie telling us not to leave for the chapel as James was still not on his way, I panicked. Not for a moment did I think I was being stood up, but I imagined something terrible had happened to him. Mammy again came to the rescue. She calmed me down, but she was likely as worried as me. Not too long after we got the go ahead, James had finally arrived. I believe it was the fastest journey to Moneyneana he had ever made.

It was Black Saturday, a day when there are parades in Northern Ireland, so I was told he got held up by the parades. But many years later, it transpired that a cousin of James's, who arrived from London to attend the wedding, accompanied James to Limavady that morning but she got lost while going to the hairdressers. James spent his time looking for her. No wonder he did not tell me that story for a long time. I would have said, 'Why didn't you leave her there?!'

James's lateness was a source of amusement for most of our married life, as the priest attributed the lateness to me and cited this in his after-dinner speech. The event was captured in a photograph by Denis Lagan, with James, Seamus and Eugene looking amusingly at James's watch before they entered the church. James, however, did not like being constantly reminded about the lateness.

Late or not, our day was not spoilt. When I entered the chapel, I could see James and the flowers he had sent me the day before sitting on the alter rails. It was Lizzie's idea to have them there, as she thought it was a lovely gesture that he should send me flowers the day before the wedding.

The parish priest of Ballinscreen, Father Deery, was the celebrant at all the weddings in the parish. He never delegated that duty to any other priest, but I insisted that

Father McGarrigle, who was our curate, would perform our ceremony. This was much to the annoyance of the parish priest, who I also really liked. Even so, I felt sorry for Father McGarrigle, who never got to do any of the joyful duties in the parish. He was a quiet, unassuming man and I wanted to make him feel important. Poor Father McGarrigle was so nervous on the day that he was sweating profusely, as he had never done a wedding before.

I felt very special on my wedding day and privileged that my good salary enabled me to have a few extras on this very significant day in my life. I remember, for example, deciding on fresh flowers, which was a departure from the customary silk flowers. I also invited the two eldest grandchildren in each of my siblings' families and there was great excitement among the young girls about getting to their first wedding. Some of them still talk about it.

After the ceremony, all the family photos were taken at the church, and the bridal party then went to a garden in Magherafelt. Although it was only meant to be the bridal party, I clearly remember Brendan accompanying us around most of the day too, while all the other family members and guests proceeded to the hotel. I was touched by his attention to me and was very happy he was there. We had Francis O'Donnell as our chauffeur for the day, with his brand-new black Ford Sierra. He was very chivalrous and opened the door for me every time I approached it, which was not something I was used to and not something that has happened many times since.

We danced for hours after the meal. James loved it. The dance floor heaved with bodies as he danced with every lady who was able or willing to get up. By the end of the day, his shirt was wet with sweat. Fortunately, he had a 'going away' outfit to change into. We did not ask the band to play a special song for our first dance as it wasn't really a thing that was done then. However, we had been to hear the band play before our wedding to make sure they were the right fit for the day. When they played a version of Eric Clapton's 'Wonderful Tonight', James said, 'When they play that song at our wedding, I will make sure to dance with you.' When the band started the song, and as James was making his way over to dance, his father stood up and graciously asked me to dance. It is a wonderful memory, and I don't regret that it was him and not James.

The music that reminds me most of my wedding is the music of Lionel Richie. It was very popular at that time and his music was very romantic. The intro music on our wedding video was 'Hello'. I get goosebumps when I hear this introduction.

All in all, it was a wonderful occasion, and some people still remember it as one of the best weddings they have attended.

Before I left for our honeymoon, I gave Mammy the money to pay for the wedding meal. It would have been a tradition for the parents of the bride to pay for the 'wedding breakfast', as it was known, but there was no way Mammy could afford it. As I wanted to give her the recognition of doing it, however, I insisted that she went to the office in the hotel to pay for it. There were 115 adult guests and 16 children, so I knew well in advance how much it was going to cost, and I had paid a deposit already. The total cost including the alcohol for the toast was £684.15.

It was customary for the newly wedded couple to leave the wedding venue when the dancing was over, which was normally at about 7 pm. Since most weddings were in the morning, it was still a long day. When the time came, all the guests came out of the hotel to give us a big send off. It was quite emotional leaving, especially for me, Mammy and Angela, as it signified the end of an era. I was starting my new life with James, and although we would always keep in touch, life had changed.

I remember a huge surge of relief and a feeling of calm when we were driving away from the hotel in our car covered with 'newlywed' decorations and tin cans trailing behind, prompting attention from passers-by as we drove through the town. For me, it was the best part of the day. At last, I was alone with James. It had been a long, hectic and enjoyable day but I was so relieved to have that part of the day over.

We pulled into a local garage to clean the car and take the cans off before we continued to The Chimney Corner Hotel near Antrim Airport. It was the closest hotel for our early morning flight and cost us £24 for the overnight stay.

We boarded our honeymoon flight the next morning, going to the Canary Islands for two weeks. It was the first time either of us had been on a package holiday.

It was a relaxing and enjoyable time, but we were also looking forward to getting home to start our new life and to get a debriefing on the wedding day from friends and family. We left so soon after the wedding that we had missed the craic about how everyone enjoyed the day.

On our arrival back, a welcome home barn dance was organised by Angela and Mammy in Derrynoid. One of the sheds was cleared out, and bales of straw were placed along the walls for seats. They had invited some of the guests from the wedding and both our families reunited to celebrate. All the grandchildren who were not at the wedding were also invited. The music played and we danced all night.

It was the culmination of a memorable four weeks in August 1984 as we began our new life together.

Settling In

Living in 'The Lane' at Ballyquin was a great start for us. We enjoyed having our own little space and all the mod cons we needed at that time for our comfort.

When I relive those early days, I am surprised how little socialising we did when there was just the two of us. We rarely went out dancing after we got married even though we had previously gone out at least once per week. We didn't go on holidays either, enjoying just a night away from time to time. I think we were just so content to be together. After all, we spent very little time together before we married as living together or even going on holiday before marriage was taboo. And, although James and I did break with tradition a few times, it was in a limited way. After our wedding, James was also really focused on work and getting the house built. We were trying to save as much money as possible.

James's homeplace underwent major renovations in the summer of 1984, just before we got married. He spent a substantial amount of his money on the house as he wanted to leave it in good condition before he started on his own house. The wedding also impacted on our savings and I had only been in full-time work one year before we got married. So, now we were starting over again, this time to build a home together.

When I had just started to accumulate savings which were being reserved for our new house, James arrived back from work one day frustrated. The engine in his Ford digger had blown up and needed replacing. This was a priority, so my first savings went to help get the digger back on track. It was acceptable throughout our lives that the needs of the business took priority over domestic needs. To me this was normal, as I had become accustomed to this growing up.

James was always very ambitious with a great drive, determination, energy and a hard-working attitude. He made overcoming obstacles and challenges look easy. He appeared to take everything in his stride. He was a problem solver. He used to say, 'Rome wasn't built in a day, but I wasn't on that job.'

When he started a job, he always made sure it was done thoroughly and to perfection, but it also had to be done at speed. He never took on a job at a daily rate. Most of his work was 'grip work', which meant giving his customer a price for the job and then proceeding to do the job as fast as possible to get the most money out of it before moving on to another job. The advantage to the customer was they knew exactly how much the job was going to cost. I used to try to encourage James to do work on a daily rate, so he was under less pressure, but he rarely did this.

When we were just married, he took on a huge project putting the roof on what was then – and maybe still is – the biggest house in Coleraine. It was for an Indian businessman who had retail and wholesale clothes shops across the country. James was recommended to Mr Guy to put on the roof, but he remained there long after the roof was complete as there were multiple problems with the house and James was capable and eager to resolve the issues which had arisen. I still remember Mr Guy calling James 'Mr James'. They had a good relationship and a mutual respect for each other, and James certainly helped out a lot. The house had an indoor swimming pool and, at one stage, when the cellar completely flooded, James had to dig drains around the house to let the water drain away. The house also had a temple, which was amazing to see in 1984 in Coleraine.

I was very happy when James was working in Coleraine in the first few months of our marriage as we sometimes travelled to work together, and he was always home at a reasonable time. Travelling to and from work together was a lovely start to our married life. However, in later years, this was not always the case as he worked long hours and away from home.

After a few months living in Ballyquin, it became obvious to us that this was not where we wanted to build our lifetime home. The plans were drawn, and we had permission to build, but it didn't feel right. We decided we wanted to get out and start afresh. James's father (Granda Tierney) was supportive and understood why we needed to find our own place. We needed space to grow as a couple and a family and we also needed physical space to grow our business. Living in 'The Lane' in a temporary capacity allowed us to weigh up what it would be like to live there, long term. There was a lot to consider, not least the shared lane, the length of the lane, the proximity of neighbours, and the fact that we would only own a site. We had no room for expansion. This was an issue, as James needed lots of space for sheds to store all his equipment and machinery.

In hindsight, this was one of the best decisions we ever made.

Dunbrock

Looking for somewhere to move to, James decided to get in touch with his great aunt Ellen who owned a farm and a small cottage in Glack. Although it is in the townland of Carnamuff, the place was always referred to as Dunbrock. Ellen was an old lady at this stage who had never married. She had been a priest's housekeeper most of her working life and was very set in her ways. She had moved to Limavady with her elderly mother (Granda Tierney's grandmother) as there were no modern conveniences in the old cottage. It was also in a rural area with no public transport, and she was isolated. The cottage and farm, that occupied thirteen acres, were derelict. James was very keen to buy this land as it would make him self-sufficient and give him space to grow his own business. James was twenty-three years old by then, and we were both mature and responsible, but even so, Ellen regarded us as young and inexperienced. So, James's father accompanied him when he went to meet with Aunt Ellen.

Granda Tierney was Aunt Ellen's favourite nephew, whom she always called 'Johnnie', so his being there would make it more likely for her to agree to sell to James and be in favour of the purchase. Johnnie added authority to the proceedings.

The sale was agreed but Ellen said we would have to pay for all the legal fees. It transpired that the deeds of the property were never transferred to Ellen's name after her mother's death, because Ellen didn't want to incur the legal costs. So, the deeds were first transferred to Ellen's name, then our name, and we paid for all the legal costs involved.

We paid £8,000 for the site and its thirteen acres in 1985. James was very proud of our first purchase together.

While we waited for planning permission to build our home, James bought cattle and put them on the land.

It was a very isolated place at first, so my excitement was tinged with apprehension. I was anxious about living there. It was a district I was unfamiliar with, too, but I had confidence in James's decision and a belief in his vision that he could make a home for us there. At that time, there were very few houses along the road leading to the farm. Coming across the Carnamuff Road from Donaghy's Corner, there was only Burns's house, which was dimly lit, and Annie O'Hara's house up a lane off the road, which was never lit up, only a faint light came from the O'Hara's window, but rarely an outside light. The road was very dark.

In the early days, I rarely went down the road towards Derry. I had no need to. I was working in Coleraine, so I always drove towards Donaghy's Corner. Years down the line, I am still unfamiliar with some of the neighbours who live down the road, but I can now count fifteen houses from Donaghy's Corner to our house, all illuminated with extravagant lighting. It's never dark along that road now and it has become a very busy thoroughfare, with delivery lorries coming and going all day long.

When we first bought the site, the land was covered with trees all the way out to the road, and there was a small overgrown path which led to the front door of the old tumbledown cottage. James, Eugene and I spent the weekends clearing it and the Ford digger which sapped our first savings paid us back a hundredfold. It withstood plenty of demolitions and excavation in the years ahead. We cut up the trees into small logs, and then I put the logs into plastic manure bags and sold them for firewood. It was the first of many entrepreneurial ideas that would be hatched in that homeplace.

James was adamant that a shed was essential to keep safe all the equipment and supplies we would need to build the house, so that was the first thing we built. It has metamorphosed many times over the following thirty years. Its first function, though, was as a haven for our mobile home when we moved it from Ballyquin to Carnamuff.

Planning permission for the house took a few months, and we started building in 1986. I still remember the footings going in in June 1986 – the day my aunt Kathleen died (Uncle John's wife).

While this was all underway, I was pregnant with Jonathan. I had had a previous miscarriage in August 1985, so we were delighted to be expecting our first child. But when the building work got underway, we were still living in 'The Lane' at Ballyquin, and James was spending most evenings in Carnamuff working on the house. James wanted to do most of the work himself, firstly to save money but also because he had a real interest in building his own house. He took pride in the finished product; he liked everything done well and had a very high standard of workmanship.

As I was pregnant and alone in Ballyquin most evenings, James decided to move the mobile home over to Carnamuff so that it would be much more convenient for him to work in the evenings. I was very pleased with this move. It was now coming into the autumn evenings in 1986, the days were shorter and the nights darker and I didn't like being alone, especially as I was getting closer to my due date. It was lonely in 'The Lane' when James was not there. I also wanted to move before Jonathan was born. So, James, Francis O'Donnell and Eugene helped move the mobile home one Saturday in December. This is when James had the 'great' idea of moving it into the shed. I was not enthusiastic about this proposal as it was very claustrophobic and dark when the big doors were closed over. But James insisted it would be a good shelter from the winter storms. I knew he was right, but I was still uncomfortable with this arrangement. I was always claustrophobic and still get attacks now and again, even if I have learned to control it.

As usual, logic triumphed over emotion and the mobile went into the shed.

When I was leaving Ballyquin for the last time on the Saturday morning, James's father, John, came to wish me well and gave me a linen tablecloth which he had got as a wedding present. I think he was a bit saddened that we were leaving and that his plan for us to live near him had not materialised. I still have the tablecloth. It was a thoughtful gesture. John was always respectful towards me, and we had a good relationship, and he visited us every Monday night for many years to come. He also showed a keen interest in our children and was very proud of all their achievements.

Mammy stayed with me for the first week when we moved and helped me reorganise all my possessions while also cleaning the mobile home. She didn't want me lifting anything or cleaning as I was almost ready to give birth. Angela was the only other person present the day we moved, but she was expecting Grace, so she was there for moral support rather than practical help. Francis and Angela stayed over that night as Francis wanted to help James the next morning.

For the first twenty-four hours there, we had no indoor running water. Angela and I still reminisce about that Sunday morning, when we woke up with no water to wash or to make breakfast. Somehow, even though we were two heavily pregnant ladies, we carried the water in with a small basin. We then went to Mass and returned to make dinner. We still do not understand why we did not go out for dinner that Sunday instead of trying to cook! Fortunately, by the end of the Sunday, we had light, heat and water, and James and I were ready to embark on another chapter of our story.

Becoming Parents

As I was overdue, I was admitted on Sunday 21 December for a routine induction on Monday morning. However, on examination we were told that I was already in labour, and I was taken to the labour ward on Sunday evening at 6 pm. The Donegal midwife, Lizzie Greer, was on duty when I arrived, and we got on well. She was older and very reassuring, but her shift ended at 8 pm. When she was leaving, she wished me luck and said she would be back in the morning, and she would come and see the baby.

It was a long night.

I was intoxicated with 'gas and air' and not fully aware of what was going on. The pain relief did not agree with me and at one point I panicked so much that my blood pressure rocketed to a dangerous level. I kept dreaming about the house we were building, and asked James repeatedly whether the roof was finished yet. James and Seamus Healy were putting on the roof at the time and the project seemed to be never-ending, so this was utmost on my mind when gas and air had taken over my senses.

At one stage during the night, James got up to leave the room and I cried, 'You can't leave!'

The nurse tried to reassure me that he would be back, but I said, 'You don't know him, when he goes out, I never know when he's coming back.' It was not unusual, after all, for

James to go out to meet someone and not return for hours. In my woozy state, I thought he would leave and forget to come back.

When Lizzie Greer arrived back on Monday at 8 am, she enquired how 'wee Mrs Tierney' had got on. She was informed that I still had not delivered, so she made a direct line to my room. She examined me and said, 'I'm getting you ready for theatre, but I'm giving you one last chance to deliver this baby.' At this stage, both James and I were over tired and distressed at the length of time this process was taking, and the baby was distressed too. We were young and inexperienced and worried. I also didn't have Mammy to call upon because Mammy was a worrier and so, when possible, I tried to reduce her anxiety. For three out of my four children, she did not know I was in labour until the baby had arrived safe and well.

I really can't remember what Lizzie did, but less than one hour after she entered my room, Jonathan was born at 9.05 am on Monday, 22 December 1986. At nine pounds and fourteen ounces, he was a big baby for a first baby!

It was not an easy delivery. Jonathan got stuck. It was called shoulder dystocia: his head was delivered but his shoulder was caught. Lizzie was able to free his shoulder, but she said she heard a crack and thought she had fractured his collar bone. Fortunately, he did not have a broken bone, but he did suffer from Erbs Palsy (paralysis of the arm). It was either that or death. It was a frightening experience, and due to severe blood loss, I needed several pints of blood following the delivery. Since I was very exhausted, I worried that I would not be able to look after the baby, but this fear proved unfounded, like many of my worries, as I recovered quickly from the ordeal.

Lizzie was very upset about his injury and sent Mass cards and wrote letters for months after to hear how he progressed. We were very grateful to her and indebted to her for Jonathan's life. We kept up a friendship with her, and James and Jonathan even visited her in Rathmullan a few times in the following years.

Jonathan was kept in the neonatal unit for a few days. When James came to visit, we both went up in the elevator to visit him. One day, on the way to visit Jonathan, we were alone in the elevator when James produced a red velvet ring box. It was an eternity ring he had got made to fit round my engagement ring. He had taken the engagement ring into the jewellers some time before to get it fitted. I never noticed it missing as I was unable to wear it at the end of the pregnancy, as my fingers were swollen, so his gift was a surprise. It was a very touching moment, especially as he had put so much thought into it so well in advance. This was characteristic of James. He was unpredictable; he never conformed to the norm of buying birthday, Christmas or Valentines presents every year, but he would arrive home unexpectedly at no particular set time and give me a present of jewellery, flowers or a simple gift. I did get Christmas and birthday presents, too, but not regularly. I learned not to expect them and knew he would compensate for it at another unexpected time.

Jonathan and I got discharged on Christmas Day. It was time to take our baby home. Ever since, I have thought that having a baby at Christmas is a magical experience. It was for me.

James collected us from hospital, and we went directly to my home in Derrynoid for Christmas dinner and a party. It was the first of many parties that our extroverted, fun-loving son would attend. I think Jonathan was born to party; he is outgoing and has friends across the world.

James was completely hypnotised by the new addition to our family and because it was Christmas, he was off work and able to spend a lot of time looking after us. This was helpful because with the experience of being a new mother, coupled with the drama of the birth, I was overwhelmed and so I appreciated James's undivided attention at that time. The timing was also fortunate because there was no paternity leave back then. Most fathers just went back to work as usual, and the mother was left holding the baby.

One drawback of a Christmas birth in 1986, however, was that the shops were all closed, and I could not get clothes and other items for the baby. I had the essentials, but it was not enough, especially as I had to change him three to four times per day. At the time, it was 'bad luck' to bring home a pram or extra baby things before a baby was born, but this was usually made up for by the fact that new babies were swamped with presents. For us, though, there were no presents because of the holidays.

One day, I was sitting down and crying when James came in. He was concerned something had gone wrong, but I was crying because I had no clothes for the baby. So, James rang his old friend, Mr Guy, in Coleraine who opened the wholesale premises for us a few days after Christmas. James did a trolley dash around the shop, gathering up multi-packs of vests, baby grows and anything coloured blue that fitted a zero to three-month-old baby boy. By the end of it, we had the back of the car laden with bags and there was no need to buy baby clothes for the next six months.

Mammy, of course, came to look after me for a week after James went back to work. She was always on hand to help, especially after new babies were born. Every one of my sisters and sisters-in-law called on her for assistance at these times. It was never even a question of if she would help; it was expected that Mammy would arrive to lend her experience, especially to new mothers.

Jonathan was a very happy baby and easy to look after. Unfortunately, though, I had to return to work when he was six weeks old as I had a new temporary job in Limavady. The starting date had been non-negotiable as it was a new post, which had been created in Limavady due to political pressure given that the area did not have an occupational therapy service. I was therefore the first occupational therapist in the Limavady area. As I was hoping this job would become permanent, I needed to take it.

We soon settled into our new routine of work and parenthood, with the added exercise programme I devised for Jonathan to help his Erbs Palsy. Every time I changed him, I exercised his arm. Though, as he grew, I never drew attention to his limitation in shoulder movement and consequently Jonathan tried everything when growing up, even learning to skip in P1, which was difficult due to the lack of rotation in his shoulder joint. He still has restricted movement, but it hasn't inhibited his ability to enjoy himself or to succeed in life.

During this period, we were still living in the caravan in the shed and the house was progressing slowly. Every evening after James came home from his daily work and Jonathan was asleep, we both went out to work on the house. We put up all the plasterboard, the skirting and door frames. It was at times like this that I was very glad we had left Ballyquin. If I had still been living there, I would not have been able to help James and I would have been home alone with the baby most evenings. The building of the house was most definitely a labour of love, and it has been my refuge ever since. To this day, as soon as I open the back door and walk in, I feel at ease.

In the summer of 1987, the caravan was beginning to feel very claustrophobic and cramped with all the additional baby gear. The house, on the other hand, was coming on well, with all the plumbing done, the kitchen fitted, the heating turned on, and a front and back door to secure the house. I had heat and light; what more did I need? So, I moved into the house before James got home from work on a sunny Saturday afternoon in August. There were no internal doors and no stairs but there was a good sturdy ladder. I moved all the kitchen stuff, as we already had a breakfast bar with its table and a few chairs. We didn't have a sofa, but we had a bed for ourselves and a cot for Jonathan. The house was warm. I was happy. In fact, there was so much space I didn't know how I was going to fill it up! I also knew that James would dedicate himself to getting it finished now that we had moved in.

James worked very hard on planning and creating our ideal home, and his attention to detail and perfection is evident in many features he built. One outstanding example are the stairs. When we moved into the house, we used a ladder to reach the first floor because James wanted to make the stairs himself. It was a big undertaking, which was going to take time. The process started in the shed, where James made a jig to hold the steel girder which he was going to mould into a curve to give the stairs a unique curvature. He then lit a large turf fire in what is now the front lawn below the front gate. I watched from the front door as intense heat and smoke encircled James while he manually pulled the steel girder around the jig to mould it into the shape he wanted. The process continued over many nights. The metal railings were then made with large pieces of mahogany screwed on top to make the banister. James made a special tool to carve the shape of the banister, which he planned for hours to achieve a smooth finish. He then sprayed the mahogany banister with varnish and sandpapered it over and over again to leave a gloss finish. He was a man on a mission, with sheer determination to produce something irreplaceable, and which will now exist for generations in memory of him. Thirty-five years later, it has never been redone.

He could easily have ordered a set of stairs, but the pride and satisfaction he gained from his workmanship and the legacy he left was worth all the effort.

A few weeks after we moved in, in September 1987, I discovered the family was increasing again and baby number two was on the way.

The Summer of 1988

The summer of 1988 was beautiful, warm and sunny. Our new home was bright and spacious, and the aroma of fresh paint and new wood hung in the air. The bare floorboards upstairs made a crackling sound in the sun's heat.

I spent my afternoons sitting outside while Jonathan played about on the stones. He walked before he was one, so he was already steady on his feet by June and there wasn't a quiet moment. With the heat of the sun combined with an overdue baby, there was little I could do except sit. James spent his time cutting hay in the fields above the house, and Mammy was staying with us as I was due to go to hospital any day to give birth. Michelle (Lizzie's daughter) was training to be a hairdresser in Limavady, so she was also staying with us during the week.

My due date had come and gone and there was no sign of anything happening soon. Mammy had been with me for a week by the time Monday evening on 13 June came around and she decided to go home for one night as she needed to get shoes for an impending wedding. She had thought the baby would have arrived by this stage and that she would have been free to return home. I was now seven days overdue but had no indication that anything was going to happen soon…

Off she went, promising to return on Tuesday.

It was warm that night and after Jonathan fell asleep, I lay down in bed with the windows open to allow the room to cool. I could hear the sound of James's tractor still working in the field, and it was getting dusky when James finally came to bed. He was only in bed for about thirty minutes, though, when I suddenly knew the time had come. I woke him up and went to Michelle's room to tell her I was going to hospital. She was now called upon to look after Jonathan.

We arrived in Altnagelvin Hospital at approximately 1.30 am and I was immediately taken to the labour ward. After my experience with Jonathan's delivery, I had decided not to take any pain relief as I felt I was not in control when I was medicated. The pethidine (pain relief) had a negative effect on me, and I didn't want a rerun of that experience.

The night progressed but the labour did not.

The staff were very aware of my previous history, so they were being very careful and monitoring the baby frequently. One nurse asked James what size he thought the baby was. They knew the baby was big, but they had no way of knowing how big. Either way, I don't know why they thought James would know!

At 8 am, it was time for the day staff to begin their shift, still with no progress being made.

The doctor was called, and labour was induced.

Five and a half hours later, at 1.30 pm, Ryan was born – weighing eleven pounds and eight ounces. I had taken no medication except a few puffs of gas and air at the very end stage. He was the second largest baby ever born in the hospital – he looked one month old! When we were taken to the ward, all the nurses came to see him and there was a constant flow of visitors asking, 'Where is this big baby?' I was checked for diabetes as this can be a reason for large babies, but I was not a diabetic. I just had a beautiful, strong, healthy baby.

When James got back from the hospital after the delivery, he rang Mammy to tell her the good news. She was shocked but also disappointed that she went home, and she was disbelieving about the size of the baby. She said, 'You mean eight pounds, eleven ounces, not eleven pounds, eight ounces!' But James reassured her that he most definitely had it right. From over sixty grandchildren born to Mammy, Ryan holds the record for the largest baby.

Mammy had returned, ready to help, by the time I got home from hospital. Though, I was more experienced with a baby by then and Ryan was easy to manage as he didn't feel like a fragile new-born.

James's Aunt Mary had given me a very regal-looking green pram with large wheels on it, which I hadn't used for Jonathan because I had no space to move it, but I put Ryan in it and wheeled him across the floor upstairs. As there was no carpet upstairs yet, the noise of the wheels on the floorboards seemed to rock him to sleep.

The first night, when Ryan woke for his feed, Jonathan was still sleeping in our bedroom, and he woke too. He bounced around the bed so excited about the baby and refused to go to sleep, crying every time James tried to put him in the cot. Ryan then became unsettled, cried and wouldn't sleep. For about one hour we had two crying babies, a tired mum and a frustrated dad. When Mammy heard the pandemonium, she came into our room and took charge. She pulled Jonathan's cot out of our room and into his own room where she put him to sleep. Everyone slept. Except me. I was the one crying now. I felt so guilty about Jonathan being taken out of our room. I felt the separation and it tore at my heart. I thought he would feel abandoned and rejected. In hindsight, I should have prepared Jonathan better for the new arrival, but I was young and inexperienced.

It was my first but not my last time to feel the separation of my children. As they grew up, I had to let them become independent, progressive individuals, hiding the heart-wrenching emotion I felt time and time again when they left.

*

I returned to work in September 1988 and both Jonathan and Ryan were left in Ballyspallen Day Nursery because there was no family member I could rely on to look after them, with them all being too far away. It was both emotionally and financially challenging to leave my two babies at the nursery, but I had to work.

Ryan's diet was very strict, as he developed eczema as a baby. I decided to not give him any dairy products, and as my neighbour milked a goat every day, Ryan was fed on fresh goat's milk instead. I also perused all the shops and visited our friend Mr Guy again to buy 'pure' cotton clothes for him. Although he had some health challenges, he was a quiet baby, had a good appetite, rarely cried and was easy to look after.

A Frightening Time

On 27 December 1988, I was busy preparing dinner for Brendan, Geraldine and Mammy as a thank you, as Brendan and Geraldine always gave Mammy her Christmas dinner. Ryan was lying lethargically on the sofa after his long afternoon nap, and I noticed he was uncharacteristically uninterested in his bottle. I was hurriedly setting the table, keeping an eye on the oven, and watching Ryan while he just lay passively on the sofa. Mammy then arrived and was immediately drawn to him, asking how long he had been lying there. I explained that I had just taken him down from his cot after a two-hour sleep, but that he was still tired. She felt his feet and said, 'The wein is not well, he has cold feet and that's a bad sign.' She startled me and demanded I go instantly to the doctors. The dinner was forgotten.

James and I headed for Dr McKenny's out of hours surgery. On examining Ryan, he asked only one question: 'Was the baby able to sit up independently before tonight?' The answer was yes. He had been sitting up, but he was now so flaccid that he was unable to sit. Without hesitation, Dr McKenny diagnosed Ryan with meningitis and ordered us to go directly to the hospital. My heart was pounding in my chest, my tongue was dry, and I began to shake uncontrollably. My mind went back to the day he was born and the difficulty I had getting him into the world. The tears started to flow. As usual, James was reassuring and positive even though he was probably as terrified as I was.

We hammered up the Derry Road, knowing Doctor McKenny had rung ahead to let the hospital know we were arriving. He had told us to go automatically to the children's ward as timing was critical. Urgent attention was required. Ryan never made a sound until they did the lumbar puncture. I was asked to leave the room at this stage, but I heard his squeal from way down the corridor. I think it would have been easier for me if I was the one getting the lumbar puncture; I felt the pain intensely. He was given intravenous antibiotics right away and James and I settled in for night duty. He was monitored throughout the night and given medication every four hours. I never left his side.

A young female doctor with long curly hair was on night duty, and every time Ryan needed his medication she was bleeped. She arrived looking tired and unkempt, and she kept pushing her hair back from her eyes. To me she looked barely awake. I stood beside her quizzing her as she prepared the medication, 'What are you giving him? How much does he need? How much have you in the syringe?' I had heard stories about tired junior doctors making mistakes and she was not going to make a mistake with my baby.

Needless to say, Mammy had stayed to look after Jonathan, but James returned home to be with Jonathan the next day, as we'd just disappeared in the night.

On the second day after Ryan was admitted, he was crying unceasingly, and I suggested to the nurse that he must be hungry.

‘No, that baby is too ill to eat,’ the nurse said.

But Mum knows best. I contacted James and told him to bring in Petit Filous yogurts, Ryan’s favourite. To the astonishment of the staff, he ate two without taking a breath. He was now on his recovery path, and I was a very grateful and thankful mother.

We were so fortunate. Everything was aligned for us to have a very positive outcome that night: Mammy arriving just in time; her experience with children; Doctor McKenny’s accurate and speedy diagnosis; and staff who were experienced and caring. Mammy had come to the rescue once again with her care and her wisdom and saved Ryan’s life. She stayed to help us and didn’t get back home until Ryan was discharged on her birthday, 2 January.

And Then There Were Three

In February 1989, I was still off work as Ryan was not ready to be cared for in a day nursery. He needed individual attention and I was too traumatised to leave him. Then, I began developing severe chest pains and felt I couldn't breathe. I talked to the doctor about this, and he suggested a chest X-ray but the results showed there was nothing physically wrong.

The children's ward was on the tenth floor of the hospital and for the week Ryan was in there, I had climbed the stairs two or three times daily as I was claustrophobic in lifts. This, combined with the stress and anxiety over Ryan's illness, meant I was experiencing panic attacks. I had also lost my confidence as a mother. Every time either of the boys showed any sign of being unwell, I found myself sitting in the doctor's waiting room. The fear of meningitis is still with me today. I now automatically feel panic if I see any potential signs of my grandchildren having that illness.

In time, as Ryan recovered, the chest pains eased. I returned to my gruelling daily routine of getting up each morning, hurriedly dressing and feeding an energetic and playful two-year-old and a six-month-old, packing their bags, dropping them off at Spallen Day Nursery, and travelling on to Coleraine. By nine in the morning, I was at my full-time job as a community occupational therapist. My line manager then was a single, thirty-something lady who lived alone in a spotless little bungalow with manicured lawns. She drove a perfectly clean little Volkswagen Polo with no sticky finger marks on the windows and no crisps strewn on the back seat. She changed her car every year, but you couldn't tell as she always bought the same colour. Her life was quiet and based around routine and she was single minded. This shone a luminous light on my multitasking, hurried and juggling lifestyle. She was always early for work and sitting composed and studious at her desk when I dashed in just on time. Thankfully, the journey to Coleraine gave me time to get my breath back and I always gave the impression of being in control. Like a duck, I was calm and unruffled on the surface, but I was paddling like heck underneath.

At twenty-six years old, James was firmly focused on building a successful business, which translated into fourteen-hour workdays, six days a week. He left for work before seven or earlier every morning and returned late, which didn't leave much time for shared childcare. Michelle was staying with me and studying as well, so at least I had company some nights when the boys went to bed.

I wasn't back at work for long after Ryan's illness when I found out I was having baby number three.

My first thought was about the X-ray I had when I was suffering from chest pain, being overwhelmed with anxiety about how this could affect the baby. To my relief, Dr McKenny reassured me that all would be well. My next thought was, 'How am I going to cope getting three babies out in the morning before work, and can we afford the childcare?' Having three children in a day nursery was not cheap. I was getting palpitations just thinking about it. I voiced my frustration to James, saying, 'I have so much to do, you are never here, I could do with some help.'

'OK,' he said, 'What do you need help with?'

I was thinking, 'Oh good, he understands and he's going to offer to do more.'

I spilled out a list of things I needed help with, and he came to the rescue again, saying, 'Ok we will get someone in to do that!'

He suggested we get someone into the house to look after the children and do light housework when baby number three arrived. This meant I could go to work without the added stress of getting three children out each morning. It was clear that James didn't expect me to cope with everything on my own, but he was not going to get involved in household duties either. Still, although he was not a domesticated man, he was progressive enough to suggest outside help. Having a nanny or even a cleaner was not something I ever expected to have as no one I knew had the luxury of this type of help. But this soon became the norm in our house, and I always had someone to help with either the children or the household chores.

I was also lucky that James had a forward-thinking attitude to women working outside the home. I knew lots of men who either expected their wives to manage everything inside and outside the home or just stay at home and do everything themselves. Equally, it was always my choice to return to work. James never put pressure on me. He was always supportive and respectful of my career.

I wanted to contribute financially and felt it was necessary; my financial contribution was a constant and regular source of income, which paid for the day-to-day necessities. On the other hand, James's more sizeable income may not have been as regular as mine, but it helped us grow and accumulate more assets, giving us the freedom to have a better lifestyle. As a result of him continuously building his business, we always enjoyed good holidays, an upmarket car and other things improving our lifestyle.

The added bonus of me working was that I enjoyed my work once I got there. It was only getting there which was stressful, especially as it was up to me. There was never an expectation that James would stay later to help in the morning or come home early to help with the night-time routine. At that point in time, men were generally not expected to do that and those who did were considered henpecked. But James had come up with a solution to the problem, and we got someone in to help.

I firmly believe now that fathers should help with childcare duties, and I am glad to see my sons at least share some of the responsibility of childcare, albeit still much less than the mothers.

In the summer of 1989, I got a taste of what it would be like to have a live-in nanny. I was about four months pregnant and still working in the community, which meant a lot of driving. Michelle had decided she wanted to go to America in September as her then boyfriend (now husband) had gone out there to work. She suggested that she would look after Jonathan and Ryan at home for June, July and August so she could save up money for her travels. It was mutually beneficial to Michelle and me. It was heaven getting up each morning, having my breakfast, going to work and coming home to a tidy house with two content and happy children.

At this point, I was still waiting patiently on getting enough money for the red carpet for the hall stairs and landing, as we had been walking on bare boards for about two years. The reason we had to wait for the carpet was because James had driven into the yard on a bright, brand new Zetor tractor from Willie O'Brien one day. He pulled up to the front window beaming from ear to ear, very pleased with his new purchase. Mammy, who was with me at the time, congratulated James and then turned to me to say, 'You will get the carpet time enough.' She always supported the business and the men.

Finally, in November 1989, two years after I moved into the house with no doors, I finally got my red carpet on the stairs and landing, and the 'Good Room' was furnished. On 2 November 1989, I was then getting the red curtains up in the hall and landing, feeling happy about finally getting the curtains. But the pleasure was overshadowed by the fact I was waiting for James to come home and take me to the hospital to give birth to Martin. I was looking forward to seeing our new baby, but emotional about leaving the other two behind. And I was apprehensive about the delivery.

Again, Mammy was there to look after the two boys when I was admitted on the afternoon of Thursday 2 November, due to be taken down to the labour ward the following day. After having two daunting deliveries, still fresh in my mind, I decided to try an epidural. By this stage, James was quite nervous about the impending ordeal, so before he arrived at the hospital for the delivery, he went to see Fr. Martin at the monastery in Portglenone to ask for prayers.

Martin's birth was different but nonetheless eventful.

I was taken to the delivery suite at about two o'clock in the afternoon and the epidural was administered. However, it only gave pain relief to one side of my body, and by the time I was due for delivery, the full effects had completely worn off because there was no doctor available to top it up! It was also too late to take any other medication, so Martin was delivered naturally with only a few puffs of gas and air.

Martin was born at 6 pm on Friday evening, 3 November 1989 and weighed nine pounds and three ounces. The smallest baby for me.

It was my conclusion that there was just no easy way to give birth, but it was always worth it.

I was very proud to take my new baby back to a fully furnished and beautiful home. No mobile home or bare wooden floors for Martin. All of James's and my long hours of work over the previous year had paid off.

Things were looking good. We had three beautiful boys, a magnificent home and plans made for the future. We always had an optimistic feeling of opulence. We strived each day to advance and progress both for ourselves and for the family. We wanted the best that life had to offer, and we were prepared to work for it. We always had the attitude that anything worth having was worth working for. We made sacrifices with our time to get what we wanted, but I can't say I regret any of it. I believe we passed on a work ethic to all of our children and a belief that they could be, do, or have anything they wanted to work for.

Granda Tierney was with Mammy in Carnamuff when James rang to deliver the news, and they decided that the third boy should be called after his mother. I was pleased and in agreement as I had not decided on a name. However, I wanted to add another name, and Graham was my choice.

We always christened the babies the closest Sunday possible to their birth. Martin was born on Friday 3 November, we came home on Sunday 5 November, and he was christened on Sunday 12 November. I had no time to register him before the christening but planned to do it soon after. After asking Felly and Monica to be his godparents, we were ready to proceed. On the day of his christening, Father Donnelly, the parish priest of Limavady – who was known for his Irish Nationalist beliefs – asked me what the baby's full name was going to be. When I said 'Graham Martin', he proceeded to the sacrament of baptism and disregarded the first name completely, without any comment or discussion, just christening him Martin. Some priests believed that children should be called after saints, so if the name wasn't in the Bible, then it was forbidden. Irish names would have also been acceptable. Priests now do not have the same dominance over their parishioners and parents would not accept this show of authority.

As we exited the church, I said to James, 'He never said Graham.' His response was, 'Oh, don't worry, I'm sure you can put Graham on the certificate when you are registering his birth.' But I was talked out of the name by the time I registered him, and I teased James that he must have paid the priest to omit 'Graham' from the christening!

Martin was aware of the naming saga, but when he got the chance to choose a name for his confirmation, oddly, he did not choose Graham. He chose Michael.

*

Having three boys under three was both exhausting and fun. They were always doing things together, and what one did the three did, but as they got older, I was aware that they needed some individual attention. So, every now and then each one would get a turn to have a secret day with me. On that day they could decide where we went and what we did. The best part was the other two did not know where we went or what we did, as it was just between the two of us. A secret day. They also had a secret drawer, which was to be opened by no one except the person who owned it. Not even me. It was their secret place. I never looked in it, but in hindsight I'm not sure if this was true of the boys.

When Mammy came to babysit the three boys, they thought they could play up on her. When she put them to bed, with Jonathan and Ryan in one room and Martin across the landing in the other, they would wait for what they thought was a safe length of time. Presuming she was away downstairs they would come out of their room to carry out some mischief they had planned earlier. But to their surprise she was sitting in the hot press, which was situated between the two rooms, saying her rosary. She would let a shout at them, and they would scarper back to their room, their plans foiled by an expert in children's antics.

The three boys spent most of their free time up in the fields as far up as McGinnis's house. They played in the river, building houses and generally getting very dirty tramping through the mountain. I never worried about them. When I thought it was time for them to come home, or if their dinner was ready, I would go out and blow the horn of the car. Within minutes the three would appear covered in muck up to their eyeballs.

During the holidays, they were accompanied by their cousins, as our house was always a popular place for the cousins to visit. If they were not up the mountain they were away working with James. And when he was in Dublin, and they were much younger, they would take turns at going down with him for a few days during the summer, as James felt it was unsafe to have more than one to look after on a busy building site. I was never very popular when time came for them to come home as I was the one who had to collect them. I recall Ryan huffing all the way home from Armagh, where James and I met to do the handover.

New Ventures

After around fifteen years of being an occupational therapist, I never really felt like I had settled into the job. I loved the patients and felt inspired to see the impact I could have on their lives, helping to support and rehabilitate them, but I never really fitted into the job situation. Perhaps I wasn't such a good employee, not being so good at being there on time or leaving at the right time. I frequently stayed late if my patients needed me and wanted the freedom to choose my own working hours. I know health boards have limited finances and need to establish criteria and waiting lists, but I didn't like to be the one to implement these rules. For example, many patients who, in my opinion, required specialised equipment, could only receive it if they met certain criteria. I wasn't thrilled with such strict regulations.

So, as my career ticked along in the background, we had a number of other enterprises going on.

In 1993, while in Dublin, James came across a company called Amway through one of the girls he met who worked in a bank. Amway is what you would call multi-level marketing – in essence, a company promoting lots of products and recruiting others to sell the products to increase turnover. It was legal and above board and there were some inspiring stories of people who came into the business and made a lot of money through it. James believed in the business concept, in the training they provided, and in its principles. Upon looking into it more, James and I wondered if it could be a good opportunity for us. Being eager to make lots of money, we decided to enter this new venture. It seemed like a manageable workload, too, because it was only supposed to be around ten to fifteen hours a week. That was not quite how it went, however, and it consumed our lives from 1993 to 1999… It ended up taking *much* more time than we originally thought, and James spent most of the weekends working on it. Combined with his own work, it meant long hours away from home and a lot of driving. But he was a great believer in Amway, nonetheless.

I wasn't so keen on the idea at the beginning and remember being asked about what my goals were at the first meeting. I said, 'My children.' I didn't have big goals of going to Florida, buying a yacht or anything like that. But still, James felt it could be a really good opportunity and so I supported him and got behind the idea.

The longer we got into Amway, the more I had to do; hosting meetings, inviting people over, learning to do makeup demonstrations, going to meet and chat with people. I was very much involved and so was all the family. The positive side of the business was that Amway provided teaching and training opportunities. They recommended that you read a book every month; that you listened to a tape every week; attended a seminar every week; and attended weekend functions four times a year. It was brilliant for networking and professional development, and they often had guest motivational speakers giving talks at their events, including Les Brown and other very successful people. Those speakers motivated and inspired us.

Our three boys also attended these motivational seminars from young ages. And I had signs up on the walls for the boys with inspirational quotes, such as: 'If you can see it, you can be it', 'Readers are leaders', and 'You can do anything, never give up no matter what'. This was what we were being taught, so it was what we taught them. On that front, it was a very positive influence on our lives and the boys still use some of the Amway teachings in their work.

At the same time that I was involved with Amway, I also did 'Colour me Beautiful' and trained as a colour analyst in Kent, which was quite costly at the time. Once qualified, I bought all the materials and set up a small salon in the dining room at home. When ladies came for an appointment, I advised them which colours would complement their skin tones, what colour makeup they should wear, and gave them a colour swatch which could be used to help choose the right colours when shopping for clothes. This complemented my work with Amway, as I had been trained to sell their makeup products as well. I was making quite good money, charging around £35 for a colour analysis appointment alone. People came in pairs, too, so I did quite well.

At that time, James was working in Dublin from Monday to Friday, busy building his business and the Amway business. We had a lot of costs to think about, from James's machinery, our mortgage, and all the usual costs involved with having a family. I wanted to do anything I could to help, so I opened a bed and breakfast at our house in 1995.

With James away during the week, I slept in the same room as the boys on the ground floor, freeing up all the rooms upstairs for paying guests. We charged £15 per night which was not a lot of money, but it was a good extra source of income. I ran the bed and breakfast myself, doing everything from preparing breakfasts to cleaning the rooms. It was fun for the boys, too, who have always been entrepreneurial. They enjoyed seeing new faces coming into the house from all over the world. Ryan enjoyed counting the money, and Martin and Jonathan chatted to the guests and helped with serving breakfast.

My decision to stop the bed and breakfast did not come until 2001, when I got a phone call one day from Martin who had just come home from primary school. I was still at work in The Disability Centre, which you will read more about shortly, and guests had arrived looking for accommodation. Martin welcomed them in and rang me to say, 'I have put them in the end suit.' It was the 'en suite' but he said it wrong. There and then I decided I needed to make my mind up with where my focus was to be. I could not have my children coming home to guests arriving and me still at work.

To add to the busy schedule, I was also involved with Unislim; a club similar to Weightwatchers that had been set up by a woman in Ireland. I ran the club in two different areas, one in Eglinton and one in Garvagh between 1996 and 1998. The boys were between seven and ten at that point, so they came out with me and helped by popping leaflets through people's doors. Even as young boys, they were always business orientated, thinking about how they could make money. They also came to the Unislim sessions with me, as James was away in Dublin working, and enjoyed collecting the money from people arriving, talking to the attendees and welcoming them in. This was a fairly successful venture, too, but it only ever brought in enough money to help buy groceries and cover other essential costs.

As you can see, it was a very busy time for us. So, apart from our 1995 trip to Australia, we didn't go on foreign holidays when the boys were in primary and secondary school. Instead, our trips mostly comprised of the Amway weekends away, where we spent our hard-earned money – they always had events in the best hotels. Most of the time we had difficulty affording to go, but we couldn't miss a seminar or weekend. So, four times a year we went to these events, sometimes held in Scotland, Cork, and other places.

*

One time, at one of Amway's events, we heard a teacher from Australia speak on stage. Her name was Lisa McGinnis and she said that her dream had always been to reach out to as many children in the world as she could, to tell them they could be anything, have anything, and achieve anything they wanted. But as a teacher, she couldn't reach the people she wanted to. One day, when she was walking across a beach in Australia, she heard a song in her head that said, 'I can do things that seem unreal, because I am a walking, talking miracle.' With the song stuck in her head, she went back to her husband, who was involved in music, to ask him what the song was. She sang three verses to him, but he had never heard of the song. It didn't exist! Next, she recorded the song, made a book and CD, and managed to reach people all over the world. We bought this book and CD for our boys, who were only nine, ten or eleven, and they would walk around the house singing, 'I'm a walking, talking miracle.'

It is amazing what you can do if you believe in it.

Another speaker who attended one of the seminars had been in a plane crash and been paralysed from the neck down and could only communicate by eye movements. He had spent months in hospital recovering. He was called 'The Miracle Man'. His story was so compelling that a documentary film was made about him. At the Amway seminar, the documentary was shown, including the whole plane crash scene and his recovery journey. When the film ended, the whole screen went black and there was complete silence. Then 'The Miracle Man' walked onto the stage. It was very dramatic. He said the power of his mind had got him through it, and he learnt to walk, talk, and do everything again. One of our team, who was with us, actually fainted at this point. The emotion and shock of it was remarkable. These were the sorts of experiences we had with Amway that made it worthwhile.

Australia, 1995

Despite the hectic lives we were leading with all our working ventures and young family, we managed to get away for a memorable holiday in Australia in 1995.

Until this time, all our holidays were in the south of Ireland in what would now be described as Airbnbs. In the years 1990-1993, I was determined that we should have some sort of holiday, so we rented self-catering cottages in Cork, Killarney, Ballybunion, and Clara Lara Fun Park in Co Wicklow. They were great fun. We packed the back of James's red Toyota Hiace van with a double mattress for the boys to sleep on, the big regal looking green pram for Martin in 1990, as well as toys, clothes and food. The boys would lie or sit in the back of the van and off we went. Mammy always went with us on these adventures. She loved touring Ireland.

After his experiences in Australia, James had a desire to work there after we married but I didn't want to leave Mammy long term. Although, we did go through the emigration process in January 1987 when Jonathan was a baby, but we were not successful. I think James hankered after Australia for a while, but we eventually realised that we had made the right decision to stay in Ireland and put down roots for ourselves and our family. However, we returned to Australia in 1995 and James enjoyed a journey of reminiscence. It was then that he agreed he had done the right thing to build a lasting home and business in Ireland.

When we visited Australia in 1995, it was Jonathan, Ryan, and Martin's first time on an aeroplane, so the trip was very exciting for them, as it was for James, who had always wanted to return. It was exciting for me too, but I was also apprehensive about taking three small boys on such a long trip…

We decided to visit Malaysia en route as James's brother Sean was there and he was keen for us to go and see him. That meant the children had to get vaccinated, but they were so excited about the trip that the necessity of injections did not deter them in any way.

Mammy was not approving of the trip. She did not try to stop us going but she did express her fears and anxieties about the boys. I got lectured on a regular basis about 'watching the weins', as she always had a vivid and exaggerated imagination when it came to potential catastrophes. I do understand, however, that this was a huge occurrence for her and that it was unconventional at that time to go halfway around the world with three small boys – just for a holiday. Although travel is much more normal for families and children now, not many would undertake this jaunt, even today.

Anyhow, once we had made the decision and the date was set, the preparations ensued. It took a lot of planning and packing for all the family to be away for four weeks. Passports had to be got, visas applied for, vaccinations arranged, and shopping was to be done. I started packing about three weeks before we were due to leave, using the spare room I had at the time. I put all the suitcases in there and just kept filling them gradually.

The anticipation grew as the date got closer, as did my anxiety.

Yet again, I was pushing the boundaries of my comfort zone, but I felt that I could achieve anything with James to reassure me and spur me on.

This trip certainly opened the boys' world and their minds. It gave them the belief that anything can be done, and that the world was their oyster. They were never scared to travel, to try new things and to look for new opportunities. Granda Tierney liked to travel as well, and always used the saying, 'Travel broadens the mind'. It most definitely opened the world to Jonathan, Ryan and Martin. When opportunities came up at school for travel, or when they wanted to expand their business in later years, travel was never an obstacle.

The boys did not want to leave Australia in 1995. We had stayed with James's sister Dympna in Sydney when we arrived; travelled as far north as Brisbane on one journey; and south to Canberra on another trip. The night before we were to return home, I was packing, and Ryan asked how long it was until we were going home.

I said, 'We are leaving tomorrow, don't you see I'm packing?'

'But you packed for three weeks before we left,' he replied, not happy to be leaving.

Although Australia holds great memories for me, many times over the next thirty-five years the decision to stay in Ireland proved to be right for us. I was also very close to Mammy and could not imagine living my life on the other side of the world when she might need me. As it turned out, she did need me many times throughout her life but particularly at the end of her life.

Changing Our Focus

With Amway keeping him and us busy, alongside his other work, James was working around the clock. It simply wasn't sustainable, as he worked all day and then all night to meet prospective clients. I don't know how many times I got in the car, drove all the way to Dublin with his suit and shoes, just so that he could get changed in the car and go straight to meetings. Sometimes he didn't even have time for dinner. It was too much and translated to a hectic, busy lifestyle for us. Really, in the period between 1993 and 1999, it was very much Amway that took over most of our time.

Sometimes the things we are attracted to in a person can be the same things that become a problem. James's ambition and drive and his tiring work ethic sometimes took over our lives. When we had a disagreement, it was usually about the amount of time he spent working, the late nights, and him rarely being at home. It became a struggle for me to cope with everything on the home front while supporting his work goals. Thankfully, James recognised this, and we decided it was time for a change.

After a lot of time and effort, it was getting to the point where this big dream we had with Amway was just not materialising. Whilst the training and experience we got stood us in good stead for what was to come in our futures, the Amway business itself just didn't work out for us. And certainly not because of a lack of enthusiasm or effort on James's or my part. We drove across the length of the country, flying to England, Scotland and Wales, bringing other people into the system too – the more people you brought into the system, who purchased the products, the greater your income would be. Unlike pyramid selling schemes, with Amway we bought the products at the same cost we sold them for, with the bonus paid on the overall turnover. As they always said, it was a people business: if you built the people, the people would sell the product. Therefore, if you had enough people in the business, you could make money. But the reality was that you needed a lot of people to be very successful.

We had always known our family wasn't complete, but after Martin was born, we had decided to wait before having another child in the hope of giving ourselves the time to reach the successes we had set out to achieve with Amway and our other work. We were completely immersed in our busy lives; from James's work, my full-time employment as an occupational therapist, the B&B, Colour me Beautiful, Unislim, and Amway – not to mention looking after the children, too. We wanted to reach a stage whereby I would be able to have the time to spend with a new baby, so we kept putting it off. But by the time I was turning thirty-six, on 23 May 1998, our attention turned once again to having another baby. I reiterated my concerns that I was getting no younger and I thought we were running out of time. Despite the pressures of work, this was something James also always wanted. We had waited long enough; we could not put our life on hold any longer.

Soon after these discussions, I was pregnant with Louise – or our 'wee pink one', as James called her – who came along exactly nine months later.

While I was expecting Louise in 1999, James was getting a bit frustrated with Amway. We started noticing that some of the people higher up weren't quite following through with what they said, and a few things started happening that we didn't understand. For example, sometimes the goalposts were moved just when you were reaching the goal. James got a bit angry about this, as he was the sort of person who liked honesty.

We had tried our best for around seven years, but we decided that was it. We called it a day.

Neither James nor I regretted the time we spent on Amway. The experience taught us how to communicate with people, how not to be scared of travel or success, and to try new things and take risks. It certainly had its benefits. But by 1999, it wasn't working out financially for us.

We used to have a big, red Mercedes and I got James a personalised number plate on it with the letters: STP (Show the Plan; Sell the Products; and Stuff the Pockets – Amway's slogan). We never did stuff our pockets. But we did show the plan and sell the products. I don't know anybody in Ireland who really succeeded, and, on reflection, I think we would have done much better getting away from it sooner. Still, it was a brave step to take to leave when we were so invested, but you have to take everything in life as an experience. There is no point in having regrets.

The way I see it is that we are here on a journey, and Amway was part of our story. It was time for the next chapter in our lives.

A Wee Pink One

I might not be politically correct today to refer to a baby girl as a 'wee pink one', but James was very much a blue and pink person. The preoccupation with gender neutrality was not something topical in 1999, at least not in our house.

Jonathan, Ryan and Martin were ecstatic when they found out we were going to have a new baby. For weeks leading up to the due date, the boys couldn't wait to get off the school bus each evening to see if the baby had arrived. There was a despondent look on their face when I opened the door, and the bump was still there. They thought that the baby would just be there one day when they came home from school. They had told their friends, their teachers, and even the bus driver about the imminent arrival of the new baby. The bus driver even bought Louise a present!

The boys were home from school on a Wednesday evening when I had the feeling all day that the time had come. When James came home from work to take the boys to Monica's house, they knew we were going to the hospital to have the baby. We left the house at 7.30 pm with Coronation Street on the TV! My excitement surpassed the slight nervousness I felt. It had been over nine years since my last delivery and the memory had faded. I was relaxed and calm. I felt mature and prepared. I had learned to control my anxiety and control my thoughts. I also was not scared of pain relief anymore. The woozy feeling no longer put me in a panic, and I took it all in my stride. I took all the pain relief offered to me, but the labour was still long. It was probably longer for the boys waiting at home though, as they thought it was only a matter of going to hospital and bringing the baby home.

Our midwife was a lady called Rita, from Donegal, and at 3.15 am on Thursday 25 February 1999 she delivered Louise into the world – our much longed for daughter.

We hadn't known the gender of the baby and when she was born, James was proud to announce to everyone that he had 'a wee pink one'.

He was very excited.

Even though we had speculated beforehand about the sex of the baby, our main concern had always been about the baby's health. Still, I know James had secretly been harbouring a desire for a daughter.

James was delighted to return home and give the exciting news to the boys. They then arrived early on Thursday afternoon, hurrying into the ward with their arms full of flowers, teddies and cards for me and the baby. They pored over her, fascinated by her wee fingers and hands. They wanted to lift her out, and they each got turns at holding her. Ryan was in P7 and due to go on his school trip in June, but at my bedside as he looked into the cot, he announced that he didn't want to leave the baby. I said, 'That's ok,' knowing well that the initial awe and wonder would have waned slightly before June. At school, they told the teachers and their friends about their new baby sister and Jonathan even wrote a poem about her.

It is difficult to put into words the excitement around Louise's arrival. James walked on air for weeks. He was certainly not working away from home now. He had returned from Dublin and his days of staying away were coming to an end. He invited every friend, work colleague and neighbour into the house to see her, as is evident by the array of photos taken with each person holding Louise.

On the day of her christening, I prepared a meal in our home for all the family. We had about thirty guests and I was proud to decorate the table with pink napkins and flowers. It was a true celebration. On the evening of her christening, two weeks after she was born and the day after we had Ryan's confirmation party, James had a 'surprise' after party. Yes, it was a surprise to me too. He invited all the 'campers' and the neighbours over to celebrate the christening.

Mammy had stayed with me since we got home from hospital, but her usual pattern when new babies arrived was to leave after the christening. So, we had all the food cleared away, dishes washed, house tidied, and the boys organised so that I would have a quiet, peaceful night after the hustle and bustle of the two previous days. But before Mammy got out the door, the new guests were arriving with gifts and drinks – ready to party. It had somehow slipped James's mind to let me know that a party was planned.

With no prior warning, there was no food and no preparation for the guests that packed into our sitting room. It was the only time that I can recall Mammy ever being annoyed with James. She had always backed him up no matter what he did. Not this time. She was cross.

All's well that ends well, however.

Mammy went home while Anne Marie, who was still with me, raided my freezer and got food organised for the guests who had now gathered in the room where Cathal McCann had already started singing. But Monica and I just sat in the kitchen as we were both worn out. After all, I had just had a baby and Monica was about to deliver her third!

James and the boys had the best night's craic, and the ad hoc party became a memorable night for everyone for different reasons.

The summer of 1999 was great. I had taken maternity leave in December 1998 and was entitled to sixteen weeks altogether, which meant I was due back at the beginning of May 1999. However, I was still breastfeeding Louise at the time, and knowing that this may well be my last chance for a long time to get an extended period off work, I decided I was taking the summer off. The time spent with Louise and the boys was precious and we enjoyed many days at the beach, with the boys also loving their time going to work with James.

Coming Home

James had worked in Dublin for a number of years by the time we had Louise, commuting back and forth on the weekends. It had been a testing time, especially as this had been during the Amway years. Sometimes, he didn't even get back home until Saturday evening if there was a big or urgent job to finish. Then he was back in Dublin by Sunday evening, preferring not to commute early on Monday mornings. The days were long for him, but he did some great work there over the years, renovating many of the SuperValu shops in Dublin and the surrounding areas. His positive attitude drove him forward, too, as he never saw anything as a problem – things were simply a challenge to be overcome. In fact, anybody who met James said that he could sort out any problem. He just had that sort of mentality. Hard as it was, his work in Dublin also helped us become more financially independent.

At one stage, James had been getting a bit tired of being away from home, so I said, 'Why don't you just come home and get a job?'

He could have got a job at any of the contractors, as everyone knew his skill and workmanship. But he said, 'I just can't work for anybody, I need to do my own thing.' He couldn't face working for contractors; he found it soul-destroying to work nine to five, Monday to Friday.

He liked doing it his own way and it paid off.

However, it was time for a change after a five-year stint in Dublin. With Amway out of our lives and Louise born in 1999, it was time for James to come back home and start building his business, focusing more on the north. He started installing automated milking parlours for farmers, which soon became a big thing in dairy farms. And he consequently began developing a good reputation for building, installing, and setting the concrete for these parlours. He was never short of work, and he had various people working for him at different times, with some men staying with him for many years. He could have up to fifteen men on the job with him sometimes.

Although he was very busy, it was good to have him home every evening, and no longer in Dublin.

The Disability Centre

In 2000, I still felt frustrated in my job as an occupational therapist in the community at the Waterside Health Centre. I wanted to leave the job, but my other work wasn't bringing in enough money. At least I was only working part-time by this stage, as I had a job share with another colleague called Joanne.

Joanne had been a colleague for years and shared my frustration with work. One day, she said, 'Martina, you know how you are always having business ideas? Why don't you set up a disabled living centre, like the one in Musgrave Hospital?'

This was a place where people with disabilities could go and try out various pieces of equipment like wheelchairs, mobility scooters, specialised mattresses, reclining chairs, etc., before purchasing them. There was nothing like this in the northwest where I lived, so I immediately knew this could be a good idea.

'Do you know what, Joanne, you and I could set up a centre together,' I said.

As a professional group, we had always talked about how we needed one of these centres in our locality. But this fell on deaf ears and the Trust never did respond.

After giving it some thought, I felt that this would be an exciting next venture for me. And Joanne said that if I did it, she would leave as well, and we could do it together. This gave me confidence to make the leap of faith. So, I went ahead and decided I was going to resign from my job.

James must have been away working at the time as I remember calling him to tell him I was leaving my job.

'When are you leaving?' he asked.

'I'm leaving by the end of the year.'

'That's ok,' he replied. 'What will you do?'

I gave him a quick overview of what my plans were, and he said, 'Go for it.'

James was very supportive, which encouraged me. He was not concerned about me leaving a 'good, secure, pensionable' job. He knew I had a drive to do something more and he was behind me all the way.

The cogs started to turn in September 2000, and I started looking for suitable places to rent. There were new units in the Vale Centre in Greysteel, which had been built after the Rising Sun Bar mass shooting in 1993. It was around seven miles away from home, so it was very convenient and ticked all the boxes. It was not very expensive either, as it was a community project backed by the European Union to revitalise the area and provide jobs and encourage innovation.

Meanwhile, Joanne was hesitant about leaving her job until she was sure everything was set up and ready to go. Joanne was very organised and always knew what money came in each month and what she needed to live on. On the other hand, in our household, there was never a set amount of money coming in as James's work was mostly 'grip' work. But we always knew we could manage. More so, I had lost interest in my job and could not wait to get out. So, as I was impatient to get started, I set most things up and consulted with Joanne along the way.

With the premises arranged, we contacted all the suppliers we had known through our occupational therapy work: suppliers of wheelchairs, beds, chairs, hoists, and so forth. We explained we were occupational therapists setting up the centre as a private business and asked whether they would provide us with products to enable us to carry out assessments. We also asked for a 25% discount if we sold their products.

If you don't ask, you don't get...

We actually got the whole of the unit filled with equipment the suppliers donated to us, including one supplier that came and fitted a stairlift. It was very exciting to see it all come together.

I didn't want clients to pay for assessments, so I got the money for client assessments from the suppliers instead. For example, they would sell me the chair for £600 and I charged the clients £700, which was the same retail price they would have paid if they bought the chair direct, but now they got a professional assessment to ensure the equipment met their needs. I didn't add on any money. I felt this was important from an ethical point of view. As an occupational therapist, I didn't want to make profits from patients. When one supplier heard this, he said I would only succeed in business if I lost my 'health service mentality'.

But I never did.

To me, health service mentality means putting the patient first. This is what I have done throughout my career and what has now become instilled in Seating Matters. It's a clinical company and the needs of the patients come first. We assess patients, see what they need, and then we get the product to meet their needs. Of course, we have to charge them, but we are providing a service our patients require.

My job in the health service ended abruptly when one day, before Christmas, I decided I had had enough. I visited a patient who was an articulate, educated lady, who sadly couldn't climb the stairs because of COPD. Her house was open plan, and her stairs had a curve, so I had to recommend a golden rail stairlift which curved up the stairs. The health service at that time didn't like installing golden rails as they weren't reusable. What they did, instead, was to put a through floor lift in. But this lady didn't want this as it would take up valuable space in her small room. So, she asked who she could write to in order to make a complaint as she was not willing to accept the decision. As I was obliged to do, I advised her how to make a complaint. When the letter was received by the relevant person at the time, he rang me up and said, 'How dare you give out my name to a patient?'

'Hold on a minute,' I said. 'There's a complaint procedure and I followed it. You're sitting in your ivory tower making rules for us to implement, and then when somebody doesn't agree with them you come and speak to me like this?'

It was the final straw.

I was really dissatisfied with my job by that point and ready to leave, so I left my office, went over to my boss – a lovely man with whom I'm still friends – and told him I was leaving. Thankfully, I was able to use the annual leave I had accrued to leave and not return. I was not staying one more day.

It was a salient moment. And time for a fresh start.

Whilst I didn't yet have an income, I knew James would provide for us in the interim.

Growing the Business

Sadly, James's father died suddenly from a heart attack the Sunday before the scheduled opening day for The Disability Centre. I had to ring Joanne and tell her the news, and we decided to delay the opening date by two weeks or so.

Louise had just turned two when Joanne and I finally had our opening day on 25 March 2001.

Everything was set to go, and we began building the business. We started off job sharing like we did when we worked for the Health Trust. I worked Monday, Tuesday and Wednesday, and Joanne worked Wednesday, Thursday and Friday – with Wednesday as our overlap day.

For the first few weeks I sat in the newly furnished, big unit raring to go, with all the equipment set up, but there was no phone ringing, and there were no customers knocking on the door. Those early days were quite frustrating because I couldn't leave in case somebody came in or telephoned. So, I was stuck there each week until Wednesday when Joanne came in. Then I could get out and start promoting the centre. I went to nursing homes and other centres, promoting our work as much as I could. Even on Thursdays and Fridays, my supposed days off, I kept promoting. I didn't go home and do whatever others do on days off – I knew I had to put the hours in to get the clients.

We had a busy open day and invited all local interested groups and individuals to view our equipment and learn about our services. We had media coverage from local newspapers and even got an interview on Channel 9, a local TV station at that time.

The business started to grow, with clients asking for assessments in nursing homes and in their own homes. At this point, I decided we needed a van to transport the equipment. We bought a new Peugeot van from Sean McKeever Cars. I was very proud of it. Soon, I knew we needed a second, and one day I said to Joanne, 'Our next van will have central locking; I'm fed up with running around locking all the doors.'

Joanne exclaimed, 'Our NEXT van?!!'

Things were moving too fast. Joanne didn't want to get into debt, and she was always concerned about whether we would have enough money to pay ourselves at the end of the month. We did always manage to generate enough money for our wages. But while I was thriving on the chase and excitement of building the business, it was nerve-racking for Joanne.

One day I went into work and Joanne said, 'I have something to talk to you about.'

'OK. What is wrong?' I replied.

'You can't be doing this – working in here Monday and Tuesday and then promoting out there on your days off.'

'What can we do?' I replied, 'We have to build up the business.'

'I am not prepared to do it and feel bad you are out there doing it.'

Joanne was a very talented artist. She loved painting on her days off. So, she couldn't spend her days off promoting the business. I didn't mind – as I was happy to do it. I told her I was happy to continue if she was happy to cover the office for the three days. I even offered to employ her, but it wasn't the right fit for Joanne, and she decided to leave around August 2002. Joanne needed certainty and security, which doesn't come easy from running your own business, especially in the early days. We're still friends now, and while she has always been very supportive of the business, it just wasn't for her.

I persevered, determined to make the business work. I started doing medical legal assessments for solicitors to generate income until the business took off. This, in itself, became a very lucrative business which sustained me financially, but it was not what I wanted to do long term.

My boys were ever enthusiastic, too, and I still remember them coming off the school bus and the first question they asked me was, 'Did you sell anything today, Mummy?'

They were only at school, but they loved being part of the business and learning about how it all worked.

When I went into care homes to explain that we provided private assessments for equipment, care home staff showed me various issues they had with chairs. Elderly people were often sliding and falling from or slumped in their chairs. This was not acceptable, especially as many spent long hours sitting each day. I therefore came to realise that proper seating was a huge problem that needed to be addressed, especially in care homes and for patients who spent many hours sitting in their own home.

Referrals began to increase as nurses became more aware of the harmful effects of poor sitting on their patients and how proper seating not only helped the patient but reduced their workload as well. I began assessing patients and ordering chairs from our suppliers that would enable patients to sit more comfortably. The company I was buying the chairs from was not keen on doing special adaptations for complex clients. It cost a lot of money and took weeks and weeks – a normal chair took four to six weeks, whereas a tailored chair could take up to twelve weeks. This is when James had an idea.

When we had orders for tailored chairs, I ordered in the standard chair and then asked James to adapt it – whether it was the armrest raised up, the footrest changed, or the back tailored. He adapted the chairs to suit whatever the patients needed. He was very good at it, being great with his hands, creative, inventive, and always with the attitude, 'Everything is a challenge, nothing is a problem.'

At this point, James said, 'Why don't we just make our own chairs?'

It was a good idea, but I was concerned about the risks. What if somebody fell off the chair, what if they developed a pressure injury and we'd get sued? I had my clinical hat on and knew all the things that could happen should something go wrong. James tried to convince me we could do it, saying if others could, we could too. It was food for thought, but not right now.

After two years, we decided to move our business to the shed beside the house. The current location was too small. If we were going to think of manufacturing in the future, we needed more space. By this stage, I had built a good team up with a receptionist, a couple of nurses to help with assessments, an occupational therapist I had previously worked with, and engineers to fix and repair chairs. I got them set up in the new Disability Centre, alongside James (although he was never fully employed, he was always there to help and provide advice).

It was a wise move. I had no rent to pay, and I was close to home, which proved to be very crucial for everyone over the next few months.

Family Before Work

Mammy had always been the one worrying about me until the tables turned when I got older. Although I was busy growing my business, she always knew I was there for her, and I would call to see her at least once per week. I rang her every day to see how she was and regularly took her to my house to pamper her. James and I took her on many holidays, too. She adored the south of Ireland, where she loved the Irish music and dancing, but most of all she enjoyed the slot machines and bingo. We also took her to Cork, Kerry, Killarney, Galway and to the Rose of Tralee Festival, where we danced 'The Stack of Barley' on the street. It made me very sad to recall this a few years later when I returned there after her death; the music was playing and, as happened so often, it provoked memories and tears.

I first became aware that Mammy was unwell in December 2004. She had a sore back and was generally slowing down, spending an uncharacteristic week in bed. At the beginning of 2005, she made a slight recovery and in May she accompanied the McCullagh ladies to Bundoran to celebrate Angela's fortieth birthday and Mary's sixtieth. We rented two houses and twelve of us spent two nights there. She enjoyed the slot machines and the fun, and she appeared very happy. It was her last holiday, but it endowed us with lasting memories. I wrote a poem after it, which I have shared here.

The Black and Brown Shoes in Bundoran

I always thought that playing slot machines was very boring

Until the weekend I spent with the Black and Brown Shoes in Bundoran

I never understood how someone could sit all day

And throw money down the drain and call it play

I could not understand how this game could give you pleasure

But the fun and craic we had in Bundoran that weekend I cannot measure

There were cheers of excitement and roars of laughter

When the sevens came up we had Chinese for after

Some players were learners others were skilled

The pots were emptied and then refilled

There were gains and losses and ups and downs

Cheers and laughter, curses and frowns

They were hard to shift 'We will go in a while'

But we waited and waited, Aelish and Geraldine had walked a mile

Mary and Brigid gave up and headed to the 'Birds Nest'

Kathleen and Angela stayed with the rest

Anna and Anne, Geraldine and Lizzie

To watch them play made my head dizzy

Sevens were spinning, bets were placed

Lizzie was wondering what horse won the race

A gambler through and through that's for sure

Could someone please get them to the door!

Can we depend on mammy to have some wit?

No! she's just like the others we can't get her quit!

The night is still young and some of us want to dance

We would if Lizzie would give us the chance.

Memories from our first trip to Bundoran with Mammy May 2005.

*

A few weeks later, on Ryan's birthday on 14 June 2005, I was in Norway with Ryan touring a factory which made chairs, looking for specialist chairs for my patients. I was not happy with those available to me in England and wanted to research other markets. I was also still hesitating about the manufacturing of chairs.

I knew before I left that Angela was taking Mammy for investigations for a pain in her stomach.

While in Norway, I got a distressed phone call from Angela to say that the results were not good. Mammy needed an MRI scan. The doctors said there was a waiting list, so it would be September before she would get one. We decided immediately that we would take her for private medical care. Ryan and I had planned on spending a few days in London on our return journey, but instead we came directly home to see Mammy and get the scan organised.

That started a succession of medical appointments, scans, a biopsy and a hospital admission to the Mater Hospital in Belfast. This ended with Mammy being diagnosed with gall bladder cancer. When I eventually accepted there was no cure, I asked the doctor how long she had left to live. He said eight, ten or twelve weeks.

She lived ten.

In the last few weeks of her life, she got very dependent on me. I went to see her every day and spent most of the day with her. All my brothers and sisters and sisters-in-law also took turns to look after her and to stay overnight. It was at this time that we were blessed to have a large, caring family and Mammy appreciated us all very much. Her sons-in-law also supported us at that time, not least by keeping the home fires burning when their wives were preoccupied with Mammy's care.

When I left her to go home at night, she appeared relaxed but often when I was at my home, I got a phone call to say that Mammy was unwell and unsettled. One morning, when I arrived back to see her, I asked her why she seemed to get worse when I left.

'It's the loss of you, you remind me of my mother,' she said.

For some reason, she felt safe with me. Maybe it was my limited medical training that gave her confidence that I knew what to do if there was an emergency, or maybe it was something else. I really don't know.

As well as physical symptoms, she was suffering from anxiety and panic attacks. The fear of the unknown made her very anxious. But I knew how to deal with her anxiety, just like she had known how to deal with mine when I was young.

There and then, we decided she should come and stay with me for a while. She hesitated at first as I had fitted out her home with a special chair, bed, mattress and other equipment to make life easier for her. She felt bad leaving it all behind. Many years earlier I had equipped a home for a very wealthy gentleman who needed specialist equipment as he was immobile. When I had his home fully equipped, he asked me to duplicate this in his holiday home, as he wanted all the same facilities there when he felt like going to his holiday home for a change of scenery. Mammy had heard this story and in fact she was with me on one of my visits to the gentleman's house, as sometimes I would call and take her for a run out in the car. She loved that. When she expressed her concern about leaving the special equipment behind, I said I would equip my house with the same equipment and when she felt like returning home it would all be there for her. Referring to the wealthy man, I said, 'If Thomas can have it, so can you.' She smiled at the idea that she was in the same league as this well-known wealthy man.

I was now running my business from home, but this was a time to put my family first. Louise was just six years old, I had three teenagers and James to look after, so it seemed more manageable to me if everyone was under the same roof. More so, it seemed that Mammy would be more content. My niece Lucia was working for me at the time, so I spent most of my day in the house with Mammy, and Lucia kept me up to date with what was going on at work. I had a good team, and I knew my time with Mammy was limited, so I made her my priority.

I knew I didn't even need to discuss Mammy coming to live with us with James. He knew how ill Mammy was and he knew how I felt about her. So, there was nothing to discuss. On 15 August 2005, Mammy came to stay at Carnamuff Road. I thought she would come for a while and then she would want to go back to Derrynoid; we did not think she was coming there to die.

I wanted to reassure her that she had the freedom to do whatever she liked, so she was often asked if she wanted to go back. Each time, she said no.

One day, I took her back to Derrynoid to see her doctor. When the doctor arrived in her home, I left them in private in case she had questions she wanted to discuss with the doctor. Angela and I went into the kitchen, and when the doctor left, Mammy said to me, 'Are you ready to go now?' So, I took her out to the car, and we left. It was the last time she would see Derrynoid.

When we got back to Carnamuff, she said, 'I thought you were going to leave me there, I heard you and Angela talking in the kitchen.' Again, I reassured her that she was still in control and could decide for herself where she wanted to be. She most definitely did not want to be left there and she never asked to go back.

Mammy had lived in Derrynoid for over sixty years, it was her home and she loved it. She spent her life there with Daddy and had reared her children there. We will never really know why she didn't want to go back in her final days. I know this was upsetting and almost incredulous for some of the family to accept.

For the first couple of weeks at Carnamuff, Mammy was in good form. The rest of the family came and went as they needed to, but at this stage no one needed to stay overnight as she was well settled.

She was using the dining room as a bedroom, so she was close to the kitchen in the hub of the house. James made her a boiled egg for breakfast and took it to her in bed every morning. She loved that but would say she 'hated giving James the bother'. After breakfast, she came out to the living room to watch TV. The Rose of Tralee was on TV for two consecutive nights at the end of August. We loved watching it as it reminded us of the days when we were actually in the big Dome in Tralee. She watched the first night and enjoyed it. Sadly, she was unable to sit up on the second night. This was the start of a slow decline. A few days later, James took her the boiled egg for breakfast and watched from a distance as she tried to eat it. She was not able to lift the spoon to her mouth. James was very upset. He came out from the room and said, 'Your Mammy is finished.'

It was a sad day.

We then started a rota to share the care and all my sisters, sisters-in-law and brothers took turns at staying over and sitting up with Mammy during the night. There was always an abundance of family members or extended family present (there were sixty-five grandchildren!). Neighbours also visited to see Mammy, and her brother John and sister Mary also visited every day during her final weeks. They were all welcome.

The house was very busy with people coming and going as they pleased, and anyone who wanted to sleep over did so. There were no rules. It was an open house. Some slept in beds, others in chairs. The kettle never cooled as they were big tea drinkers. Everyone brought food and there was always someone cooking, so no one left without getting fed.

Everyone was there on the night we knew Mammy was nearing the end. James spent the night making hot whiskeys, especially for the men as they were finding it difficult to cope. Mammy had been a strong influence in everyone's lives and losing her was not easy for anyone. She died in the early hours of Friday morning on 30 September 2005, six-and-half weeks after she arrived.

We later realised that Mammy was born and died on the same dates as St Thérèse of Lisieux, her favourite saint and one she always had a picture of. She was called St Thérèse The Little Flower and was born 2 January 1873 and died on 30 September 1897. While doing some research for this book I learned her father also died on 30 September 1958.

It has to be said that I was very proud of James, Jonathan, Ryan, Martin and Louise for the way they not only accepted Mammy's presence, together with all my extended family, but with how they welcomed them too. When she had first arrived to live with us, it was for an unspecified length of time. During that time, they gave up their beds, their rooms, their chairs, and their living space. Her arrival had also coincided with the beginning of a new school term, which in itself can be a challenge, but they got on with their work and their school life and I never heard one complaint or disagreement. Louise was six, so she was collected at school by whoever was available at that time – it was rarely me! Her bed was occupied by whoever got there first and each night she slept in our bed.

On the morning that Mammy died, I went upstairs to tell Louise that her granny had gone to heaven. We had been preparing her for this day for a long time. She looked out the window and said, 'There are no cars.' She had become accustomed to the yard being full of cars all the time. Then she said, 'Can I have my room back now?' It was such an innocent response to the situation. When I told my brother John about Louise's reaction, he said he wished everyone could accept death like a child.

One day, when Mickey finally accepted that Mammy was not going to live, he asked me whether I was taking her back to Derrynoid when she died. Of course, there was never any doubt in my mind that she would be waked in her own home and buried next to Daddy in Moneyneana.

On the day she finally left Carnamuff, all her old neighbours from Derrynoid, friends and family came out to accompany her home. They formed a solemn line at my front door as she was carried out by James and Sean Kelly. As the coffin was being carried out, I was looking around to find Mammy. It had become a habit of mine to look out for her and for a split second I forgot she was the one in the coffin.

A Welcome Visitor

I was faced with an unfamiliar stillness in my home on my return from Mammy's funeral. The hustle and bustle of the previous six weeks was replaced with an unusual silence. The dining room had been cleared to allow the undertaker space to prepare the coffin. There was an emptiness that I thought I could never fill. The pace of the past few days had caught up with me and I felt weary and drained of energy, but I had James. He understood how I felt as he had been there a few years earlier when his Daddy passed away. I put on one of Mammy's nightdresses and went to bed.

The next morning was even more strange. I had nothing to do; the phone was not ringing for an update on Mammy, there were no cars on the street, and the house was empty apart from my own weins. It was Monday morning, but I had no plans. I didn't open the office that day. It felt like no one needed me. My back was aching from having stood for such long periods the previous two days, and I was sitting at the dining table lost in my thoughts when the front door got a loud rap. I thought it unusual. I opened the door to see Paddy and Teresa standing there. Paddy had woken up that morning the same way as I did. Not sure what to do with himself, he thought of me.

'I knew it would be hard for you waking up to an empty house, so I just did what I have done the past few weeks, I just came out,' he said.

It was one of the most thoughtful moments I experienced in my life. I was touched by his kindness. He was sad but he still took time to think how I might be feeling. I have never forgotten that moment, and I still feel emotional even when I'm writing about it eighteen years later.

Seating Matters

In early 2008, Louise was almost nine, Martin was around eighteen and still at school, Ryan was almost twenty and had left school to work with James and Jonathan was twenty-one.

When Jonathan was in his AS-Level year, he decided he was going to leave school after his exams to start working for The Disability Centre. At seventeen, he got a licence so he could drive the van and I agreed for him to start but told him that he should then reassess what he wanted to do after a year, as I wanted to make sure he felt no pressure to stay on. He started delivering chairs all around Northern Ireland for me at first, then further afield. The chairs arrived on a Tuesday, got packed into the van on a Wednesday, and then he started delivering. He enjoyed the freedom of getting away in the van and even started to bring in orders.

Up until 2008, we were still buying in chairs, and I had become the main seating supplier in Northern Ireland for a large company in England. In fact, the majority of chairs being used by the health services in Northern Ireland came from 'Martina at The Disability Centre'.

It was very rewarding to see the success of all the hard work.

But that's not to say there weren't hiccups along the way.

Both Joanne and I had formerly been employed by the local Trust, and they were the most resistant to using The Disability Centre as their supplier of chairs, even though the manufacturers of the chairs told them we were their representatives in the area. They previously purchased directly from the manufacturers, rather than me, and didn't like this new system. So, the manufacturers came over to Greysteel and we had a meeting with the procurement department at the Trust. It transpired the problem was not with the procurement department, but with a head occupational therapist who had gone into management. I had previously worked with her, and she was the one stopping us getting the orders.

I remember saying to the head of supplies, 'Someone else is making the snowballs but you're having to throw them?' She didn't say anything, but we had established what the problem was. This lady didn't like the fact I had gone out on my own. She tried to stop it for a while, but in the end, they had no choice but to buy the chairs from me.

The business continued to grow. James paid for and renovated the shed; tiling the floor, dividing it up, and creating the offices. So, the whole initiative was, of course, joint – just as we had always helped each other and been involved in what the other was doing.

We then started to expand into Dublin. There was another company in the south of Ireland who was supplying the same products as me in the Dublin area. I didn't think this would be an issue but when the other company found out we were in Dublin, they were not happy for us to be operating on 'their patch'. I met with the man running that business and told him that there was enough work for everybody there – it was a huge city, after all.

I continued working in Dublin. Aelish came to Dublin to help me out. She was considering returning to nursing after a period of absence. The work at The Disability Centre dealing with patients and helping with assessments gave her the experience she needed to reregister as a nurse. It was great to get the help and it was a win-win for us both.

We had been discussing going down the route of manufacturing and having our own brand of therapeutic chairs for some time, although I had my reservations. I eventually succumbed to the idea, however. Initially, we were going to do it slowly because it was going to take time to get the designs right, secure the insurance, test the chairs, and so forth. In the meantime, I decided The Disability Centre was going to get an injection of growth; I brought on four salespeople and bought them each a new car. I had a whole plan of areas we would cover.

Then, on 6 February 2008, I got a message saying the manufacturer who supplied our chairs wanted to meet. I thought that sounded very good; perhaps they wanted to meet to find out about all our plans to expand and learn what I was planning to do for the year ahead.

The representative told me he was flying into Belfast, and we agreed to meet at the airport.

I will never forget that day.

I was so excited and nervous to meet them that I was rushing around and managed to fall over in the shower and hurt my back. There was a black bruise on it for weeks. It didn't matter – nothing could stop me. I made my way to the airport and sat down, waiting for him.

Then, a representative from the manufacturer came over to my table and handed an envelope to me.

'I just wanted to hand deliver this to you.'

'Ok,' I replied, curiously.

Upon opening the envelope, I was shocked to read the words: 'You are no longer a distributor of our product.' Our contract was up at the end of March. It suddenly became apparent to me that the other supplier in the south, who was much more influential financially at that time, had put the pressure on the manufacturers.

I sat there with all my business plans, devastated.

I got home and cried A LOT. It was James's birthday, so we went out to the Riverside Theatre in Coleraine. When we were out, James said to me, 'Never you worry about it. Never you worry. We will just speed up the process of our own chairs.'

I didn't see how it could be possible; we had so many orders and assessments that would turn into orders. How could we fulfil all those orders in time? It would take time to get our chairs to market even though we had, at least, already started the process.

James calmed me down. He was good with this sort of thing.

We calmly assessed what we had to do. I went through all the completed assessments and buying orders. We ordered the chairs we needed to fulfil the current orders and any potential future orders, which was a big investment. We were taking a chance that the assessments carried out would all convert to orders. The shed was full of chairs. I had enough to keep me going until we got our own products launched.

Then, a few days later I got a phone call from an occupational therapist who said, 'Martina, I don't know how to tell you this, but we are not able to purchase chairs from you anymore. The manufacturer has just sent out a letter to everybody in the Trust to say that you are no longer a supplier.'

I was so confused. They had told me I still had until the end of March. Their letter to the Trust also made it look as if I had done something wrong. It was incredibly stressful for me – not to mention I had a shed full of chairs we had invested in.

Again, James was great, and his support was invaluable: his attitude was 'Keep your head down and get on with it'.

We always had a thirty-day credit facility with the manufacturers but throughout this period, they kept sending me bills for the chairs I had bought. Yet, they'd sent letters out telling occupational therapists that they couldn't buy them from me. I refused to pay. They subsequently threatened court action. On the bottom of their invoices, I noticed it said, 'The chair remains the property of the company until paid for in full.' Yippie!! I rang them and was delighted to report, 'I think all these chairs belong to you. If you want them, come and get them.'

They begrudgingly sent a van to collect the chairs. I certainly wasn't going to pay for them when I couldn't sell them.

However, my problems were not over. I had no products to sell. I had patients who needed chairs and referrals coming in every day. I had unfulfilled orders.

The period from March to May 2008, from a business perspective, was very challenging. It seems like a blur now. All I know is that it was hell for leather at the factory. James was on board, and his contacts meant we had good suppliers for the various parts of the chairs. The design of the chair was registered by FR Kelly, the work was done mainly by Martin, and we were good to go. But we needed to get the manufacturing ramped up. We employed an upholsterer and sewers, and a few other production workers, but otherwise we subcontracted out most of the other work to contacts

James had in the industry for the woodwork, metal plates, welding, powder coating, etc. It was all done in haste, but we succeeded. By this time everyone was on board. Ryan had come to help as well, and Jonathan was keeping the existing business going as best we could.

In the middle of all of this, we somehow managed to get away.

James always wanted to go to Canada to do the Rocky Mountaineer Train cruise through Alaska to see the glaciers, so in 2007 we had pre-booked to go in May 2008, just the two of us. This was going to be our first holiday without the children. Because we weren't taking them, I decided we should go first class and go on the best of everything. However, by the time May came around, there was such turmoil with our business that I thought it was a bad time for a holiday. But James made a good point: perhaps it was the best time for a holiday.

After all, it was all paid for, so off we went.

We treated ourselves, and in hindsight I'm so glad we did. James was never one to worry about money, always saying, 'We'll figure it out. We'll get it.' So, even though finances were tight, and things weren't as rosy as we had expected them to be, we had a lovely time. I'm so glad we went because I have wonderful memories from that trip.

Nice as it was, the factory and the chairs were never far from my mind. On the day we got back, one of the girls who worked for me said, 'You really need to come into the factory. The upholstery is all wrong on the chairs.' She was really stressed, which wasn't exactly the best return from the holiday. We came back to reality with a bump but managed to sort through the issues one by one.

Martin was still at school when we were designing the chairs, but he had contacted a company who were the main suppliers of motors for specialised clinical beds and chairs across Europe.

When the representative from the company arrived at the office, he told the receptionist he was there to meet Martin.

'He's not home from school yet,' she said.

This must have come as quite a surprise to him.

When Martin hopped off the school bus and met with the representative, he couldn't believe it. To this day, each time I meet this representative, he tells the story of Martin turning up to the meeting with his school bag! He said that initially he thought someone had done this for a prank.

Martin was head boy of the Limavady Grammar school, a top student, so he decided he was going to get four A's at A-levels just to prove he could, before leaving school. I told him that if that was the only reason he was staying, he shouldn't feel he needed to prove himself to anybody. He had proved himself many times in the past.

The next morning, Martin decided to put a suit on instead of his school uniform. He then went into school and told the headmaster he was leaving. The headmaster listened to Martin's plans, then he stood up, shook Martin's hand and wished him well. He knew Martin was going to be successful and he was not depending on a university degree to achieve that success. Martin has since been back at the school to speak to students and has also been the keynote speaker on leadership at Association of School and College Leaders (ASCL) conferences in both Northern Ireland and the UK.

*

Remarkably, we launched our chairs in June 2008 at a hotel in Belfast. We invited all the occupational therapists in Northern Ireland and the distributors who would potentially sell our chairs. We brought on two distributors at the launch who are still working for us today.

It wasn't easy and there were some issues with the chairs in the early days. We had, after all, been operating in a very pressured timeframe. Time was of the essence. Delay in getting our product out meant our customers were likely to source products from other suppliers and we needed to act fast. However, as the saying goes, 'People don't care about the problem, they care about how you deal with it.'

If we had a problem with a chair, like a wheel becoming loose, we fixed the problem or brought them a new chair. The teething problems at the beginning were therefore dealt with in the right way. Thankfully, though, even if the manufacturing side needed tweaking, the designs were safe and so patients were never at risk and no falls or injuries occurred.

After we began making our own chairs, we called ourselves Seating Matters at the Disability Centre. But that was a bit of a mouthful, so we cut it down to Seating Matters. The name came about because I was passionate that seating did matter to our patients, who have always been at the core of our business.

The next curveball came later in 2008 when the manufacturers who had previously supplied me with chairs decided they were going to sue me for copying their products. A letter soon arrived saying they were taking us to court. It was a stress we didn't need. This went on for months with solicitors' letters being exchanged back and forth. From the outset we had registered our design with FR Kelly, so we were confident the chairs were a new design. We had also made clinical changes to the chairs based on my experience to better meet the needs of the patients. Indeed, we had been adapting them for years to improve outcomes for the patients. Nonetheless, having a legal challenge hanging over me didn't make for a stress-free life and caused sleepless nights. We could not afford the cost of a lengthy legal battle and just wanted to get on with the business.

With all of this going on, we went on a Bob Proctor cruise around the Caribbean, which had again been booked long before all this aggravation. James and I wanted Louise and the boys to experience the motivational cruise, which was a bit like the Amway motivational talks we had gone to. It was so good to get away and get inspired, motivated and rejuvenated. And I will never forget the moment when we were disembarking from the cruise. I was walking off the gang plank behind Martin when his phone bleeped. He answered it and with delight in his voice he announced, 'Mammy, they have decided to withdraw their case.'

The feeling of relief swept over me. It wasn't until that moment that I realised how much this had been dwelling on my mind. I felt euphoric, a weight had been lifted, and we were ready to take on the world of seating.

Going Global

In 2009, the boys weren't happy with the speed at which Seating Matters was expanding. One bank holiday weekend, we travelled home in separate cars after visiting their cousin, Maranna, who had had her eighteenth birthday. The boys clearly had a chat while driving because when we arrived home, they announced, 'We're going to sell chairs in England.'

'When?' I asked.

'Tomorrow.'

'Tomorrow is a bank holiday!'

Jonathan and Martin were determined to give England a try. Ryan, however, was staying at the factory. He had his mind made up about what role he was playing in the business, and it wasn't getting out in front of customers or patients. His interest lay in the manufacturing and setting up processes to make the task easier.

We had some buy-to-let houses in Tyneside at the time, which wasn't an ideal location to start a business like Seating Matters, but we didn't have a base anywhere else in England. So, the boys decided to move into one of the vacant houses. The week before leaving, Martin had set up meetings in Scotland with equipment providers and care homes. He would be travelling across Scotland anyway, so he wanted to make best use of his time.

Sean Mullan, who was in the same year at school as Martin, and who had been a friend of the boys for several years, also decided to leave school to manufacture chairs in the factory with Ryan. When he heard of the plans to expand the business in England, he saw an opportunity for himself and joined them.

Suddenly, three of them were heading to England to sell chairs. They had no money and a below-par van, but they persevered and set up in the north of England.

In Northern Ireland, people knew me and would happily try 'Martina's chairs' but in England, the boys were up against other well-established companies – including the manufacturer, who, until a few years before, was my main supplier. It was very difficult for them to begin with.

Nonetheless, they persevered by showing our chairs to as many potential clients as possible – in person. There was no email marketing, it was boots on the ground and knocking on doors. The boys set up appointments, taking the chairs out to the patients and the customers, and also set up 'Lunch and Learn' training events. I travelled over at least twice every month to help them, training the clinicians and giving as much credibility to the brand as I could. It took time to establish the brand and for clinicians to trust a new company, but the business started to emerge and grow.

Sean, who started with a second-hand van, living in a dilapidated house with Jonathan and Martin in Teesside, with very little income from the chairs, is now a successful distributor in London with five people working for him.

Jonathan, Ryan and Martin naturally fell into positions they felt comfortable with within Seating Matters: Jonathan has always been a natural salesperson; Martin is good at selling too, but his strength is in the legal side of things, clinical research, and finance – he is very much the person to dot the i's and cross the t's; and Ryan looks after the manufacturing.

Gradually our chaotic manufacturing system was replaced with an efficient, lean system of continuous improvement initiated by Ryan. He researched how to manufacture efficiently and reduce waste and came across Paul Akers who had written the book 'Two Second Lean'. It was the start of a Lean journey that has transformed our business and allowed us to create the best therapeutic seating available today for our patients.

Jonathan has gone from delivery driver at seventeen to leading a global team of distributors and salespeople across the world to distribute the therapeutic seating. At this time, we have business throughout UK and Ireland, Canada, USA, Australia and New Zealand, with opportunities emerging in UAE and Europe.

I'm proud to say that we manufacture the best therapeutic seating in the world and we are transforming the lives of hundreds of people every year.

There are also over fifty employees from Seating Matters arriving and leaving Carnamuff every day; containers leaving this homestead for Australia, Canada and Europe; and visitors from across the world coming to view and tour our factory. It's a world apart from the place we drove up to in 1985, covered with moss and trees and bushes. The thirteen acres will soon be concreted over, too. It's a testament to James's vision and foresight; this growth could never have happened in 'The Lane'.

Seating Matters is an outstanding success across the world, including in Australia. I believe James's influence, ambition and foresight, at a young age and throughout his life, has contributed to this success. Australia was always talked about when our family was growing up and was a special place for James and for me, so it seems fitting that our family business should be a success in the land where James chose to kickstart his own career. Today, as I edit this book in 2023, I am sitting in a beautiful hotel room in New Zealand where I am due to deliver training and meet new customers over the next few days. I am amazed that the business has taken me across the world and there is no doubt that the decision I made twenty-three years ago to leave my job and follow my heart was the best decision I ever made. It has impacted my family and thousands of people around the world. It just proves that you are never too old to start something new.

Work Hard to Succeed

'The only place success comes before work is in the dictionary.'

Vince Lombardi

James lived by this motto and said it many times. Work was everything to him. Even when he was very ill and receiving treatment, he needed to get the boots on and get out to work. When he was diagnosed but in remission, as you will soon learn more about, I asked him if there was anything he would like to do or anywhere he wanted to go, and his reply was he just wanted to get to work.

He instilled in me and his family that hard work was important and the route to success. I regularly meet people who reminisce about James and without fail they will say, 'He was a hard worker.' It's difficult to say where this drive and determination came from. His upbringing was not affluent, and he didn't have much money, but he was ambitious from as early as I can remember him. Even when I met him, he always appeared successful and well off. He had a 'can do' attitude to everything and as he often said, he would 'never let anything beat him'.

When he got ill, he struggled with not having control over his life. For the first time ever, he felt he just could not do what he wanted. He was restricted by pain, medication, treatment, doctors' appointments, and fatigue. He kept going as much and as long as possible, but this was proving to be a battle that was difficult to win.

My views on hard work, however, have changed over the past years. I still believe you must work to achieve your goals, but how you think and your belief in your self is equally important. Struggle is not necessary. We were brought up to believe that we needed to struggle and sacrifice to get what we want. I now believe that everything we need is already here and we must believe in ourselves, have faith, visualise what we desire and keep moving forward towards our goal. Yes, we still need work, but not to sacrifice your health and your family along the way.

James was not a good employee and, as it turned out, neither was I. We both felt very restricted by working for others and our enthusiasm, creativity, drive, and independence were curtailed in a nine-to-five Monday to Friday job.

Besides the monetary reward, James really enjoyed his work and took pride in a job well done. He would work all day and all night if necessary (and did so on a regular basis), rubbing up a concrete floor just to get it perfect and to move on to a new job as soon as he could. He didn't like staying in one place for too long. When reminiscing with his work mates and colleagues, as well as the farmers or contractors who engaged him for work, the one thing which was always unmistakable was the fun they had too. The 'craic' was great. They never talked about how much money they made, only the fun, the adventures, and the practical jokes they played when they worked with James. They often recalled the long hours with fondness.

It is often quoted that success is doing what you love and getting paid for it and I believe that if this is true, James was very successful.

From Sunshine to Darkness

Before we booked our first trip to Florida in 2003, we decided to tarmac the yard around the house, as we had been putting it off for some years until we could afford it. There was always something more urgent that the money was needed for. After all, it was quite a large area and would cost us £10,000. However, James and I set our goal, agreeing that we would only book Florida if we knew we could afford to do both. That's all we needed: a goal. We always worked well together when we had a shared goal.

We achieved both, but true to form, the work around the yard only completed the day before we left for our holiday. James said he planned it that way so no one would be driving on the newly laid tarmac for two weeks. It was a plausible story, but like the shoemaker's family, anything that needed to be done around the house was always left to the last minute. I had established The Disability Centre two years prior, in 2001, and it was difficult leaving it in the hands of employees for a full two weeks, but this was something I really wanted to do for my children and James. When we were involved in the Amway business, Disney World was a carrot that dangled every year if you reached a certain level in the business. But, as you read, the goalposts almost always changed just when we thought we were getting ahead and reaching our target. So, I was determined that James and the children would enjoy a fun-filled, no expense spared, holiday to Florida to live out the dreams of that tantalising video shown to us at every Amway seminar.

It was a dream come true for us all and one we wanted to repeat at some time in the future when Louise was a bit older – although she loved it at the time, and we felt a great sense of achievement taking the family there, it was a trip we thought she would not remember when she grew up, being so young. She was only around four when we went.

It was July 2011 when we finally booked our return holiday to Disney World in Florida. We were full of excitement for our second trip. This time, Olivia, who had been going out with Ryan since she was sixteen and was now a part of our family, accompanied us too. Luck would have it that the trip would coincide with her twenty-first birthday, so we organised a memorable birthday dinner. We had a magical and enchanting trip, eating at different restaurants every evening and enjoying Disney World's daily firework displays. Louise was twelve and enjoyed the big rollercoasters with the boys and Olivia, while James and I wandered around the parks, enjoying the weather and our free time. Neither of us were very interested in the rides and we felt relaxed and content that the children were old enough to look after each other.

Finally, we felt as though we were getting to a point in our lives where we could unwind. Not only was Louise older and more independent, but we were more financially stable than we had been in previous years. I was very relaxed, and we even discussed ideas about going on more holidays on our own in the future now that I didn't have to worry so much about leaving the business for two weeks at a time. It was a relief to have good employees who could look after things while we were away. After twenty-seven years of marriage and having brought up four children, we were reaping the rewards of our hard work.

One of the 'must sees' when you go to Florida is the dolphin show. We were all looking forward to it and hoping to get a front row seat, so we arrived at the Dolphin Resort early, just after a heavy rainstorm. Unsurprisingly, the steps leading down to the front of the arena were still wet and slippery, which caused James to fall as we made our way to the seats. He was wearing sandals, so blamed the unfamiliar footwear. Despite him telling me he was OK, he had clearly hurt his back and I could see that he was walking very cautiously throughout the rest of the holiday.

With our holiday over, we returned to our daily routines, the commotion of family life and running the business. I noticed that James was still very tentative when he was walking or getting up from a chair, so I asked him about his back again. He then admitted it was still sore and that he was puzzled as to why it was not improving. He was taking pain relief but, typically, would not go to the doctors.

As the following months passed, his back was not improving. Even so, he continued working hard and even enjoyed travelling to Prince Edward Island in Canada with Martin in November 2011. It was clear that he was in pain, which Martin was aware of too.

When Christmas came along in 2011, Louise and Olivia decided we should all wear Christmas jumpers for the first time. James and I bought matching jumpers and enjoyed a very memorable, fun-filled, and happy time. Little did we know that it was the calm before the storm. We were about to enter a time in our lives filled with great pain, suffering and loss.

After Christmas, James went to the doctor to investigate the cause of the pain. They sent him for X-rays and gave him strong pain relief but did not diagnose anything of particular concern. I was worried about how much medication he was taking to manage the pain, but he needed it just to function. Our GP was difficult to reach and did not appear concerned that a strong man like James, who was never previously in his surgery, should be suffering so much pain. James even had difficulty walking. I was very angry about this for a long time, but eventually let it go – I had once heard that holding onto resentment was like taking poison and expecting the other person to die. In essence, resentment destroys the person who is holding onto it.

James's fiftieth birthday was on the horizon on 6 February 2012, and I wanted to treat him to something special. He loved cruises and since we had done the Mediterranean a few times, Alaska, the Gulf of Mexico, and the Caribbean, I suggested a cruise on the Persian Gulf, taking us to Dubai and Abu Dhabi. James was attracted to the idea of something different, so it was agreed. As was the accepted practice when going on holiday, I did the booking, the preparation, and the packing. It was never a point of discussion – just the way it was always done.

As we walked to the terminal building at Belfast Airport, James turned to me and said, 'Do you have my passport?' It was so hilarious. We were about to board a plane! Fortunately, I did have his passport and everything else he needed, including a good stock of pain relief.

We had wonderful new experiences, learned about Middle Eastern culture, visited mosques, and enjoyed riding camels on a trip to the desert. James even went on a four-wheel drive experience into the desert – abandoning me with a bus load of strangers with whom I was going on a shopping trip. I didn't mind being deserted, it was his birthday, and I was just glad he was having a good time.

James spent a lot of time on the ship enjoying the hot tubs as he felt he was getting relief for his back. I knew by this point he wasn't well, but I had no idea how serious it was. Little did we know it was to be our last proper holiday…

On the way home, James walked slowly through the airport and made no attempt to pick up the suitcases from the carousel. This was not like him. He had always been there to do the heavy lifting, but things were changing. I was still hoping the change was temporary, but I would soon find out our lives were changing forever.

James's mobility worsened after the holiday, as did the pain. He was still attending the doctor, but the doctor was not really taking the situation seriously. He also attended the ED department at Coleraine Hospital, where it was again reported that there was nothing of concern. He was also seeing a private physiotherapist and chiropractor.

Life for me was still very busy. I was travelling to England two or three days every other week to do training and to attend events. James, on the other hand, was spending less time at work and a lot of time at home, which was very worrying. Ryan worked at home most of the time and so was there to see this, and one day he told me he was worried about Daddy because he had not left the house. It was time to get to the bottom of this problem. I accompanied James to the doctors the next day and was brushed aside by the GP. He was most unhelpful.

On 19 March 2012, a chiropractor referred James for a private MRI scan on 22 March.

James lay in the back of the car to and from the appointment in Belfast as he could not sit upright. He even had trouble getting onto the scanner. After the appointment, we were told that the results would be sent to our GP, but we had not yet reached home when James got a call from the GP asking him to go and see him first thing in the morning.

I remember James saying that it had taken a trip to Belfast to get the GP to sit up and take notice, but I knew the news was not good. The GP was too quick to ring. James did not think this was strange, however, and was just glad the wheels were finally moving.

I did not sleep one wink that night. There was a very dark cloud hanging over me and I had a heavy feeling of dread. Things were not right, I knew it. So, I prayed and prayed and prayed. I kept repeating positive affirmations. I wrote the affirmations down and tried very hard to focus on a positive outcome. It was a very long night for me. James, though, was asleep. The medication and the long journey had knocked him out.

The next morning, I couldn't eat or even drink a sip of water. My insides were shaking, as they are now while I recall that day.

James seemed oblivious to what was about to unfold. So, seemingly unaware of how serious the situation was, he had his breakfast as usual. I was dreading the worst, but still trying to convince myself that I was overreacting.

The appointment was at 9 am. The GP was waiting for us in the corridor outside his surgery.

It was definitely not going to be good news.

The doctor said he had got the results of the scan and that James had cancer. Worse, it was very serious. We did not speak for a while. I felt the room was revolving around me. My mouth was dry, my stomach was turning over, and I thought I was going to have a panic attack. I looked at my big, lovable husband and felt my world was ending. But I needed to be strong for him.

I asked the doctor if that meant James would need chemotherapy or radiotherapy.

'All of the above,' he said.

The prognosis wasn't good.

The doctor was sorry about how it had been handled and asked if I wanted to talk about it. I had nothing to say to him. All I could manage was, 'At this minute, I just want to get my husband treated.'

'What do we do now?' I asked.

'You need to go to Altnagelvin Hospital for an assessment and proper prognosis,' he said, 'but, since it's Friday, you could leave it until Monday if you prefer.'

'No. We are going right now.' I said.

Professor Morris

The doctor phoned ahead and told us to go directly to the Sperrin Room for an 11 am appointment. Even hearing that phrase made me feel ill. I knew what the Sperrin Room was. I had delivered chairs there for patients before. In all my years of business with that unit, I never once imagined that one day I would be taking James there.

I can't remember James speaking at all. We left in silence.

When we got to the car, I was trying to be strong. I never cried or let James know how I felt. I was trying to work out what was going through his head.

'Let's go home and get ready,' I said.

'No, we will go to Mass at 10 am in St Finlough's Chapel,' he replied.

So, we did. I heard nothing during the Mass, and I remember nothing about it.

When we were coming out from Mass, two men were building a new grotto beside the church and I don't know if James knew them or not, he probably did, but he stopped and talked to them as if it was a normal day. I was in a trance, standing there until he finished talking.

We went back to the house and Ryan was there. He asked what the doctor had said, and we told him we were going to Altnagelvin for investigations. We didn't tell him any more than that. We weren't ready to talk and needed to know more before we caused alarm and stress to our 'weins'.

We set off on that first day; the first of countless visits to the hospital. A very long and difficult journey lay ahead of us.

When we were going through Greysteel, James said, 'I always thought I would be a Granda one day.' It broke my heart, because I knew he loved children, and he would have made a great Granda.

'You need to be tough,' he then said. I was – at least, I was when I was with him.

We arrived in the Sperrin Room to find out that the main consultant was on holiday. His replacement for the day was a semi-retired consultant haematologist, Professor Curly Morris, from Belfast City Hospital. He immediately took us to the consultation room, as it was very quiet. He told us he had been about to leave for Belfast when he received the referral from the GP. He looked at the scan and said it was either one of two things: bone cancer, for which he had very little treatment available; or multiple myeloma, for which there were several treatments. But there were no guarantees. I was praying again. Please let it be the second. I believed that having a chance of treatment would help James fight the rest. He always said he never let anything beat him. All we needed was a chance – get him on the road to recovery, and we would do the rest together.

Professor Morris instructed the nurse to get a bed ready.

'Oh, is James staying in?' I asked.

He gave me an incredulous look. 'Of course he's staying. Your husband is a very sick man.'

He spent the next two hours taking an array of blood and urine samples, etc. He was constantly in and out to go into the laboratory next door, his white coat swinging as he sped from one door to another. Professor Morris was a man in his sixties, he wore round glasses, and had white wispy hair which blew in the wind as he walked.

A drip was then put up and James was given morphine for pain. Finally, James felt comfortable for the first time in months. Then, after hours of testing, Professor Morris came in and explained that James had multiple myeloma. He had kidney failure, too, and his kidneys were operating at only ten percent, which is a common complication of multiple myeloma when it hasn't been diagnosed early. Coincidentally, Professor Morris, who was substituting for the consultant haematologist that day, was a world-leading expert on myeloma. He told us he was at the cutting edge of research into treatment.

The first step from there was to get James's kidney function to improve. So, he started treatment for his kidneys right away. If there wasn't significant improvement by Monday, he would go onto dialysis. Chemotherapy could not begin until his kidneys could tolerate it. Professor Morris told me again that James was a very ill man, and it was fortunate we arrived at the hospital when we did. He praised the GP for making a swift referral, because James would not be alive if we had left it until Monday. I was too distressed to say it was me who made the swift referral, and that if we had taken the GP's advice, James would have died. I was just grateful we had got this far. James was comfortable and he was getting treatment. I was exhausted, but everything was going to be ok.

At the time, Jonathan was in England, Martin was in Canada, and Louise, who was only thirteen, was at school. Ryan, who had been at home, told Jonathan and Martin that Daddy was in hospital. I was not ready to say the word 'cancer' to anyone yet, but the boys had already worked it out. After all, Jonathan knew the ward James was moved to – Ward 43 – as he was familiar with the Altnagelvin Hospital. I still don't remember who told Louise.

Now, ten years on from that earth shattering time, I feel that I should have talked more to Louise about what was going on, but I didn't want to upset her. I thought we were going to overcome this challenge as we did every other challenge in our lives. We always had a positive attitude, we believed in our own ability to change what was happening, and this time wasn't going to be any different. I had read and listened to many stories about how people overcame cancer and life changing illness. If they could do it, James definitely could.

So, I tried not to dwell on the worst-case scenario and disregarded the pessimistic outlook of others – including those in the medical profession.

Jonathan and Martin came home right away. Whenever there was a problem in the family, everyone needed to be together. No questions asked – both simply returned within a few days. James hadn't wanted to tell Martin as he didn't want to upset him. He also didn't want him travelling home. But we knew there was no way we were going to convince Martin to stay in Canada when he needed to see his Daddy.

I was booked to go to Canada the following weekend to do a week-long round of seminars and James was insisting that I continue with the work arrangements. He was feeling better due to the pain relief and also because of the fact he knew someone was looking after him. He had been let down by doctors until he met Professor Morris. Still, he was not fully aware of what the following weeks had in store. There was no question about it; I knew the Canadian trip was not going to happen. I was still waiting for Professor Morris to come on Monday to decide about treatment and the possibility of dialysis.

James made a good recovery in the first twenty-four hours and his kidney function greatly improved. By the time Monday came, and Professor Morris visited us, he was very happy with the improvement in kidney function and decided he did not need dialysis. Chemotherapy would commence right away, which seemed to be a very positive step forward to me, and the first step on the road to recovery. I also told

Professor Morris that we were prepared to pay for treatment if he felt there was anything available outside the NHS that would give James a better chance of recovery and survival.

'Not at this time,' he said.

This reverberated through my head… 'Not at this time' meant to me that there may come a time when we needed to look further afield, but for now I put these terrifying thoughts out of my head. I was going to deal with the situation as it was – here and now. Professor Morris had a tried and tested treatment plan. If the plan worked for others, then we were certain it would be the solution for James.

James spent one week in hospital, and we were all very positive about the outcome, firmly believing that everything was going to be OK.

James then returned home with a plan to go to the Sperrin Room twice a week for treatment; two weeks on and one week off. But he still had to attend on the week off to get his bloods done so they could monitor his progress and plan the next cycle.

A new, fully adjustable bed was bought and put in the downstairs bedroom. Everything James needed was going to be bought, no expense spared. James appreciated this very much and was very gracious, but as soon as possible he insisted on getting back upstairs and sleeping in his own bed so he could have a sense of normality.

Seeing James in a Different Light

The main focal point of our home is the kitchen table. The dining room which was temporarily used by Mammy as a bedroom had now been opened into the kitchen, giving a larger spacious area. I never knew who would be sitting at that table any day when I walked in the back door as it was an open house. For the next few weeks, we had constant visitors at our home calling to see James.

I did not realise how many friends James had. Nor how much impact he had on other people's lives. We spent hours talking to his friends around the kitchen table. He really enjoyed this time and was delighted to see everyone. The craic was great, and the family enjoyed hearing the old stories and yarns from James's earlier days, as well as his work adventures. I pointed out to my children that it was great to be able to sit there with James and listen to everyone tell him how great he was, to hear funny stories, and hear of the times he had helped them. We had been totally unaware of how much time James had spent helping others. I told our children that this usually happens at a wake when the person is no longer there to be appreciated, so James being present for that was priceless. I will be forever grateful for that time and for the two years that followed, however painful they were to go through. This time was precious. It gave us all time to learn more about James, to tell him how much we loved and appreciated him, and to allow him to do the things he really wanted to do.

When James had the opportunity to reflect on his life and his future, all he really wanted was to get on with his work and see the business flourish. I suggested holidays and cruises, but he was not interested. We had travelled quite a bit in the past, so he was now happy to work, to go out for dinner with me or the family, and to enjoy a few nights away in a local hotel.

It may seem strange to say, given we had been married for twenty-eight years, but this time gave me an opportunity to get to know James better.

I knew James as my faithful, thoughtful, loving, and sometimes romantic husband. He was an ambitious man who was always motivated to do, be and have more. He was courageous, happy to take risks, and certainly not afraid of hard work. He was a family man, eager to spend time with his children, albeit usually in a work capacity – he took the boys to work as soon as they were potty trained and able to walk! He was not really a Daddy who changed nappies, but he was happy to do anything else. Louise was the apple of his eye, the icing on his cake. He was so proud of her and, as far as I can recall, there was never a cross word spoken to her. He reacted differently with her. I'm not sure if it was because he was now an older father or whether it was because she was 'his girl', but the first time he stepped foot in Limavady Grammar School was for Louise's open night. He hated school so much – he never went to the boys' parent's evenings throughout the entire decade of their schooling. Don't get me wrong, he was always keen for them to go to school and learn. He just didn't like school so much. Still, he was happy to go for Louise and had attended some of her Nativity plays, too, when she was at primary school – again something he did not do for the boys, as he had always been working instead. It must be said that there weren't many fathers who attended school activities at the time.

I saw another dimension to James when he got ill. I saw a man who cared for others outside his own family. I was a busy working mother, a wife, a daughter, and a sister to twelve siblings, and that was my world. James's view of the world was wider than this. He cared for people and treated those who worked for him and his customers like his family. If they were having family problems, he guided and counselled them. If they were having financial problems, he supported them.

We heard stories of James doing work for customers and not taking money from them until they could afford to pay. For example, one farmer needed his milking parlour finished but was struggling with cashflow problems until he could get the parlour operational. The farmer offered James a cheque for the completed work, but James said he would wait until the farmer had received payment for his milk. This was at a time when we were still struggling to build Seating Matters, but James could see the stress the farmer was under, and he did not want to exacerbate his problems.

As you can well imagine, James's customers became his friends and often relied on him for more than work advice. They trusted him.

One man told me a story about when James was concreting his shed and the client's teenage daughter came home to tell her parents she was pregnant. The mother got very upset, and an argument ensued. The father did not know how to handle the overwrought situation between the daughter and her mother, so he came out to James who was in the shed and asked him to go in to help. James had been working at the home for weeks and had developed a relationship with the family, so he could be trusted. They had recognised a genuine, caring, and wise person who could put the tense situation into perspective. James spent time talking to them, settled the situation down, and helped everyone involved to see a positive outcome to what they perceived as a devastating state of affairs. The remarkable thing about this story is that I knew where James was working, I was acquainted with the family, but he did not come home and tell me about the family's situation. I never knew the girl had had a baby until the father told me many years later.

For the record, it must be said that until relatively recently, it was frowned upon for a single girl, especially in the Catholic tradition, to have a baby. It was felt she brought disgrace upon her family and had sinned against God. Some people still hold this view, and it is still against Catholic teaching, but a baby is welcomed with love despite the status of the mother or the parents for the majority of people nowadays.

There was another time when a young girl got pregnant, and the family were very upset. James went to see them and consoled them by saying, 'A baby is God's way of saying the world must go on.' Once again, this story was related to me many years after the event and the family told me that his visit and support gave them great comfort. As you can see, he had a way of dealing with situations in a caring way – without letting it impact on his own life. There were so many stories like this that were told at that time, which helped me develop an even greater insight and respect for the man I had known for thirty-five years.

Alternative Treatment

From March 2012 to August 2012 James continued attending the Sperrin Room in Altnagelvin Hospital twice a week for chemotherapy. Meanwhile, I researched everything we could do to speed up his progress and ensure his full recovery. I contacted a herbalist in Maghera and she advised me on a variety of different changes we could make to James's diet to help his recovery. She recommended that he became totally vegetarian; no dairy products, no wheat products, no sugar, which included potatoes as they have a high sugar content. James loved his desserts and biscuits… No processed foods were allowed, organic foods only, and she recommended a regime of vitamins and herbal medicine. She advised me to grow wheatgrass from seed and juice it, too. James needed to take this freshly squeezed wheatgrass juice every morning before he ate his breakfast. She said it had to be drunk within ten minutes of being juiced or it would lose its nutritional value. She believed the benefits of fresh wheatgrass was undervalued and she had experience of people who had great results from taking it. These changes were very dramatic. I enticed James to visit her to see if she could convince him to change his eating habits, in the hope that this would benefit him long term. He was not easily convinced, although he did like the lady and was very respectful of her views. He agreed with some of them, but the change was too much for him on top of a recent diagnosis. His life was already in turmoil, and he was still reeling from the shock. So, we left her clinic.

I was ready to start a new dietary regime to support James, so we stopped in the nearest restaurant for lunch, and I ordered a fresh salad. James ordered deep fried fish and chips! I knew the battle was not going to be easy. I was desperate to get started immediately, but I needed James on board. So, I started slowly.

I introduced changes which were more palatable at first. No dairy products, and only organic food. Rice milk instead of cow's milk. Fortunately, this was available locally in small cartons. Thankfully, James liked it. No matter where he went, I had a carton of rice milk for him. I was overzealous about everything. I wanted everything to be done perfectly. I wanted James to have the best chance of survival and I was going to do everything that needed to be done. When we went to the hospital for his treatment, I packed his lunch, refusing to allow him to eat the hospital food. The staff, although polite to us, did not approve of our alternative approach to treating the cancer. They had no faith in a nutritional approach.

I cut chicken and red meat out of our diet but kept fish, just to please James and to coax him to cooperate with the new regime. Luckily, James liked fish and he was happy with that. Plenty of fish and organic vegetables were piled onto his plate daily. Like most Irish men, James was very fond of potatoes and dinner was not a dinner without them, so we agreed on reducing rather than abolishing. He never ate pasta or rice because he considered them to be 'foreign foods'.

My shopping trip to the local supermarket was now taking twice as long, as I needed to read all the ingredients. Plus, the local shop did not have much in the way of organic food, so I shopped in Derry – twenty miles away. At first, I was extremely stressed at trying to source the proper food, and shopping was now something I dreaded. However, after some research and talking to various people, I soon had a system in place. The most important thing was that not only was James eating healthier, but everyone in the family joined in to support him. The house was now a sugar free zone. Looking back, I recall Louise not being overly enthusiastic about the dietary changes. She did go along with most of it but was allowed to revert to her old eating habits from time to time.

It was all a very stressful time, with James being my priority, and I now know that Louise, along with everyone and everything else, was neglected at that time. It was a period of shock and disbelief that James had cancer, but also a period of determination that he was going to get through it and survive. I think my thought process was to focus on him and get him fully recovered. After which, I could make up for all the people and things I had abandoned. This also included my work.

Wheatgrass

I was determined to grow wheatgrass, but there was a detailed process if I was to get it right. We needed to use only rainwater or distilled water, so I bought a distiller. The soil needed to be organic, and everyone I spoke to had different methods with many do's and don'ts, which confused me greatly and caused me a lot of anxiety. I had so much faith in the wheatgrass. I really believed it was a cure, so I had to get it right.

With everything in place to begin growing the wheatgrass, I started growing and soon had trays of grass in the kitchen, on windowsills, on the floor, and on the worktops. I then bought a large trolley with shelves to hold the accumulating trays of grass. I bought the most expensive juicer and got ready to juice.

It took fourteen days from planting seed until the grass was ready for juicing. As one tray of grass was needed every two days, I needed to be constantly planting seeds to have enough grass available at the right time. If the grass grew too long, it lost its nutritional value, so there was an opportune moment when it was just right. I constantly worried if I had the grass just right, or if I had cut it too quickly, or if I had left it too long. James's life depended on this, and it was up to me to get it right. The strain was immense. I don't think anyone realised how much I worried about this at the time.

We then heard about a man called Danny McDonald in Dunaff, Donegal who had refused conventional treatment and claimed that wheatgrass cured his stomach cancer. He was sort of a celebrity in the wheatgrass world, being interviewed on TV and in newspapers.

Danny was also an expert at growing wheatgrass and people came from all over Ireland to meet him, get inspired, and learn how to grow it. He gave many people hope of a cure, so we, too, set sail on a two-hour journey to Dunaff to find out more.

Danny was a farmer living with his elderly sister in an Irish country cottage on the western edge of Donegal. The Atlantic Ocean was his next-door neighbour. James related to this elderly man who was convinced by his story. He encouraged James to persevere with the wheatgrass juice when James told him he was finding it very difficult to swallow. I was very relieved at that time as I was clinging to this for a cure.

I then became the expert wheatgrass grower in my area. People who were diagnosed came to me to see how to grow it and to get advice.

Improvements

For the remainder of 2012, I dedicated myself to James. I accompanied him to every hospital appointment, I ensured he was eating right, and I administered his medication. He was dependent on me for all of this and was well and truly out of his comfort zone. Suddenly, he was no longer putting on his boots, grabbing his lunch box, and heading out to work. His new life meant attending the hospital on a twice-weekly basis and sleeping a lot more due to the medication.

James's health was beginning to improve, with his first treatment cycle completed. The morphine patch kept the pain at bay, and we were happy with how everything was going, but we still had a long way to go.

By this time, in May 2012, we had established a routine when he came home from the Sperrin Room. James took the steroid tablets and his pain medication right away while I made lunch, as he never liked taking medication on an empty stomach.

Then, one day, he appeared in the kitchen with his working boots on.

'Where are you going? I asked.

'Work,' he said.

I looked at him in disbelief and exasperation.

'You CAN'T go to work. You need to rest,' I implored.

'I've laid about long enough and I'm going out to work.'

Things were just starting to improve, he was getting more mobile, his pain was under control, but he was a long way off being able to work. He was going to cause a setback; I was furious and concerned. I pleaded with him to not go, but he went.

I just wanted him to take his time and allow himself to recover, but he was frustrated and impatient. The fight back had begun; he said he was not prepared to 'lie down and die'. This caused a bit of tension between us. I was doing everything to help get him better, I was worried, I was weary, and I was infuriated because I felt that he was working against the plan for a full recovery. Then, I realised he just needed to be out with his workers; to drive a digger for a while and generally start to feel a bit like his old self. The humdrum of hospital visits, doctors, scans, blood tests, treatments, medication, wheatgrass and no sweets was beginning to affect him mentally. He never admitted this or showed signs of anxiety or depression, but it was natural that he should feel irritated and annoyed by the sudden and unexpected change in his life. He very much wanted to be in control of any situation he found himself in. But now he wasn't.

He never showed any signs of panic when in a challenging position and he prided himself in 'never letting anything beat him'. But this was different. Probably for the first time ever he had lost control of almost everything; his health, his time, and even what he ate.

Being aware of this, I said to him one day, 'How do you feel? You have never cried.'

'What is there to cry about?' he replied.

So, James continued to do what he wanted to do, and I tried to understand why he was doing it. It was not easy. I stressed about it all the time.

*

As the summer of 2012 progressed, so did James. He steadily got stronger and was responding well to the weekly treatment.

Lourdes had always been a special place for James, and he had been there many times as a volunteer. So, as James was getting stronger, we decided to go there on a week he didn't have any treatment, which also coincided with my fiftieth birthday. We planned the trip ourselves and it was incredibly uplifting, with James being in very good form, and me being confident that the pilgrimage, along with the treatment, was going to be our solution. He rested well while there, and I wandered off by myself to pray well, too. I implored Mary and Jesus to cure him. One day, he spied me deep in prayer in the Basilica and was touched that I was praying so fervently for him. My only wish was that he would live. I could not imagine a life without him.

When we got back home, he continued to work and did a little more each week. That summer, he, James Eakin and John Donnelly, wired Patrick McGinnis's mountain. It was a huge undertaking for someone receiving treatment twice weekly, but he paced himself, the weather was favourable, and he enjoyed the craic with John, who was a character, full of jokes and pranks.

Patrick McGinnis was a sheep farmer who lived very close to our home. He had a lot of sheep and was in his eighties at this time. He was brought up in an era of austerity and was very careful with his money, even though he was a wealthy man with no dependants. He was keen to get the wiring done to keep the sheep fenced in – the existing wire was rusty and ruined from years of exposure to the elements. He had wanted to reuse as much of the old wire as possible, but James convinced him to replace all the old wire with new. Ultimately, Jonathan benefitted from that investment in 2021 when he bought McGinnis's Farm after Patrick's death. It had been a long-standing desire of James's to buy this large mountain farm when it came on the market, as James knew Patrick did not have an heir. So, it was a bittersweet purchase because for as long as we lived in Carnamuff, it was a foregone conclusion that James would make every effort to buy it when it became available. Since Patrick was more than thirty years James's senior, it seemed reasonable to expect James to outlive Patrick. This was not to be.

Harvesting Stem Cells

A stem cell transplant was on the cards as a possibility from the start of James's treatment. Professor Morris said he had a first line treatment to start with, to get the myeloma under control, but that a stem cell transplant was the best chance of long-term success. James was responding very well to the first line treatment, although he was never discharged and continued having his bloods taken every week, even after finishing his treatment.

We hoped the transplant could have been avoided, but Professor Morris was adamant that it was his best chance. Although he gave no guarantees, he indicated that there was evidence to suggest that if the transplant went well, James could get between two and ten years of treatment-free life.

The preparation started in October 2012 with the harvesting of the cells and James was put on medication to increase his own bone marrow cells. He then went to the City Hospital and had the stem cells drained out. When they were harvested, they were frozen so that they could be put back into his body at the time of the transplant. This part of the process was very successful and problem free, so we were buoyant to have it completed. They had enough cells collected for two transplants. Everything was going well, and we were happy.

James was put on a waiting list for the transplant.

A Rolex

Ever since we first met, James had always wanted to own a Rolex watch at some time in his life. Every time we were away on holiday, he went into the Rolex shop and quizzed the salesperson about the watches. He tried them on, asked lots of questions – including the price – and then he would leave. I continually prompted him to buy it, but he always said, 'No, not now. I will get one sometime.'

After this procedure in Belfast City Hospital, James and I went to Killyhevlin Hotel in Enniskillen for a couple of nights recuperation. And I decided the time had come for James to finally have his Rolex. In the past, he had been to look at Rolex watches in Lunn's, Belfast, but I always felt he was not well received and had therefore vowed that he would not buy one from them. So, I researched who the official dealers were in Northern Ireland and found Mercer's Jewellers in Enniskillen. James, meanwhile, was unaware of my plan.

On our first morning in Enniskillen, I suggested we should go shopping and drove straight to the jewellers. It wasn't difficult for me to convince James to try on a watch, as he had done this many times before. The owner of the shop was impressed by James's knowledge of the watches when James asked for different designs and models. Then, James said, 'That's the one I would buy if I was buying.' He knew the exact watch he wanted.

'We will take it,' I said.

James threw me a questioning look.

'You've looked long enough at the watches, it's time to buy one.' For once, he did not walk away or resist, and the watch was bought. We then went across the street and bought a full new outfit of clothes for him. He was very pleased with the purchases of the day, and everyone was delighted for him when we got home. They knew it had always been one of his aspirations.

Stem Cell Transplant

We patiently waited from October to December to get a date for James's transplant and it eventually came. New Year's Day 2013 was the day allocated for us to go to the City Hospital for the transplant.

We decided to celebrate the New Year in style as, after all, it was going to be a new start for James and all the family. So, we went to a New Year's party at The Belfrey Hotel near Derry. Jonathan, Ryan and Olivia, and Martin and Louise went with us. We had a great night. James was in very good form, and we managed to keep all worry about the forthcoming treatment well to the back of our minds.

The transplant was basically administering a high dose of chemotherapy to destroy the cancer cells but having good cells depleted at the same time. This caused James to be extremely susceptible to infection as he was neutropenic. James was in a single room for four weeks, with only me, the boys and Louise allowed to visit. I stayed in the Wellington Park Hotel in Belfast for the full four weeks as it was walking distance from the hospital. I kept a vigil by his bedside for at least twenty hours per day in the early stages, as he was extremely sick and anxious following the transplant. He had severe mouth ulcers, he lost his hair overnight, and was unable to eat. For the first time – understandably – he showed signs of anxiety. Although we were warned about the side effects of the treatment, it did not make it easier to deal with.

During this time, I became a hypochondriac as I was petrified I would get a cold or infection, which would make James ill. I kept eating vitamins and garlic to build up my immunity, knowing how important it was for me to be there for him every day. The thought of not being able to visit him was inconceivable.

One evening, when James was beginning to recover, I was kissing him goodnight when he said, 'There's an awful smell of you.' It was the garlic.

He was never afraid to say what he thought. And that's the lovely compliment I got for looking after his health.

This brought me straight back to our third date. I was still relatively shy and reserved about the relationship when he looked at me and said, 'You've got a big nose.' I had never thought about my nose before that, but I've been aware of it ever since! He never said it in a belittling or criticising way, it was just an observation. As you can see, he sometimes had a very direct way of speaking – but it was not meant to hurt.

Towards the end of his stay in City Hospital, he was beginning to feel stronger, and his appetite was returning, but he was getting very down and frustrated by the confines of the room. He was supposed to get discharged on a Monday, I think it was 28 January, but the nurse said he had to wait another day for blood results. He huffed and wouldn't talk to me.

Jonathan called to see him on his way to the airport and James said very few words, he was not happy.

'It's just one more night,' I told James.

'That's alright for you to say,' he snapped, 'You haven't been sitting in this room for a month.'

I knew he was at the end of his tether. This was not like him. He had never complained, all the way through.

I then had an idea. Until then, he had had very limited visitors due to infection control, but I decided it was time for a visitor. I rang his Uncle John who lived in Belfast. He was a lovely and gentle man who cared a lot for James. They had worked together many times, I had often stayed with him and his wife Josey when I was a student in Belfast, and they were the most welcoming and caring people.

John arrived that evening and for the first evening since James was admitted, I felt I could leave him. He was delighted to see John. I left them alone and they chatted for hours. His spirits were lifted. It was the best therapy he could have got. He was discharged the following day.

Aside from close family, we had limited the visitors for the first few weeks after his discharge from hospital, as we were waiting for his immune system to recover. But James was constantly chatting to his friends and work colleagues on the phone. When he eventually got up and went out the back door, he saw a sign we had put on the door, saying, 'Visitors restricted due to risk of infection'.

I had got it printed on Belfast City Hospital headed paper to make it look official. He was not pleased that we had disallowed visitors, as he thought it was impolite, but we had done it to protect him – otherwise the house would have been filled with well-wishers every night.

Glimmers of Hope

2013 was shaping up to be a very good year. We were pleased that the transplant had worked. James was off treatment but still attended every week for blood work and a review of pain medication. My life was beginning to resemble normality. I was back doing training for Seating Matters, travelling to England on a regular basis again, and we were doing research with the Ulster University on the Seating Matters chairs.

James's first day back at work happened without planning. Large windmills were being erected in Loughermore Forest on the Barnailt road and were being transported to the site on huge lorries. The driver of one of the lorries was following his satnav, which took him onto the Nessagh road just above our house. It was a very narrow road with soft edges and the lorry got stuck. The side of the road gave way and the lorry slid over with its heavy load, toppling it into the ditch. The road was blocked. The driver was angry. And no one could get the lorry out. The news of the ongoings up the road reached James. This was music to his ears. He loved this type of challenge; he was ready to get the boots on and go to investigate.

He arrived at the scene and after surveying it for a while, he had a plan of action. Of course, he never left the site of the collision until he had the lorry out, the load was on its way, and the men involved were brought to my kitchen for tea. He was in his element.

In May 2013, I decided to go to Lough Derg in thanksgiving for James's recovery. I went for two nights and returned home on Monday to accompany James to the hospital as usual for his weekly check-up. However, as I had been up fasting and praying for three days, James told me to go to bed for some rest. I did that and when James returned from hospital he said, 'Your prayers are working, my bloods were completely clear!'

I was elated. I could not have wished for better news. After a full year of treatment and worry, my prayers were being answered.

Later that summer, James wired the mountain on the Birren road for Eugene. He was keeping busy and even if his work was less manual, he was enjoying it.

Ryan and Olivia were planning to get married, although no engagement had taken place, and they had bought their first house in Limavady on Scroggy Road. It was a good house but needed modernising. Again, this was an opportunity for James to do what he loved – getting fully immersed in a project and seeing it transform. He spent the end of 2013 and the beginning of 2014 working on their house.

A Crushing Set Back

Regrettably, our optimism was short lived. In November 2013, we were told the myeloma was back. The transplant failed and James was to begin treatment again in the new year, 2014. It was devastating. Being told you have cancer is shocking and overwhelming, but to hear that it has returned is totally crushing, especially when you have had the best treatment available, and when you are feeling very positive and with such high hopes for success. All the hopes, prayers, change of diet, treatment, and transplant – it was all for nothing.

We decided not to tell anyone until a decision was made about when treatment was to commence. We travelled back from the hospital that day in silence. What could I say? It had all been said before. Be positive. You will overcome this. You can beat this. It all sounded so futile now, so I said nothing. James came into the house and went straight upstairs to change before putting his working boots on. That's how he dealt with everything. Work.

He went to Martin's Farm and got on the digger. He was putting in drains. I let him go alone. I just circled the kitchen, my head was spinning, my heart was pounding, and the fear and anxiety which had subsided for a few months had re-emerged with a vengeance. This time, it was worse. Another transplant was not on the cards because it was too soon after the first.

Our options were beginning to run out.

After a few hours, I decided to go down to Martin's Farm to see how he was. I took some lunch for him. When I reached the digger, he stopped it and said, 'I knew you would come down, I was waiting on you.'

He'd had a few hours to ponder.

'We will just give it another go,' he said.

The first person I told was Jonathan at the Occupational Therapy Show in Birmingham. It was not an easy conversation. Every time I attend the Occupational Therapy Show now, I think of that day.

It was coming up to Christmas. Ryan and Olivia had got engaged. James wanted to throw a party for them. We were to remain upbeat and cheerful – where there is life there is hope. We had a great party and a great Christmas.

It was our last. 2014 was not going to be an easy year.

*

James started the new year working in Ryan and Olivia's house, but we knew what was around the corner. A new cycle of treatment. The same treatment he had got before the transplant. This time, James was not so compliant. He was half-hearted about the treatment. And I felt there was an understandable annoyance that he was back at the start and the outcome was so uncertain.

Then, early in 2014, he got a very severe flu and chest infection. I was worried because, for the first time in those two years, he stayed in bed for a week. He was very ill.

Since he was not keen to recommence treatment, we decided to try the nutritional approach again, but this time we were going to need the professionals for help. We had been told about the Hippocrates Health Institute in Florida, from which there were many stories of people using the nutritional approach to reverse their condition or at least go into remission.

So, we got in touch with a lady in Dublin, Bernadette Bohan, who ran a weekend called 'Hippocrates Style', in Cork. She was a cancer 'survivor' and had written a book called 'Eat Yourself Well'. Being an alumni of the Hippocrates Institute, we booked in to see her one weekend. En route, we stopped off in Carlow to see a tailor called Michael Johnson, who was famous for making suits for the President of Ireland, Michael Higgins. James wanted a tailor-made suit for Ryan and Olivia's wedding, which was planned for December 2014. Having had a fitting, James was on good form and looking forward to the first wedding in the family.

We arrived at the venue in Cork with great expectation, but once again I was anxious about how it would all go. I really wanted this to work, as I knew we were running out of options. I then got a phone call from Ryan who told me there was a bomb scare outside the Seating Matters factory. A pipe bomb at our front gate? The factory had been evacuated and the bomb squad were there doing a sweep of the area. Ryan and Louise, the only two living at home at the time, were relocated to the Roe Park Hotel for the night. Louise had an exam the next day. This added greatly to my anxiety. Why was there a bomb at our house? Who put it there and why? There were no answers. Initially, I did not tell James because I wanted him to settle in at the venue in a relaxed manner.

That evening, when we met with the group who were there for the nutritional weekend, the leader asked us to say why we were there. What were our concerns? What did we hope to achieve from the weekend? It was all couples; one was ill and the other was a carer or partner there to support them. James did not speak in the group. He was more a one-on-one person. Later, when we were all chatting, everyone thought I was the one who was ill. James, at this stage, was looking very well. He had recovered from the illness he had earlier and, as usual, he was comfortable chatting socially to people. The strain of everything, including the bomb, was etched on my face. We had arrived on a Thursday evening and by the time we left on Sunday night, I had lost seven pounds in weight. I really could not swallow the food that weekend, with the stress of everything building up inside me.

We returned home and were keen to hear an update on the bomb situation but there was no explanation. The bomb squad had come in and made it safe. The conclusion from the police was that it was destined for somewhere else, but the plot had been abandoned.

Following that weekend, we were strongly advised by Bernadette Bohan to go to The Hippocrates Health Institute in Florida. I later found out she got a fee for recommending new clients.

We were just so desperate to try everything, and James was really no longer keen on chemotherapy. So, it seemed like a good next step. This health institute was known as a retreat and lasted for three weeks. Jonathan accompanied James and me to Florida, as I was going to stay one week only as a guest, and Jonathan was happy to spend the three weeks with James. I needed to get back home and have all the wheatgrass, vegetables and sprouts grown for James's return. If I stayed for three weeks, it would take me another two to get all the food organised and grown, and James's new diet plan would be two weeks behind. I needed to be organised. It was going to be a challenge. No cooked food. All raw organic vegetables and, wheatgrass.

The weekend before we left for Florida, all the family travelled to London to the O2 Arena to attend a Tony Robbins motivational seminar weekend called 'Unleash Your Power'. Martin flew in from Toronto to join us. One of the challenges of the motivational weekend was to do 'The Fire Walk'.

We all walked across the red-hot coals, coached by Tony Robbins, which was said to be 'a powerful expression of moving beyond one's fears'. We had always believed in the power of our mind to overcome obstacles. But, until now, all our obstacles were work or money or business related, and this was the first time we had a health challenge to deal with. We thought we could treat this challenge like every other one we overcame.

James walked across the coals without any bother. He was strong-willed and determined.

The next day, we flew business class with Virgin Atlantic from Heathrow to Florida because it was the only way to travel. James's back was very painful if he sat for too long. We arrived on 23 March 2014, two years to the day since we first met Professor Morris. We did not tell the medical profession we were going to Florida as they would not have agreed and would have disapproved of James travelling outside the UK. Fortunately, though, James did not catch any infections while he was away. I was particularly careful, especially on the aeroplane, and ensured I was fully loaded with antibacterial wipes and sanitiser.

I think James would have described Hippocrates as a place of torture. For a man who loved his food, this was a nightmare unfolding. A completely vegan diet. No cooked or warm food. No animal products at all, including fish. No breakfast. Lunch and dinner consisted of raw green vegetables and sprouts. No fruit (as it contained sugar), as the thought process was that 'sugar feeds cancer'. No potatoes or bread, either, due to their sugar content. James was allowed nuts and almond milk, which he lived on for most of the time.

His only escape was getting out to a vegan restaurant once or twice, where he ate cooked vegan food. It was not allowed, but he was eating it anyway. The hot tubs, sauna, massages, and reflexology were about the only pleasures that kept him going. Jonathan seemed to enjoy the food and embraced the culture. There were a lot of vitamins recommended, with daily intravenous vitamin C and wheatgrass ingested religiously at least twice per day. The people running the centre passionately believed there was more therapeutic benefit to be gained for the people needing the wheatgrass if they grew and juiced it themselves, so everyone was encouraged to go to the kitchen every morning to juice their own wheatgrass. James was never going to follow this routine. If it was left to him, there would be no wheatgrass consumed. He tolerated it, but I think he was doing it for me more than himself. I had put my heart and soul into this regime, clinging to the hope it would be a success, but it was a tough journey for James and me.

He used to say, 'Will I live longer, or will it just feel longer?' After one week, I left Hippocrates ten pounds lighter. For the first time as an adult, I was wearing size eight clothes and they were not tight.

I picked James up from Belfast Airport on Sunday 13 April. He looked thin and tired. I thought he would have been more buoyant. I was excited to see him and enthusiastic about the new path ahead. He appeared despondent.

He was happy to be back home, but he was finding it very difficult to comply with the regime. He also did not want to resume chemotherapy. Everyone in the family had pinned their hopes on this last nutritional solution. The staff and the director of Hippocrates Health Institute, Dr Brian Clements, had given us a lot of reasons to be hopeful, telling James that myeloma was easy to cure. Apparently, 'you could sneeze it away'. James was uplifted by this statement.

But the journey was not going to be easy.

James struggled with most of the recipes and the healthy drinks. It got to the point where I had to go outside and physically climb up the steps of the digger to bring him his food, as he refused to come in and eat. He was losing weight fast. I was constantly urging him to eat the food, but it was a losing battle.

One day, his sister Anne Marie came up and I just broke down and cried.

'Nothing is working. He won't eat the food and he won't go for chemotherapy.' My strength and patience were wearing thin.

The one thing James did have faith in was the intravenous vitamin C, so I researched where this could be found locally. We sourced a clinic in Belfast on the Cregagh Road that was run by a controversial doctor, Finbar Magee, who was defying general medical practice by providing alternate solutions to conventional treatments. Our first appointment was on 6 May, and we attended this clinic twice per week from then. James liked Finbar and once again was uplifted by the positive vibes coming from him and his staff. James still agreed to be monitored by the hospital and get his bloods done. Although he was no longer receiving treatment, he wanted to know if the vitamin C was working.

For a few months after our return from Hippocrates, his condition remained static. He was eating some of the healthy options, drinking wheatgrass (daily), receiving vitamin C twice a week, eating the recommended vitamins, and attending kinesiology. On top of that, he was using the infrared sauna every day, which we purchased when Hippocrates advised us on its therapeutic benefit. James loved the sauna. He also bought a hot tub, but we did not have space for it, so he planned on building a special room to house the sauna and the hot tub. He was still looking to the future.

There was still evidence of the myeloma, but it had not drastically increased. We were pleased with that as we knew the new approach was going to take time. Everything seemed to be going well. James was going out to work, mainly at Ryan's house, Martin's farm, Jonathan's pillars on the Dunbrock Road, or up at Loughermore where he was getting the electricity in to the sites.

We still had a great belief in the power of the mind to overcome difficulties, something we had learnt from those motivational seminars on the Bob Proctor cruises. In fact, it was on a Bob Proctor cruise where we met Paul Martinelli, an internationally known speaker, educator and mentor who knew the power of human potential, and how to use that potential to attract whatever you wanted into your life. So, we decided to invite him to our home and mentor James for a week, to enable him to use the power of visualisation and positive thinking to overcome the disease and the negativity associated with cancer. James was very agreeable to this, so we booked Paul into the Roe Park Resort for a week. James met with Paul for five full days. He seemed very happy each morning going to meet him and each evening we met for dinner. I did not ask what they talked about because I was just happy that James had an outlet to express himself, and an opportunity to increase his belief that he had power over his own destiny.

We were all very euphoric about this development.

We believed James would overcome all the odds.

June 2014 was a positive month. James was working, we were going to see Finbar Magee twice weekly, the nutritional plan – although toned down a bit – was still a healthy diet with, of course, wheatgrass every day. Seating Matters was going well, I even went to London for a weekend with Louise. We were getting there, slowly but surely.

Killybegs, July 2014

Despite the positive month we had in June, I noticed James's condition had slowly begun to deteriorate. On 6 July 2014, we were preparing to go to a barbecue at Angela's house. He was exhausted, pale, lacked energy, and was extremely subdued. So, I suggested we cancel the visit. He was insistent that we go, much against my better judgement. We spent a happy afternoon there, but the next day James was admitted to hospital.

He had known that day would be his last visit to Angela's, and he did not want to cancel.

He remained in hospital for one week.

Angela and Francis went on a cruise after the barbecue, which James had encouraged them to book, as he had always enjoyed them. While he was in hospital, he was on the phone to Francis to see how he was enjoying it. Sadly, from that time on, he was constantly in and out of hospital – getting home at night as often as possible.

Most of July 2014 saw James in hospital with recurrent infections caused by neutropenia. We had done everything possible to keep his blood up, but the disease was overtaking us.

Then we heard about a healer, Catherine McLean, who lived in Donegal. Paddy Duffy, a lifelong friend and work colleague, had mentioned her a few times and had great faith in her. Coincidentally, another patient who was attending

Finbar Magee's clinic with myeloma was also seeing her and held her in high regard. He had been in remission for years.

We tried so many times to reach her by phone but without success. Our situation was getting serious. We were running out of options, and I was desperate to get James to see her.

Paddy Duffy said he knew where she lived, so I convinced him to take James to her home in Killybegs. Perhaps they could knock on her door and she would help?

They set off on a two-hour journey to Killybegs. I calmed down. I thought she would help. I was wrong.

They went to her door and her husband greeted them and said she was not available. They left with no appointment but were reassured she would be in touch. It transpired, however, that she had just received news of the death of a young boy, and she was too distressed to talk to them.

Eventually, we were given an appointment to meet Catherine McLean on 18 July 2014.

James and I had planned to go to Harvey's Point near Donegal Town for a cabaret evening in the summer of 2014. It was something we talked about many times over the years but had never got round to. I had it booked for early July 2014, but we postponed due to James's regular admissions to hospital. So we gave the tickets to Ryan and Olivia. We then rebooked it for 16 July to coincide with the visit to Catherine.

Before we arrived at Catherine's house, my preconceived image of a lady healer in Donegal was of an old lady wearing black clothes, encircled with a pious aura, and with rosary beads in her hand. The lady who greeted us was much younger, modern, and approachable. A total contrast to what I had expected. We went inside and gave a summary of James's condition, telling her what stage we were at in the treatment process. She said she could not guarantee that she would heal James, as that was up to God. She said she would do all she could, but the outcome was not determined by her. That was OK with me. I thought, we just need a helping hand here. I then left so James could talk to Catherine in private.

They talked for one hour as I waited in the car outside. She then signalled for me to come in. The first thing she said was, 'Stop the wheatgrass.' I was shocked but sort of relieved as it had always been a battle to get James to take it. I thought she knew best; I was ready to cooperate with whatever she recommended. She said, 'Give him good, nourishing food.' Then, she asked for us to return the next day.

We stayed overnight in Killybegs and both enjoyed a lovely meal without worrying about nutrition. James was in great form, uplifted. He really liked Catherine. I was in great form, too. I was unaware of the conversation that had gone on between them, but I presumed it meant James was going to get better. After all, that was the only outcome I could perceive or endure.

From that day on we saw Catherine every week. James would have walked over hot coals to get to her. He was most definitely being enriched and heartened by visiting her.

For one of James's appointments with Catherine, which I didn't know was going to be his last, he was an inpatient in the Sperrin Room. But he was determined to go no matter what, so he instructed me to be in the hospital on time and to have his clothes and shoes with me.

When I arrived, he got up, got dressed, and marched down the corridor and past the nurse's station without saying where he was going. The sister on the ward shouted after him but he strode on. I traipsed after him, apologising for him.

'He can't leave, he's neutropenic,' she said.

As he raced along the glass corridor, I knew there was no turning him.

Meeting Catherine was the best thing to happen to James and all my family, but I was unaware of the impact or lasting effect she would have on us.

While we were still seeing Catherine, Professor Morris was not happy with how things were going. The day I dreaded had now come.

'I have exhausted all my options,' he said. 'Remember you offered to pay for treatment if it was going to benefit James? Well, that time has come because I have nothing left to offer him.'

He told us about medicine available in the USA. James could travel to the USA for treatment, or we could buy the treatment and he would administer it in Altnagelvin Hospital. I knew James was neither physically nor mentally able to travel, so we said we would buy whatever was needed.

Professor Morris ordered two cycles of a drug used in the USA to treat myeloma that wasn't available on the NHS. He started his first cycle on 4 August. Because the side effects were unknown to the medical staff, James was an inpatient while the treatment was being administered. He stayed Monday to Wednesday for three weeks. He received one cycle. Then he was off treatment for one week beginning 25 August. This was working out very well for us as it was our thirtieth wedding anniversary on the 25 August, and we had planned to go away to celebrate.

While he was getting the treatment, James had an immediate positive reaction. One day, he even said to me, 'This is really working, I don't have a single pain or ache.'

For the umpteenth time in this unpredictable and heart-wrenching journey, I was feeling optimistic. No, overjoyed.

James got out of hospital after the third week of treatment and went straight to work. He was building the pillars at Jonathan's farm on the Dunbrock road. On Sunday 24 August, we had planned a family meal in Derry to celebrate our anniversary and the family had arranged a three-night stay for us in Co Cavan following the celebrations. James, being James, was so absorbed in building the pillars that we were late for our meal. He just did not want to leave the work.

After the meal, I drove to the Farnham Estate Hotel and we arrived to champagne, strawberries and flowers in our room – all courtesy of the family. We were going to relax and have a memorable thirtieth anniversary. We both deserved it. It had been a turbulent few months.

Then, I noticed James's lip was bleeding.

The End of the Celebrations

The celebrations were over before they began. I knew the symptoms were due to low platelets. James, however, stubbornly said nothing was wrong. I did not sleep that night. James did. I kept an eye on him until morning.

When he woke, he was adamant that we continue our holiday. He wanted to persevere so as to avoid spoiling the occasion for me. But the holiday was already over for me. We went for breakfast and then on a tour he wanted to go on before afternoon tea in the Slieve Russell Hotel.

On our return to the Farnham Estate, I convinced James to let me ring the Sperrin Room. He was initially against this as he knew they would insist on admitting him. As suspected, they advised us to return to the ward immediately.

I explained to the hotel receptionist that we were checking out early as James was unwell. They refunded the three nights.

James said we would go back at another time. That was not to be.

James was admitted to the Sperrin Room on 25 August, our thirtieth wedding anniversary. For the first time, I sat beside his hospital bed and cried.

'You must think I am bad if you are crying, it's not like you,' James said.

I told him I was upset because it was our anniversary. I still had not fully realised that it was coming near to the end. But it was getting more and more difficult to keep positive as every time we thought we were making progress, another block appeared.

This was to be James's last hospital admission; even though he did get home again, he was never discharged. A bed was kept for him, and he could come in when he needed, and go home when he felt well enough.

Even with this arrangement I still did not grasp the seriousness of the situation.

A week after James was admitted, Professor Morris asked to meet with me. I met him with Jonathan on the afternoon of Monday 1 September. He said James had one week to live.

I did not believe him.

He said I should use the next week to say anything that was left unsaid, and I was fortunate as many people do not get that chance. He said he would see him next Monday, 'If he was still there.'

Then he left the room.

Jonathan said nothing, only looking at me to see how I was reacting.

'Do you really believe that? Do you really think Daddy is not going to be at Ryan's wedding?' I said. 'I don't believe it.'

Then I left the room to return to James. As I passed the nurses' station, they had their heads bowed, no one wanted to look me straight in the eye. We had built a great rapport with them over the last two years. They were very dedicated and caring nurses. James was a favourite of theirs, as he always asked about their families and helped with various problems they had. He got to know them.

I went straight over to them and said defiantly, 'You might have seen this before, but you've never met the Tierneys.'

I was not giving up. I was going to show them we were different.

When I got back to the room, James said he didn't want to talk. We had never discussed death or dying before, and this time was no different. He still wanted to know if there was anything the doctors could do. Continuing the treatment from America was not an option, it was too toxic for him. They started him on a form of chemotherapy, but I now know it was just to please him and me.

My head was spinning again. My heart was pounding. Louise had just started her first day of the new academic year, which was her GCSE year. How was I going to tell her this?

I didn't believe it anyway.

Doctors were not always right. They did not believe in the power of prayer. There were so many people praying for James that we knew things had to work out well.

As a family, we started the Surrender Novena – a nine-day novena.

I convinced myself and my family it would work. This is what the prayer said:

'Why do you confuse yourselves with worry? Leave the care of your affairs to me and everything will be peaceful. I say to you in truth that every act of true, blind, complete surrender to me produces the effect that you desire and resolves all difficult situations.

Oh Jesus, I surrender myself to you, take care of everything!' (10 times)

Each night we said this prayer. We prayed all week.

James was allowed home every night to sleep but he went into hospital each day, usually for a top up of platelets and pain relief. I know now that there was no treatment being given, but I did not ask the question at the time.

Someone stayed with him all the time he was in hospital.

It was a long and painful week for everyone. We had a lot of visitors, and the house was busy each night. The evening of Thursday 4 September, Anne Marie and Monica visited. They were very tearful and upset. I didn't like this. When they were leaving, I followed them out to the street and told them not to be crying in front of James as it would make him think he was dying. They just looked at me and said nothing. It was a look of disbelief.

Friday 5 September arrived, and we were still waiting for the miracle. I contacted Catherine McLean in Donegal. It was unusual for her to leave her home to visit people, but she agreed to come to James. Her husband took her to Derry where Jonathan met her. Again, her visit to James was private. No one was in the room while she spoke and prayed with James.

When she was leaving, all three boys accompanied her to Derry. They wanted to know what she thought. I don't know what she said but her presence always brought a sense of peace to us. James was happy to see her.

It was Saturday 6 September. We were getting a new front door installed and James knew the man fitting it, so he invited him in for breakfast. We all ate at the kitchen table. Then James went to Limavady to see Ryan and Olivia's house, which was still being renovated. Their wedding was just three months away. He also wanted to price a job. Jonathan and Louise went with him.

He was due to return home before I took him to hospital for his treatment, but while he was in Limavady, he said to Ryan or Olivia, 'Just take me straight to the hospital.' He wasn't feeling well. Over the course of that week his abdomen had begun swelling and he was finding it uncomfortable to sit. Ryan and Olivia accompanied him to the hospital. I stayed at home until he returned.

Some years later I saw a photograph of James, Olivia, Ryan and Louise in Limavady that day, and I could not believe how ill James looked. At the time, he was still the same James to me. I really can't understand yet how I was so irrational to how ill he was. As I look at that photo now, with his worn-out face, I wonder, 'What was he thinking at that moment?'

When he returned from hospital that day he could not walk upstairs, so he lay on Ryan's bed in the ground floor bedroom. After a few hours, he was able to get up and rest in the sitting room on his recliner chair. Eugene and Paddy Gilloway came to visit him, and he seemed to enjoy a bit of craic. He ate a pancake. I then suggested he go to bed.

'You go on up, I will be up later,' he said.

He wanted to sleep upstairs but he wasn't sure how he was going to make it up the stairs. He did make it up, but it was his last time to climb the stairs. The stairs that he had taken so much pride in making. Only his sheer grit and determination got him up those stairs that night. And he was determined not to need help.

It was obvious to me that he was in great pain, so I pleaded with him to go to the hospital for pain relief. But he would not concede, continually saying he was ok.

Eventually, he gave in and said that I could ring the out of hours doctor. The GP arrived and gave him an injection of morphine. All the time, Jonathan, Ryan, Martin, Louise, Olivia, Elizabeth, Sean Mullan and James O'Donnell were downstairs nervously waiting to see what was going to happen. One of them would come up to see how James was every now and then.

James was sweating profusely but the morphine was beginning to act, and he was more settled. He kept chatting. And it was then, in that moment, that for the first time since his diagnosis, I gave in that James was going to die. I suddenly realised that he was holding on for me.

I had never come to terms that he would die. It was unthinkable until now.

I called Jonathan and, as we stood in the corridor leading to our bedroom, I said, 'We have to let him go, it's not fair on him.'

Jonathan agreed. Maybe he had come to the realisation before me, but he never said.

I went back into the bedroom where James was resting, and spoke to him, saying, 'James this is not working. I have to let you go. I will never forget you, but it's not fair on you. I am only being selfish, wanting to hold on to you.'

'I will never give up and I will never leave you,' he said. 'Get into bed and don't worry about it tonight.'

I got into bed beside him and snuggled up to his back, just like I had done for the previous thirty years. And slept.

7 September

He woke early on Sunday, 7 September. I asked him if he was in pain.

'It's not excruciating,' he said.

I asked him if I should call the doctor again to get a top up of morphine.

'No, I think we should go into the hospital.'

I wanted to keep him at home if it was feasible, if I could manage his pain, but he had other ideas. In death, as in life, he was determined to have it done his way. So, I rang the hospital. They still had his bed saved for him. They were expecting the call.

All the family gathered into the bedroom. Sean Mullan and James O'Donnell were out on the landing waiting for James to come out of the bedroom. It was an anxious and uneasy gathering. James looked up at everyone and said very quickly, 'Fourteen eyes looking at me.' He still had not lost his sense of humour. He was keeping up a brave face.

Ryan asked him, 'Daddy, what do you want us to do?'

I'm not sure what Ryan meant by this question, but James's response was, 'Make plenty of money and enjoy it.'

He was now sitting on the edge of the bed with everyone round him. I was sitting on his right side with Louise beside me. The three boys were directly in front of him, and Olivia was standing with her back against the wardrobe door. Elizabeth, who was still getting to know the family, was standing just outside the bedroom door looking in.

James said to her, 'Come you in, too, you are part of the family.' He always knew what to say and when to say it, even at this very poignant moment.

I then asked him where he wanted to be buried. He had done work at two graveyards in the parish. St Finlough's and Christ the King. Since death was never discussed before, I had no idea if he preferred anywhere particular for his final resting place. I wanted to make sure I got it right.

'St Finlough's,' he said. He was calm and peaceful.

Olivia and I started getting him dressed for the hospital.

'Who would be best at dressing a patient, an OT or a physio?' he asked.

He had been around an occupational therapist for over thirty years and knew there was always a bit of competition between the professions. It was, again, his way of keeping the conversation light. Since his abdomen was distended, I thought I would put a pair of soft, elasticated, tracksuit bottoms on him for comfort. He was never a tracksuit and trainers man.

'What are you doing with those aul tartles, have you no good clothes?' he said.

I took out a pair of good trousers, but I could not get the belt fastened because of the swollen tummy. He was happy with them. I then put on his Barker shoes to match the trousers. He loved good clothes and especially shoes.

He was ready to go.

During the night, while everyone was doing a vigil in the kitchen, the boys had planned how they would get James down the stairs, as it was obvious that he was in a lot of pain. Walking may be unrealistic. They had a large white sheet, and the five boys were going to carry him.

James had other plans.

With his Barker shoes on, he stood up, dashed across the landing, and bolted down the stairs. I was in hot pursuit – afraid he would fall. Martin had the car pulled up to the front door and he got in without assistance. He had left his home in a flash with his independence intact. He knew it was his last time. As Martin drove down past Dunbrock Road, James said, 'I didn't get Johnny's pillars finished.'

I remember no other conversation en route to the hospital.

*

The hospital ward knew we were on our way. Martin had called them. We arrived about 9 am. When we reached the door of the hospital, the nurse who had always looked after James was waiting with a wheelchair. She opened the car door and James swung his legs round and placed his two feet firmly on the ground.

'Look at you,' she remarked, 'Lovely shoes and all dressed up.'

'Aye,' he said, 'And she was going to put aul tartles on me.' She looked at me and we both smiled.

The final day had come.

James was taken up to the now familiar room and a syringe driver was inserted to control the pain. Within a very short time, he was asleep and comfortable. The nursing staff were so kind. They knew us well by this point and we had developed a mutual respect. I was told that as soon as I noticed James in any kind of discomfort, I was to alert them, and they would deal with his pain. I had previously been told by Doctor McKenny, my family GP, when Mammy was dying, that she should never be in pain. She wasn't, and James would not be either.

Since James's diagnosis I had accompanied him to every hospital appointment, I looked after his diet and his medication, and at times when he was overloaded with information, I took responsibility for his care. I just had one last act to perform. I needed to make sure he had a peaceful, pain free end. I was fully committed to making sure James did not suffer. It was too late now to worry about overdosing with drugs. Everything that could be done was done. Everything that needed said was said. He deserved a peaceful and pain free release. I was also aware that although he was not saying much, he could hear us, and we only talked about positive things while we were at his bedside.

All the extended family had now been informed that James was in hospital. His brothers, sisters, mother, and all my family. The first to arrive were Angela and Francis. James O'Donnell had kept them in the loop about developments during the night. Angela arrived with a crucifix. It is very customary in the Catholic tradition for a dying person to hold a crucifix and rosary beads in their hand. I have kept this crucifix and held it every night for about six years after his death. It was like holding his hand and it has given me great comfort. I hope it is in the palm of my hand when my time comes.

The hospital room was filled with people throughout the day. People flowed in and out quietly, sat for a while, and prayed. It felt very peaceful.

In the afternoon, the sun shone through the large window. The staff had given us an extra room for the overflow of visitors, and refreshments were brought in.

There are a few moments that are etched in my memory from that day. At various times throughout the day, James woke up. One of those times, he woke up and my brother Felly had arrived with Brendan. James looked over and said, 'Hello Felly, what are you all doing here? Have you no work to go to?'

'It's Sunday,' I told James.

'That doesn't matter, I would soon get you something to do.'

Work was still in his head. This caused my brother to think that he was still going to recover. Felly said to me, 'He might be OK you know.'

'No Felly, this is it,' I said. 'There is no coming back from this.' Felly still could not conceive that this was the end for James. I, on the other hand, had finally surrendered.

It was a distressing day for everyone. Saying goodbye is heart-breaking. James's mother was an inpatient in the Waterside Hospital at that time and not very mobile. She was brought to James's bed in a wheelchair by Monica. She prayed for a while and when it was time for her to go, she needed help to stand up. Monica and Anne Marie stood one on either side of her to support her, and she kissed James goodbye. It was a sad moment for everyone in the room.

Another time that James woke up was when he sat straight up in the bed and kissed me directly on the lips. He said nothing and just lay back down.

The final farewell.

He did not sit up after that.

I called in the nurse whenever I observed him getting agitated. They were so attentive.

The light of the sun started to fade in the room and at six o'clock I could hear church bells ringing 'The Angelus'. I was still sitting, holding James's hand and wetting his lips. I asked him if he could hear the bells. I got no response.

Catherine in Donegal wanted to be kept informed about James. Jonathan rang her and she asked if she could come to the hospital to do a healing. We were very happy for her to come. She had always been a source of strength for James. He needed all the help he could get right now. So did we.

She arrived just as Monsignor McCanny was there conferring James the last rites. They greeted each other, then Monsignor left her alone with James.

As with every other occasion, I also did not stay in the room. She spent a few minutes praying with him, and when she came out, she said, 'He will pass peacefully soon, I have done a healing on him.' For anyone who did not know Catherine or the gift she had, this may have sounded very unreal. How could James be healed at this stage? I had come to realise that there is more to healing than just physical healing, and I was very reassured that James had been healed spiritually – he would have a peaceful transition to the spiritual world.

As the evening passed, there was less and less response from James. The natural light in the room was now gone and replaced with a dim light above the bed. I was getting very tired. I was also very concerned about Louise and the boys and how they were going to react when the final breath came. They had been so attentive and never strayed too far from his bedside.

At one point, I was very frustrated, and I said to my sister Geraldine, 'God would not let me keep him and now he won't take him and give him rest.' I just didn't understand why this was happening. We had been in this room fourteen hours at this stage. We knew what we were waiting on, but the stress and anxiety of knowing what was ahead was overwhelming at times.

It was nearing midnight when the nurses came in to check on James. They said his clothes were very wet with sweat and asked if I wanted them changed. I had done this in hospital so often over the previous months, as he hated being wet, and so I thought it would be more pleasant for him if he had dry clothes. They told me to go and have a break and that they would change him.

I had just moved outside the room when they called me back.

As soon as they went to move him his breathing changed, and they knew the end was very near. We summoned the immediate family and those who had sustained us over the course of the day. We all held hands round the bed and reassured him we were there.

Then he was gone.

The light of my life had finally gone out.

It was just after midnight. Monday 8 September. One week after I met with Professor Morris.

As he had predicted, he had one less patient to see on Monday.

A Celebration of James

No matter how long you wait on someone to take their final breath, there is still an element of shock when it happens. The finality of it is very hard to process. I was numb with disbelief that the person I loved, who was larger than life and full of energy, was lying unresponsive in this bed. For a brief moment I thought I was dreaming, then I thought I was going to have a panic attack. But I pulled myself back to reality and realised I had children to support and a job to do. James would be very annoyed if I let him and them down. I kept my composure. There was no hysterical crying. We were all calm, exhausted, and resigned. The nurses said we could stay as long as we wanted, no pressure to leave. We remained in the room, but I have no idea for how long. Time meant nothing now.

When I was waiting for James to pass, every minute felt like an hour. Now he was at peace, time stood still.

We arrived home. The news had spread and there were lots of people in the house as we had to prepare for what we now know was the biggest wake ever seen in this area. Furniture was being moved around to make room for lots of chairs. The big dining table was moved out. But as I didn't want the house completely overhauled, I asked for the furniture in the sitting room, a cream leather suite, and a grand piano to be left. James was very proud of his home, and I wanted it to look as normal as possible for James's final farewell. He was an extrovert who loved social gatherings. This room had hosted many parties, but the largest gathering ever was about to take place.

On Monday afternoon we went to the funeral home to bring James home. We were escorted into a little prayer room for private viewing. He was dressed in a brand-new suit I had bought for a wedding we were to attend in July 2014 in London. I had great hopes that we would be there, but James was too ill. His hair had grown back well from the chemotherapy and because it was new hair, it was wavy and felt so soft to touch. He had a red tie and white shirt and looked so handsome. It tore my heart to know I would soon never see his face again.

The wake and funeral were huge. People queued for two or three hours to get into our home to pay their respects. The queue extended across the yard and out to the road. Cars were parked in the nearby fields.

I stood beside James's coffin with his two sisters for two full days until late in the evening to greet everyone. People came from miles away, all with their story to tell about James. They were feeling very sorrowful about his untimely passing.

As the queue grew longer and longer, one of my sisters suggested we speed up and not talk so long to each person, but I couldn't do that. They came here for a reason, and they needed to be heard. Because James had been out working two weeks previously and driving a tractor, most people thought he was doing well, and were shocked to hear he had passed away.

Monsignor McCanny visited our home on several occasions during the two-day wake and wanted to know more about James. He knew his work ethic well from the work he had carried out in the parish, but he wanted to know more about the person James was, and what he was like as a father, husband and friend.

After hearing our thoughts and taking from his own personal experience of James, he chose the passage from Matthew's Gospel in his homily to reflect James's character:

For I was hungry and you gave me something to eat.

I was thirsty and you gave me something to drink.

I was a stranger and you took me in.

I needed clothes and you clothed me.

I was sick and you looked after.

I was in prison and you visited me.

It was a very fitting tribute, for in life James had fulfilled all of those statements. He was always bringing people into the house for tea and food. I knew several men with alcohol addiction whom he supported. He visited people in hospital. People in prison. He supported people through grief and family tragedies. He also brought workmen from Latvia into our home when they had no living accommodation. All of this was done discreetly and most of it I was unaware of until I was told about it from the family or the people he had helped.

*

I stood in the graveyard on a warm and sunny autumn day for hours after the burial, surrounded by my family, to receive more people who wanted to express their sympathy and condolences. The heat of the sun felt comforting and warm, and I was unaware I was getting sunburnt.

We then proceeded to the Drummond Hotel where a dining room was filled with family and friends waiting for the immediate family to gather. It was what James would have wanted. Everyone there getting a warm meal. They had supported and sustained us over months, weeks and days, and this was our way to say thank you.

I said grace before we ate and spoke to everyone in the room before leaving.

It had been a long three days.

We then left the crowd behind to begin our lives without James.

Two Weddings and a Funeral

The days after the funeral now seem like a blur. I wandered around aimlessly unable to focus on anything. After all the never-ending trips to hospital, the worry and anxiety about James, the large wake and funeral, and so many people to talk to, I was utterly exhausted. I had no motivation. I was lethargic and weary. I wasn't sleeping at night. When the bedroom door was closed, that's when reality hit home. I felt alone.

My concern had now turned to Louise and the boys but particularly Louise. My attention had been so firmly focused on James for so long that I felt I had neglected her. She was fifteen years old and had just started her GCSE year. She wasn't very communicative about her feelings. She just kept saying, 'I'm OK.' I knew she wasn't, but I could only ask and hope that she knew I was there for her. I tried to spend as much time as possible with her. Jonathan, Ryan and Martin were very good at involving her in their day-to-day activities, and I put no pressure on her to go to school. To me, this was not a priority. When she felt like going, she went, when she didn't feel like it, she stayed at home with us. A long time after she told me she didn't want to go to school at the time because all her friends and teachers were carrying on as 'normal' as if nothing had happened. Her world had fallen apart but everyone was getting on with their lives. When she was home with us, there was a camaraderie. We were all in this together and we were going through it together. She needed to be with those who understood what she was going through.

I tried to be upbeat with the boys and encourage them to keep working.

Ryan came in one day, maybe a week after the funeral, and he said, 'I don't know what to do.'

'Why?' I asked.

'Because I don't know what Daddy would want,' he said.

He felt lost, too.

I told him he had to do things his way. Whatever he thought was the right thing to do, he needed to just do that. He would be guided by his Daddy.

Although I brought them up to be independent, until now they had always had James for advice or a backup if things didn't work out. It was not just me who had to adjust to life without James and I was very conscious that I needed to show them the way. I had to walk the walk. I was reminded of my brothers who were in a similar situation forty-three years earlier when Daddy died. At the time, I had thought my brothers were old men, now I realised that in their twenties, children still needed the guidance and experience of their father.

Ryan's wedding was the first big event. After the Month's Mind Mass, held about four weeks after the funeral, I decided to throw myself into preparations. The Month's Mind Mass provided an opportunity to remember James once again in a prayerful way with family and friends. It was also the first time to reconnect with some people since the funeral. Afterwards, we had tea and refreshments in St Finlough's for about 200 people. I really liked seeing everyone again, and felt I was keeping James at the centre of life by talking about him with his friends and family again.

It was now October and I needed to decide what I was wearing to the wedding. I had already made my mind up that I was getting my outfit designed, so I contacted Eamon McKay, who was recommended to me by my beautician. Geraldine and I made a trip to Dunloy to meet him. Eamon was an eccentric, small and talented man who was very excited about designing my dress. I immediately got on well with him, but he had come with a warning as, apparently, he is always last minute about getting the work complete. I was told, 'You will be running to him on the last few days getting the final fitting.' I didn't need that stress, so I explained my situation and told him I was feeling quite anxious and asked him whether he could have it completed at the beginning of December.

One of Eamon's customs was to spend at least one full day at his client's home. I think he did this as he loved the craic, the food and the company. Eamon lived alone in a small bungalow. He had cared for his mother until her death, and I think he was quite lonely. He loved experimenting with different food dishes and loved his wine. On each visit I made to him for a fitting, we started first by going for a coffee. His work was also his social life. When the time came, we arranged a day for him to spend at my home. Since Eamon did not drive, Geraldine collected him from his home and brought him up. I invited Angela to join us too, just to take the pressure off me. We spent a day measuring, fitting, and sewing. Eamon took lots of breaks, ate lunch, smoked a few cigarettes and had a glass of wine, but we made great progress. By the end of the day, I had a dress to try on, albeit unfinished, but it was taking shape. Eamon kept his word, and my dress was complete by 1 December.

Leading up to the wedding we had lots of visitors coming with presents. The wedding guest list was very large as many of the extended family and friends had spent so much time with us over the previous few months, and Ryan and Olivia wanted to include them in the celebration. That is when I noticed Paddy, my brother, was not in good form. Paddy was always someone who arrived with an upbeat attitude and was great craic. He would sit all night drinking tea, smoking and talking. He loved to ceili. During the run up to the wedding, he visited me twice with different members of his family. He was always very caring and supportive towards me and had great empathy for what I was going through. However, I noticed he was quieter than usual, so I asked him if he was ok. He said his stomach was sore and that he had heartburn. I gave him a hot whiskey as I knew he always liked one before bed. It seemed to pick him up and he became more engaged in the conversation taking place around our dining room table, but I was concerned about him.

The night before the wedding we had a quiet family evening and I reassured Ryan that the next day was a day to celebrate. 'We have cried enough,' I said, 'and we are going to enjoy your wedding – that's what Daddy would want.'

The wedding day arrived. Olivia, who had been part of our family since she was sixteen, was soon to become the first Mrs Tierney of the next generation. Olivia had been through the ups and downs with us over the years, and I was very happy that Ryan had a lifelong partner in her.

We were all gathered in the chapel, and while we waited for the bride to arrive my stomach was doing somersaults. I wanted to be brave but listening to the beautiful music was testing my resolve. I was sitting alone in the front seat until Angela arrived, as the three boys were on the altar and Louise was bridesmaid.

The Mass was said by Bishop Lagan, Olivia's uncle. The first thing he did when he came out on the altar was to acknowledge James's absence. Although it was difficult and I had to fight back the tears, it was a relief. It meant that I didn't have to worry about James's name being spoken again until the wedding ceremony was over. It was a very compassionate way to deal with the emotional situation. Tears were averted and the ceremony continued.

I was still thinking of Paddy's health that day and I felt more aware of my own mortality and the mortality of others, so I devised a way to get a photo of my all brothers and sisters together. The opportunity was lost, however, because although John came to the wedding in the chapel, he did not attend the reception.

A short time after the wedding, Paddy's son James rang me and told me Paddy had cancer of the oesophagus. This explained the stomach problems and the heartburn. I was distraught by the diagnosis coming so soon after James, and I felt so much empathy for the family and what they had in front of them. However, over the next weeks and months, I supported and encouraged them as best I could.

2015 had begun on a bleak note, but again I needed to get the spirits up as there was another wedding on the horizon. Martin and Elizabeth were due to get married in Syracuse, New York in May 2015. In 2011, Martin had met Elizabeth on a mission to Haiti following the earthquake. Elizabeth had been to our home on a number of occasions to meet us, but she got a baptism of fire at James's wake, where she met hundreds of people, including all the cousins, aunties, uncles and neighbours. All in the space of two days. It must have been mesmerising for her.

Thankfully, a few days before James went into hospital for the last time, Martin and Elizabeth arranged a phone call between James and Elizabeth's parents, as by now Martin knew they were never going to meet in person.

In 2015, it was time to visit Eamon again, and plans were made to get another dress designed and made for the forthcoming wedding. This time I told Eamon we were shipping it off one month before the wedding to ensure it was completed in plenty of time.

Like I did at Ryan's wedding, I put on a brave show. It was more difficult as I was meeting some of Elizabeth's family for the first time who were aware of James's passing and wanted to acknowledge it and talk about him. When his name was mentioned, I felt the physical pain of his loss in my heart, but I needed to hide my emotion and keep my composure. If I started to cry, I wasn't sure I could stop, and I didn't want to make the other person feel uncomfortable. I shed the tears in private.

I was very conscious that this was also a difficult time for Martin. His hopes of having his Daddy at his wedding had been crushed, so I needed to step up and be strong. On the day of their wedding, Elizabeth had four grandparents and her mother and father, and Martin only had me.

Martin and Elizabeth married in Syracuse on 2 May 2015.

A few months after their wedding I was rummaging through old documents when I came across a diary I had kept, recording our first family holiday to Canada in May 2000. I was astonished to read it and remember that we had been to Syracuse before. For that holiday we had hired a huge motorhome and travelled for miles through Canada, but James had also wanted to cross the US border, so we entered the USA, which was a first for all of us. As usual, James had just kept driving, but as it was a Saturday night, we eventually parked up in Syracuse. The next morning, we found a chapel for Mass, after which we were invited downstairs to a reception room for tea and buns. It was a treat we remembered as this was not a practice we were used to in Ireland. In the little red diary, I had recorded that: 'We arrived in Syracuse, New York. We went to Mass, the priest invited us for tea afterwards.'

Maybe it was even the same chapel in which Martin got married fifteen years later.

Martin was delighted to hear that his Daddy had been in Syracuse. It felt good and was a wee sign from James that he was – and is – still with us.

The day after Martin and Elizabeth's wedding we were told that Granny Tierney (James's Mother) had fallen in the care home in Limavady and had been taken to hospital. She was very ill. Monica, Anne Marie and Peter, who had been with us in Syracuse, cut their holiday short and returned home. We did not tell Martin, as he was going on his honeymoon to Europe.

I returned home a few days after the wedding and spent the next two weeks in and out to the hospital again. There was a vigil kept around her bed twenty-four hours per day. Granny Tierney passed away on 16 May 2015. Martin and Elizabeth were told a few days before she died, and they returned from their honeymoon.

Another wake and funeral so soon after James was a very upsetting time for everyone close to the family. It felt like déjà vu as the same people we had met during the past few months had returned once again to pay their respects.

Martin and Elizabeth returned to Rome after the funeral to complete their honeymoon as they had arranged to meet the Pope. It was an event they did not want to forego.

When they returned home to Limavady, a wedding reception was planned for them so uncles, aunts, cousins and friends who could not travel to New York got the chance to celebrate with them. I also accomplished one of my goals at this reception. With a bit of effort and cajoling, I eventually managed to get all my brothers and sisters neatly in a row for a photo. It was more significant now than ever before, as I had an unsettling feeling that it might be my last opportunity. It was. Paddy passed away in October 2016 and this was our last photo of the thirteen siblings.

I am writing this now not to get pity or for the reader to feel sorry for me, but to reassure you that there *is* life after death. It is a very difficult journey, but I can now say that I have come through this better than I ever thought possible at the very start. I once heard a saying:

'When you are going through hell, don't stop.'

And that is what I did. I kept on going; looking after my family, setting myself small tasks at first, and trying to keep busy. I wrote a short poem in the early days called 'One Day at a Time', because that was how I got through. In fact, some days it was one hour at a time, but I got there in the end.

One Day at a Time

It's a phrase that's overused and said without much thought

Buts it's the only way to handle pain that's what my grief has taught

You can't look down the road and wonder how you are going to cope

You can only live in the present and keep alive your hope

I know it isn't easy, your mind will wander away

But catch your thoughts at that moment and bring them back to today

Get something to divert you and keep a busy mind

And allow your tears to flow from time to time

Tears will heal your heart and soften the pain of your grief

And allow yourself the time you need to adjust to your new life

They say life goes on but you feel trapped in time

We haven't any choice it really is 'Just one day at a time'

January 2015

I can't imagine anyone loving another person more than I loved James, and although it was tough letting him go, I have survived. I now live a happy, fulfilled life – something

I never thought could happen without James. Like the poem says, 'The waves still crash over me every now and then, but I know I will survive'. My faith that he is still with me has helped me enormously but having my family around me has been the greatest blessing. My family gave me something to live for. A reason to get up each day and a reason to be happy.

Reflections

I would consider myself to be a rational, informed and enlightened person, who, when faced with a situation, could come to a knowledgeable and sensible conclusion about it. I visited many sick people over my thirty-year career and could recognise when someone was not going to make it. I did this when Mammy took ill. We took her to the doctors, we got investigations done, we got a diagnosis, and I asked for a prognosis. We were told she had eight, ten or twelve weeks to live. I was devastated and heartbroken and could hardly believe the day I had feared most of my life, especially since Daddy had died, had now come. However, I accepted this and proceeded to make her comfortable. I attended to her every need and cared for her in any way I could, as I tried to prepare myself for the inevitable outcome while supporting my siblings to do the same. Some of them were more aware or accepting than others. Some of my brothers could not take in that Mammy was going to die.

Six years later, when I was faced with James's diagnosis, I reacted in a totally different manner. It was out of character for me. I never let the thought of him dying enter my head. I could not accept he was going to die. I totally convinced myself that we – as a couple and as a family – could overcome this challenge. When I met with other patients in the hospital who were ill and dying, I would feel sorry for them, but I thought they had 'given in' too early, that they didn't fight hard enough, that they listened to too many negative stories, or that they had nothing to live for. James was different. We were different. James was not going to die. He was going to be the miracle everyone talked about. We still had so much to do. When we were together, we acted like teenagers and talked about all the things we would do in the future. We were still young; life was not supposed to end this soon. We still had a future to enjoy. So, when he was diagnosed, I totally committed myself to finding a solution. No stone would be left unturned.

My reaction was possibly common for people in my situation. Others who have found themselves in similar situations may have reacted the same. I think it is a coping mechanism. Maybe its denial. I recognise it now in others.

Grief is unimaginably difficult, especially when it is your soulmate you have lost. The days after the funeral were filled with emptiness, loneliness, fear, disbelief, and anxiety. I felt paralysed. I could not even focus on making a cup of tea. I could not sleep; I walked about in a trance all the time trying not to show the grief I was feeling to my family. They were dealing with the loss of their father, after all, and I could not add more burden on top of that by having them worry about me. We went through the motions of going out for dinner and talking to people, but all the time there was a well of tears just waiting to flow out from my eyes. I held back until I was alone, and then the flood gates opened. I was in a very lonely world. I missed James's physical presence. I missed his support. If ever I had a problem, he was there for me. Now I was facing the biggest challenge of my life. He was gone. Or at least, that's what I thought in those early days. I needed his strong arms to hold me and his confidence to reassure me, but I had nothing to lean on. Everyone around me was grieving, everyone was struggling in the sea of grief.

I had family to support, and Ryan and Olivia's wedding was approaching in a few months. It was going to be difficult having our first family occasion without the main man. I was adamant the wedding was going to be a happy event and something to celebrate. It would be a lasting memory for Ryan, Olivia and all the family so it could not be clouded with tears and sadness. Still, I knew Ryan was worried about how we would all make it through the day, especially me, and I was not going to be the one to let him down. I was going to do this for him and for James.

I attended grief counselling very early on and started a spiritual journey of trying to understand why this had happened, and whether there was a bigger picture to this all.

Was there a reason why James was taken from us?

Was it all in life's plan?

Is the day we are born and the day we leave this earth predetermined?

My attention had been drawn to Esther (Abraham) Hicks in 2008 when I was on the first Bob Proctor cruise. Her book 'Ask and it is Given' was on sale and I bought it. I was always fascinated by her spiritual teaching, but listening to her now, after losing James, resonated with me and gave me comfort and an insight into death and dying that I had not previously considered.

Firstly, Esther never referred to dying as 'death'. She says, 'There is no death, there is no ending to who you are, there is just a continuing and expanding of who you are, when you make your transition from physical to the spirit you are still all of who you were before and much more.' After listening to and reading her work I did not like to use the word 'death' when speaking about James, as I knew his presence, his spirit and his influence was all around us. I have only used the word 'death' while writing this book, as it was the common way to refer to the process of transitioning from the physical to the spirit world.

It is very difficult to accept the loss of someone's physical presence in the early days of grief. We are physical beings, and we depend on our senses, touch, sight, hearing, taste and smell to make sense of our world. We rely on seeing, touching and hearing our loved ones to reassure us that they are there for us and there to help. When these senses are no longer available to communicate with our loved ones who have passed away, we feel desolate and alone.

As I began to open up to the idea that James had not gone away, my grief began to subside. I listened to Esther Hicks' recordings about the spiritual world and afterlife and realised it was not that different from what is read at a requiem Mass. In the Catholic Church, the priest reads the following: 'Lord for your faithful people, life has changed not ended, we gain an everlasting dwelling place in heaven, in him who rose from the dead, our hope of resurrection dawned'.

In Monsignor's Homily at James's funeral, he said, 'For James, life has changed, not ended. Now that he is no longer trapped in a physical body, think of the greater number of people he will be able to help.'

This had not been explained very well to me while growing up in the Catholic faith. I needed to understand more. My life's companion was no longer beside me and I wasn't prepared to accept that that was it. That his life was over, he was no longer part of our lives, and we must get on without him. I could not take this onboard.

Having Catherine from Killybegs as a support and a mentor helped me and all the family immensely at this time. She is Ireland's answer to Esther, as she had a profound belief in the spirit world and what happened after we make our transition.

My first visit to Catherine took place a few weeks after James's funeral. She has the gift of bringing peace and calm to an anxious soul. She calls it a healing. At first, when I heard about her, I thought she physically healed people. While she may have that result for some people, her greatest power is bringing relief to those who are in distress. I felt better every time I left her.

It was during my first visit to her after James's funeral that so much of what happened between her and James made sense. She told me that on his first visit, James acknowledged he was not going to get better, that the end was nearing. His main concern was not for himself but for me and the children and how we would cope. I also think it was his idea to stop the wheatgrass. He just got Catherine to break the news to me. In hindsight, this was the right thing to do. After all, the reason I accepted it was because I thought it came from Catherine. I was still grasping at the nutritional solution, but James was out ahead of me. He knew it was not going to change the outcome and he just wanted a good meal. I am perpetually grateful for this decision, as he enjoyed great food and desserts for all the weeks that remained of his life.

I have already explained in this book how determined James was to see Catherine and how hell or high water was not going to keep him away from her. I realised after my first meeting with her that he was not only getting so much spiritual support from her, but he was also paving the way for me and his family to get spiritual support after he passed. He was lining up our aftercare. Catherine had a huge insight into our family from listening to James, and she developed a very special connection with him, which she says has supported her in some of her own life challenges. I attribute much of my healing from grief to Catherine, and I believe she was brought into our lives not just for James but even more for us to understand and cope with his physical absence.

Like Esther, Catherine has always reassured me of James's presence around me and my family. She always said he was very near and looking out for us. I most certainly believe that he has inspired all the successes my family have achieved since he made his transition. He championed everything the boys and Louise did while he was here with us, and he was extremely proud of them. I now feel his presence in all the decisions they have made since. I am confident that they agree with me on this.

It would sound unusual to the average person if they heard me say, 'I don't know what I would do without James,' but I say this to myself every day. I really don't know what I would do or who I would turn to if I didn't have James. He inspires me, he strengthens me, he guides me. I am not saying that I would not like to have him here with me, I still miss his company and his strong physical presence, but I know he has not gone away. From where he is now, he can be even more effective; he has a wider view of what is going on and he can help so many more people.

In 2018, I went on an Esther Hicks Cruise with Angela. Esther comes out on stage to talk to everyone without a prepared speech, taking her cues from the audience. People who want to ask her questions need to put their hand up and she then chooses who will join her on stage. I was eager to go up, but also nervous.

On day two, after some hesitation, Angela persuaded me to put my hand up. We were at the back of the theatre, having just returned from lunch when I put my hand up. Esther pointed towards me, but I was unsure if she was pointing at me, as there were so many in front of me with their hands up. She gradually eliminated all the hands and then pointed directly at me, asking me to come up. I was shaking with nerves and excitement. There were about five hundred people in the theatre.

I sat on stage facing Esther, who stood in front of me. With my face projected on two large screens for the audience to see, I explained to her that my husband had made his transition, and then asked, 'How do I get over missing his physical presence?'

'When you stop looking for him where he isn't,' she replied, 'and start looking for him where he is, you will feel a whole lot better.'

It had reinforced my belief that although James was no longer in physical form, his presence was in everything we were doing. I just had to talk to him, relax, and wait for him to answer. I cannot tell you how often I have received answers from him. When we pray to God we are usually asking for a specific answer, but I have learned that we must ask, and then let God decide on the best outcome. It is the same with James. I talk to him about whatever I'm concerned or thinking about, and he will find a solution.

From the experience I have had with James's illness and transition, I have now concluded that although we have free will in our lives, the date and time of our transition is predetermined. Everything we did to avert or prevent James from making his transition was all part of the journey we had to take to allow us to feel we did everything possible for him. Guilt on top of grief just compounds the problem. We had no guilt, we did everything possible, but it did not change the outcome. James knew the outcome long before I gave in.

I read a lot about grief in the weeks and months after his transition and the best description I have come across is in the following passage:

Grief is Like a Shipwreck

As for grief, you'll find it comes in waves. When the ship is first wrecked, you're drowning, with wreckage all around you. Everything floating around you reminds you of the beauty and the magnificence of the ship that was and is no more. And all you can do is float. You find some piece of the wreckage and you hang on for a while. Maybe it's some physical thing. Maybe it's a happy memory or a photograph. Maybe it's a person who is also floating. For a while, all you can do is float. Stay alive.

In the beginning, the waves are 100 feet tall and crash over you without mercy. They come 10 seconds apart and don't even give you time to catch your breath. All you can do is hang on and float. After a while, maybe weeks, maybe months, you'll find the waves are still 100 feet tall, but they come further apart. When they come, they still crash all over you and wipe you out. But in between, you can breathe, you can function. You never know what's going to trigger the grief. It might be a song, a picture, a street intersection, the smell of a cup of coffee. It can be just about anything…and the wave comes crashing. But in between waves, there is life.

Somewhere down the line, and it's different for everybody, you find that the waves are only 80 feet tall. Or 50 feet tall. And while they still come, they come further apart. You can see them coming. An anniversary, a birthday, or Christmas, or landing at O'Hare. You can see it coming, for the most part, and prepare yourself. And when it washes over you, you know that somehow you will, again, come out the other side. Soaking wet, sputtering, still hanging on to some tiny piece of the wreckage, but you'll come out.

Take it from an old guy. The waves never stop coming, and somehow you don't really want them to. But you learn that you'll survive them. And other waves will come. And you'll survive them too. If you're lucky, you'll have lots of scars from lots of loves. And lots of shipwrecks.

Although I believe James is still here in spirit, it is still hard to live without his physical presence nine years later, and every so often the waves still crash over me, but I know I will survive.

*

In December 2015 I was in Canada with Martin, meeting customers and doing seminars. I woke early one morning. It was still dark, and I lay in bed thinking. James was on my mind as usual, and I started to come up with a poem which I thought would help Louise and the boys deal with James's passing. It was still very sensitive and raw for us all. The words just started to flow, so I took out my phone and started to record the words. Over breakfast I read the poem to Martin, and he said, 'Where did you get that poem?' I told him it had just come to me early in the morning.

When I returned home, I added a few finishing touches and then gave it to Jonathan, Ryan, Martin and Louise as a Christmas present. I also gave it to close family members. I had a picture of James attached to the poem which I had printed and framed. It read:

Something for you to look at now he can't be seen but not to cry over what might have been.

He's all around you everywhere helping you each day, just talk to him as you always did in the same familiar way.

He's not away, he's always near but you must relax and listen if you want to hear.

He's sending you his love in many different ways, so stop asking why and go on with your days.

Don't worry about what he's missing, because he sees and knows it all. He was always a step ahead of us anyway. He was always on the ball.

He didn't sit round and question the things he lost or people who passed away, he got up and made it happen and focused on today.

He was a great example of never giving up, he kept on going even when times were tough.

His time here on earth was well and truly lived, he did so much and helped so many and had so much to give.

He took time to think of others even when his day was full, he had time to listen and lend a hand and give a man a 'pull'.

He'd want you to think of others too on your journey ahead and do good when you can instead of turning your head.

There's more to life than me and you there's a world that needs our care, I know he would go the extra mile if he was there.

He was always in a hurry to get the job 'read up' and move on to the next place to see what needed done.

He had no regrets and rarely looked behind, he was always moving forward to see what was next and what he could find.

So it really shouldn't surprise us that he went ahead of the rest, he still has work to do in heaven and God wanted only the best.

So this is the legacy he left us 'Keep moving on, don't look back with regret'. He would not be very pleased if we didn't get on with the job, keep his huge memory alive and never forget.

We all have a part to play while we are here on earth, you're here for a reason from the moment of your birth

Sometimes we get confused and wonder why we're here, especially when we lose someone who was very dear.

But don't let James's passing give you a reason to doubt, it's clearer now than ever what it's all about.

His years were shorter than we would have liked, we thought he still had much more to do.

But he's done so much in his short years, so he's left the rest to you. We must finish what he started he has shown us the way.

And build his memory bigger every day. He's just stepped aside to let us grow; but he hasn't gone away!

He's there beside us when we need him, we just have to say. He told me 'I'll never leave you, and I won't give up.'

I now know what his meaning was. It helps me to cope.

So when you feel you miss him just smile at him and say, 'I will keep on going for your sake because we will meet again someday.'

And always remember when we're feeling sad, we are just reliving good memories and the love we had.

He is my inspiration.

*

I have tried to use my experience with life and death to help others travelling along the same path. I am aware that not everyone deals with death in the same way, but I try to give people hope, faith and understanding. When Geraldine's son, Paul (my Godson), died when he was just thirty-nine, on 13 November 2018, it was a very difficult and challenging time for everyone - especially for Geraldine and Sean. I have tried to be there to support them and even if our circumstances are different, loss and grief have a way of binding us together. I hope I can be a beacon of light for them and others who grieve.

The Letters

While James was in Australia in 1982, I received a letter from him every week and I wrote one to him every week too. I so looked forward to his correspondence, and I read and reread the letters many times. He also admitted that he lived for my letters. After all, he was young and far away from home. Many times, when I'd receive his letter, it was started one day and finished the next, as he would fall asleep writing it. He worked very long hours and lived mostly in camps set up for the workmen in the bush. Australia was undergoing development in the 1980s and there were hundreds of men, young and old, from all over the world working there to build dams and road networks.

I had always kept the letters, and many years later James said, 'Burn them aul letters', but I couldn't. They were an important part of my life story, recounting a very poignant time for me. I had kept them safe until then. I reassured him, 'No one will ever find them, I have them safe in a drawer.' However, around about 2004, I was looking for the letters one day only to discover they had disappeared. I could not understand how this happened. Where did I put them? I searched and searched but to no avail. I was hesitant about telling James I could not find them as he thought they should have been destroyed. Over the next few years, I would keep looking, hoping they would make an appearance. But they never did, and I never told James they were missing.

Life then got busy, James got sick, and the letters were momentarily forgotten. Then, one day after James had passed, I saw a box in the hot press that looked out of place. 'What was in that?' I thought.

On opening it, I was astonished to find the letters. I was puzzled. I had been in this spot many times and that box was never there. Who had put it there? I asked everyone in the house, and no one had an explanation. Then Martin said he saw the letters in the box in the roof space when he was putting away the Christmas decorations in January 2014, when I had been in Belfast City Hospital with James, and the boys and Louise had taken down the Christmas decorations. I have NEVER been in our roof space. It's not a place I like because memories of the roof space in Derrynoid when I was young, with the occasional mouse, had put me off ever attempting to enter the roof space. So how did the letters get there and how did they get into the hot press?

The only explanation I can surmise is that James hid the letters in the roof space at some time in the past in case someone would read them, and never told me. But he knew they were sentimental and important to me, and he wanted me to have them after he was gone. So, he went to the roof space and retrieved them. But I still don't know how or when he was able to get into the roof space that year when his back was so sore, and he was so ill. It is not easy to access. I also reached the conclusion that he knew the end was in sight for him the day he took them down. It makes me a little melancholic when I think about that, wondering whether he read them and if so, how did he feel? I will never know the answer to these questions, but he knew I would feel better having the letters close to me.

After I found them, I read them night after night with mixed emotions, but I am grateful now to have these precious memories.

New Life and a Growing Family

Every year brings highs and lows and 2016 was no different. However, the biggest high since James's passing was the birth of our first grandchild and the announcement that another grandchild was on the way. As James always said, 'A baby is God's way of saying the world must go on.'

So, I rejoiced in our grandson's arrival. James Patrick Tierney (Junior) was born on 5 May 2016.

There was never any doubt what the first grandson would be called. I believe Ryan and Olivia had always planned on calling him James, but now it was more poignant. It seemed very natural to be talking about James. He brought new life and a reason to keep going and build a future for him. I was also delighted when Martin and Elizabeth revealed that they, too, were becoming parents. Their baby was due on 6 February 2017, James's birthday.

2016, however, was also a difficult year for the extended family. Paddy's condition was deteriorating and from the very recent experience I had with treatments and cancer I knew the outcome was not going to be positive. We supported him and the family as much as we could. Paddy had spent his last few months in hospital as he required constant oxygen. We took turns to sit up with him to give the family well-earned rest, something I was proud I had the courage to do, coming so close after my experience with James.

John Eugene Tierney arrived a few days after his due date, on 8 February 2017. Again, it was an occasion to celebrate. John is called after his two great grandads, James's father, and Elizabeth's grandfather Eugene, who had passed away in January 2016. It was Elizabeth's first close family member to pass, and it was a fitting tribute to her grandfather. Martin and Elizabeth had been living in the USA since their marriage but had always planned to start their family here in Ireland, so they moved back to Limavady in August 2016 to prepare for the birth. They lived in one of our rental houses in Plantation View Limavady until a more spacious home came on the market at Crossnadonnell, Limavady, which they purchased. Just this year they have moved again into their lifetime home on the Carnamuff Road.

I was very happy to become a grandparent, but I couldn't help thinking how much James would have loved it – something he had said himself when he was diagnosed. Although the experience was tinged with a little bit of sadness, I chose not to dwell on this.

"Peace is the result of retraining your mind to process life as it is, rather than what you think it should be." Wayne Dyer.

I would have liked the children to get to know James, but I also knew he was still with us in spirit, and it was up to me and everyone else to keep his memory alive. The grandchildren talk about him all the time and from a very early age each one of them could point to his picture and say 'Granda James'.

He is never forgotten.

*

Our grandchildren all have very different personalities, but they are a light of hope and joy in my life.

James is a wise, practical, and creative wee boy. John is sensitive, intelligent, and caring. They are so much fun and love spending time with each other. I was determined that the grandchildren would get to know me and be part of my life. Mammy had set a very good example of how to be a granny. She was light-hearted with them, approachable, not too strict, but when needed she could put her foot down (one of her famous expressions). If I can emulate her then I have succeeded as a granny.

The following year, in 2018, I was blessed with the addition of two little granddaughters. Martin and Elizabeth's first daughter Martina Rose was born on 4 April 2018 and Maria Grace, Ryan and Olivia's daughter, was born on 10 May 2018. They were born just a few weeks apart, so they were christened on the same day. I was honoured to have a girl called Martina, who is known as Rose. Rose is a quiet, sensitive wee girl, who likes lots of hugs from Mammy and Daddy. Maria, on the other hand, is full of mischief and fun. My mother would say she was 'full of devilment'. They are both good friends but like all children, they do have their moments, such as 'She's not my friend' being a regular grumble when they are playing. Still, for the most part they interact very well together.

Our family was expanding rapidly and there was never a dull moment when Martin and Elizabeth's second little lady, Anna Elizabeth, came along on 22 November 2019. Fittingly named Anna (sometimes we call her Annie), with her golden curly hair she could get a part in a movie of the same name. She's an independent little lady with a strong will, and holding her own has never been a problem. She is confident and loving. She will often compliment me on my nails, my clothes or my lipstick. She misses nothing.

On 18 June 2021, the precious and much longed for second son of Ryan and Olivia, Oliver Anthony Tierney, joined the family. At this moment he is just about one year and nine months old, but he is already developing his own wee character. He has a cheeky grin, bright button eyes, a happy nature, and is a joy to have around. I love his energy and determination.

Olivia was pregnant with Oliver during the Covid-19 lockdown, during which Jonathan and Ann announced their wedding, which was to take place in Cincinnati, Ohio. Ann and Jonathan had met two years before their wedding, and I was pleased Jonathan eventually met someone he wanted to settle down with. Ann had been over a few times to meet everyone and also spent Christmas with us in 2019.

The original date for the wedding was December 2020 but due to travel restrictions, the wedding date was changed.

The new date was 9 April 2021. Travel to the USA was still restricted and we could not travel there direct without a two-week quarantine. Since we did not want to spend two weeks in a quarantine hotel, the plan was to travel to Canada, stay there for two weeks, and then fly to Ohio. Everything was very uncertain, and the regulations were changing regularly. However, it was decided that Ryan, Sean, Louise and I would go to Toronto and submit to the quarantine. Elizabeth and Martin were exempt from quarantine as Elizabeth was an American citizen.

While we were travelling as essential workers, linked to the mask production we had undertaken during Covid-19, Olivia could not go as it was not possible to take the two children, and she could not leave James and Maria behind for almost three weeks. Everyone was annoyed about this, but we had no choice. Ryan was certainly not happy.

We all arrived in Jonathan's house in Canada for a lengthy two weeks, waiting to cross the border to America. We were still unhappy that Olivia was home alone and missing the wedding, and Louise decided she would figure out a way to get her over. I'm not sure what she did, but she worked on it for hours and ultimately applied for a special circumstance, citing Olivia's profession as essential. Lo and behold, Olivia got permission to travel direct to the USA. We were all ecstatic, but especially Ryan. It wasn't all plain sailing getting through customs, and I believe it was very tense, but suffice to say she arrived, seven months pregnant and looking amazing, two nights before the wedding. She was there for the rehearsal dinner and the wedding and returned with Ryan the next day.

It really made everyone's day having her there and she was delighted. We did, however, miss James and Maria.

I had arrived in Ohio a few days before everyone else to meet Ann's family and have a look around the venue for the wedding. I had a memorable few days with them both and Ann arranged for Jonathan and me to have a beautiful meal on our own in a very upmarket restaurant. It was the same evening that Olivia was to arrive, and it was the perfect end to an unforgettable day.

On 9 April 2021, Ann Ostendorf became the newest member of the Tierney family. Their wedding day was beautiful. The sun shone all day. The church was magnificent. Dorothy Papadakos provided us with memorable music. It was clear that Jonathan was very happy, and he smiled all day. He was also very relieved that all his close family did eventually make it to Ohio to be part of this special day. Of course, James was never very far from our minds on another significant day for the family. He was spoken about during the speeches, which caused a lump in our throats, but the pain of loss had subsided with the passage of years, and we could talk about him without breaking down in tears.

Jonathan had planned on staying in America for a few years to get the business established, but the changes in work patterns during the Covid-19 pandemic allowed him to bring the date forward. He had been working virtually from his house in Canada for almost two years prior to getting married, which gave him the flexibility to continue his work remotely from Ireland instead. So, in August 2021, Ann and Jonathan came to live on Tartnakilly Road, Glack. And just before Christmas 2021, they announced that a baby was on the way. They were truly excited about the impending birth and on 26 July 2022, Sarah Ann Tierney arrived, our seventh grandchild. Sarah is now almost eight months old, and she is a treasure. She is so pleasant; we never hear her cry, and she has the most beautiful smile. She has two doting parents, too. I am excited to watch her grow and develop, and every time I see her, she has reached another milestone.

This section on my growing family would not be complete without including Sean Mullan.

Sean was in Martin's year at school but has been a friend to all three boys, and when they get together now, they recount some of the predicaments and scuffles they got into throughout their teenage years. Seemingly some of the antics and practical jokes were not for my ears at the time. I was oblivious to their pranks and frolics, but it was all a bit of fun and, as far as I know, no one has had any lasting damage from their experience! Sean has been connected with our family over the years, through good times and bad, for as long as I remember. I have already spoken about his presence with us on the night before James was admitted to hospital. He has been someone we could always rely on if we needed help.

He started his Seating Matters career in the factory and then moved into sales, accompanying Jonathan and Martin on their maiden voyage to the UK. He has since established his business in London and is a trustworthy advocate for the company. So, Sean has been associated with the Tierney family for all of Louise's life. Though, there was very little communication between them when she was growing up, as he was just one of the boys' friends.

Louise turned sixteen in February 2015, a few months after James passed, so she started going out with friends at the weekend. I knew this was part of growing up and she was just having fun, but I worried about her during that time. The boys had all left home and James was not there to pacify me when it got late and she wasn't home. Thankfully, this phase passed, and I got more relaxed about her going out at the weekends. She was a level-headed girl who knew the boundaries.

I can't remember exactly when the relationship between Sean and Louise changed, but they started to become friends. Ryan was married, Martin and Jonathan were away, and when Sean called at the house, Louise was always pleased to see him. When she was going out for the night, he would sometimes offer to take her home instead of her getting a taxi. I was always relieved when, as she left for a night out, she would say, 'Sean says he will take me home.'

I knew she would be home safe.

Sean's father, Gerry, became ill in 2017 and Louise had a lot of understanding for him and his family as she had been on this journey herself a few years earlier. During 2017, Louise and Sean became good friends and sometimes went to the cinema together. I was beginning to suspect that the relationship was reaching a new level, but every time I brought the subject up, she protested that, 'We are just friends!'

During the time of Gerry's death on 8 November 2017, Louise was on hand to help organise the wake. Jonathan, Ryan and Martin were in Japan, and she was there for Sean. She was a great support for him as he knew he could rely on her.

Over the next few months nothing seemingly changed, they were still friends and enjoyed each other's company.

Early in 2018, Jonathan needed help in the USA. He was working on a contract with a large hospital in California but needed someone with expertise to demonstrate the chairs and sell the benefits of them to the staff. Sean agreed to go for three months. During this time, Louise was at college in Derry and still not sure what she wanted to do. By March 2018, she had planned on opening a bridal shop, but before she went full-time into the business, she wanted to travel for a few weeks. She went out to Jonathan in Canada and helped him in the office, but from there she would fly to a different city at the weekends. On one of the weekends, 27 May 2018, she met up with Sean in Nashville. Did they have it planned? I don't know. But after that weekend the relationship was sealed. They were finally a couple.

I picked her up her from the airport on her return. Sean was still in California, and I vowed to myself I would not ask about her visit with him, as previously she became indignant when I made suggestions about their relationship. We chatted about this and that and we filled each other in on what had taken place during her travels. After about an hour, I said, 'And how is Sean?' Then she told me.

I had suspected that something was brewing for a few months. It was not a surprise to me, and I am very happy for them both.

Louise

Louise deserves a chapter to herself because she loves her independence. As a baby, she was the apple of everyone's eye but especially her Daddy's. Her brothers were also very protective of her and would help her in any way they could. They were very attentive to her, especially during and after the period when James was sick.

Even as a very young child she was very mature and independent. When Mammy lived with us during her illness, she became very frail. One day Mammy was trying to pick a pancake up from the plate and her fingers couldn't grip it, Louise noticed and gently slid the pancake out to the edge of the plate so her granny could get a hold of it. It was remarkable that she noticed the struggle Mammy was having and was mature and compassionate to help her in a discreet way. She was six years old.

It was Mammy who relayed this story to me, and she said, 'That's an amazing wein, how she knew to do that.'

Louise never liked being told what to do. When she was about two or three her famous lines were, 'Don't you bossy me' or 'You're not the boss of me'. Either could be directed at her brothers or me, but not often to her Daddy as far as I recall.

When Christmas was approaching in 2005, the adverts had started on the television and Louise had her list ready for Santa. One of her sought-after toys that year was Annabelle, an interactive doll who could talk and tell the child when it needed to be fed and when it needed its nappy changed. Louise watched as the child on the TV played contentedly with the doll. Each time Louise was asked, 'What is Santa bringing?' Annabelle was the highlight.

Christmas morning arrived and Louise was delighted to see Santa had fulfilled the request. She unpacked Annabelle excitedly and started to investigate how it worked. We put the batteries in, and she was ready to go. But a short time later Annabelle was abandoned. I was busy getting the dinner organised when I noticed Louise had moved away from the doll and was engrossed in the other toys.

'Where is Annabelle?' I asked her.

'She is lying down there,' she replied, pointing to the corner of the dining room.

'Why are you not playing with her?' I asked, having thought she would be obsessed with this doll all day.

'I don't like her; she tells me what to do ALL the time.'

It made me laugh. It was so typical of her. She would not even allow the doll to 'bossy' her. It goes without saying that the abandoned Annabelle had to find a new home.

When Louise was young, she sat and played with her toys for hours by herself, talking to the dolls and lining them up. Needless to say, she was the one making the rules and giving the orders. One day, Cathal McCann observed her and said, 'Does she not get lonely on her own?'

'She's never alone, she's surrounded by her make-believe friends,' I replied.

Her independence is a trait she still carries with her today and it has been her strength.

Louise, being the youngest and the only girl, could have chosen an easy passage through life. For example, there were opportunities for her to work in the family business. She did work there temporarily during her holidays and at a time when she was not sure what direction she wanted her career to take. During this time, she proved she was capable of any position she worked in; she worked in customer services, accounts, order processing, and she attended exhibitions and helped set up booths. There was nothing she could not do. She could easily have taken a full-time job in the family business and earned a decent salary. She could even have carved out her own position. But, just as she could not abide being told what to do as a child, it followed that as an adult she was going to do things her way.

When she was fifteen, she said she wanted to get a job in the local hotel. She wanted her own money. This was a family run hotel, so they allowed fifteen-year-olds to work there. I took her down to the hotel and asked if she wanted me to go in with her.

'No,' she replied.

I waited outside in the car and when she came out, she had successfully secured her first job.

Many times, I have been approached by parents of adult children asking me if I could give them a job. My first thought is, 'Why can they not ask for a job themselves?' If they haven't got enough interest to go looking for their own job, then I would hesitate about employing them.

Louise was not letting me speak for her. She was capable and confident.

Louise got amazing results in her GCSE's, which she did in the months following her Daddy's passing. It was not easy. No pressure was put on her from me, but I know the pressure came from herself. She was determined to do well. After she received her results, she decided she did not want to do A-Levels but instead applied for a business course at the Northwest Regional College in Derry. She liked this course as it gave her more freedom and independence than the A-Level course allowed. Again, she did very well and could have gone to Queens University in Belfast to do a degree in Business. She still had time to consider her options before deciding.

In March 2018 I was on a cruise with Angela and was lining up ready to disembark when I got a phone call from a very excited Louise. While I was on holiday, Ryan and Louise had brainstormed what business she could start. It should not be a surprise to anyone that she wanted her own business, it was in her DNA; she was another one who would not be a good employee – just like her father and mother.

They had come up with the idea of a bridal shop and Victoria Ivy was the name. Louise did almost everything herself to set up the business, and, when requested, any of the boys would lend a hand. They fully supported her in any way they could. At first, I accompanied her to bridal shows, but it was evident from the start that she had a flair for the bridal business, and she soon became an expert at choosing the dresses on trend, knowing what her customers would buy. The following year, Jonathan saw a bridal shop for sale in Ballymena. It was a shop with designer labels and was a going concern. It was an opportunity too good to miss and again she was encouraged and supported to buy the business. I admired her drive, her ambition and her capacity to take a risk. She was twenty years old, running two shops, and learning on the go.

Running your own business is never easy. The 'buck always stops here' and there are times you wonder why you put yourself through all the trauma. But if you are cut out for being your own boss and making your own decisions, then that is part for the course. The benefits will always outweigh the downsides. Louise has employees now and is quietly running her business in the way that suits her.

Louise and Sean have now been a couple since 2018. It does not surprise me that she has settled with someone a few years older than her because she was always wiser than her years. It took Jonathan, Ryan and Martin some time to get their head round their wee sister being with one of their friends, but they know it is a good partnership and they are happy for them both.

At last, I no longer have to worry about Louise, and Sean is now officially part of our family.

I have contemplated the reason we had such a large gap between Martin and Louise. I believe it was all predetermined so I would have Louise at home for a few years to allow me to adjust to being on my own. When James passed, Jonathan was working in England, Ryan was about to get married, and Martin was in Canada planning to get married. If Louise was born just after Martin, she may have already flown the nest, too. I was very grateful to have her company for the ensuing months. It gave me a reason to get up and go on and encouraged me to be brave for her sake. The sad side of this is that Louise suffered the loss of her Daddy at fifteen. She was and is so special to him. He admired her independence, her strong will, and her individuality. He was so proud of her.

After she was born, I thought I should have one more child to keep Louise company, but James never came round to the idea. He was complete when Louise was born. She was everything he ever wanted in a daughter. She may not see him now in the physical form, but he is guiding and protecting her every step of her journey.

The biggest change in my life since James made his transition was not my sixtieth birthday in 2022 but adjusting to living alone when Louise left home.

Flying the Nest

Louise did not have the experience other girls her age had of going to university, moving away from home, and living independently. It was no surprise then that she wanted to buy a house and live independently before settling down and having a family. At the beginning of 2022, she started looking for a suitable house and had quite quickly set her sights on a new development in Limavady. The whole process seemed to happen smoothly and efficiently and soon she had signed for a brand-new house.

She moved in gradually. There was no moving out or moving in ceremony. Her bedroom at home has been left untouched and is ready for her when she wants to come back and stay over for a night, and she also has a bedroom in her house for me.

I know this transition was not easy for her. It is not easy being the only daughter, and she probably feels a sense of responsibility towards me. But it was something she wanted to do, and I admired and supported her decision.

I have been lucky to have her for so long and the eight years since James's passing has allowed me the time to adapt to becoming more independent and figuring out what I want to do for myself. I am happy for Louise; she needs to find her own way. Living here at home with the Seating Matters business so close was also difficult for her to get time or privacy alone because my house is always busy.

Since she has moved out, we now spend more quality, well-planned time together. Our relationship has matured, and I am enjoying having her as a friend as well as a daughter. I know she will always be there for me, but I like my freedom too, so I will try to never become too dependent on her. Louise has been there for me at every turn, such as when I recently broke my wrist, and during the times I have had a few minor health challenges over the years.

I am adjusting to having the house to myself, and I have rearranged it to suit me. Like Louise, I am now enjoying my newfound independence. Another new chapter in my life has started, and I am looking forward with eagerness and excitement to what lies ahead.

A Blanket of Love

It took six years before I could change anything in our bedroom because it was my safe place, surrounded by James with all his clothes, shoes and belongings exactly where he left them. I would open the wardrobe door and look at his clothes all hanging clean, neat and untouched. For the first few months, I would rummage through his pockets to see if there was a wee note or secret message left for me, but everything he left me was all around me. He had left no secrets. I could not clear the wardrobe as it felt like I was throwing him out of his own house – and then he would be gone forever. I felt he deserved the space he had worked so hard for, and seeing his clothes brought me comfort, even if it was tinged with sadness. Every shirt and jacket told a story: his work clothes sparked with concrete that stubbornly wouldn't wash out; his favourite warm work shirt with the frayed collar; his beautiful, chequered shirts that reminded me of when we were young; the dress suit that reminded me of the cruises and holidays; even his wedding shirt. Then there were the clothes he wore to hospital every week. He always dressed well going there, and in an effort to distract him and me from why we were there, the nurses always remarked on his shoes or jacket.

I did not want to give his clothes to a charity shop and there was no-one who I cared enough about who fitted into the clothes. Eugene got a pair of shoes and jeans, and Brendan got a coat, but James's shirts and trousers were too big for most men I knew.

Then, unexpectedly, one day when I was looking into the wardrobe, I had an idea. I could make a memory blanket. There were certainly enough clothes. But sewing had not been one of my strengths, in fact James would often tease me, saying, 'You could do anything, but sewing on a button is not one of them!'

It's amazing what you can do when you really want to – 'When the dream is big enough the facts don't count.'

I looked up sewing classes and attended a few led by a former Amway colleague Patsy Gribben. I borrowed a sewing machine from Brendan's Geraldine and then cautiously tried to sew. Then lockdown 2020 arrived. There were no shops open, no travel, no visitors, and no grandchildren to look after. So, I ordered a sewing machine and taught myself to sew. I spent hours, night after night and day after day, cutting the clothes into small squares and matching them up and making different patterns with them. As I cut, I cried, and I remembered. I thought of Dolly Parton's song about the coat of many colours, 'Sewing every piece with love', but instead of a coat, I made a patchwork blanket that I was so proud of. Each piece holds a memory and tells a story, and when I need it, I just wrap myself in the blanket of love.

Going Solo

My experience with illness, death and grief over the past ten years has bolstered my determination to make the most of my life and to appreciate it as a gift. So, after coming to terms with the major change in my life – going from being part of a couple for the previous thirty-five years to being a single person – I decided I was going to embrace this new life and see what I was capable of doing all by myself.

Life is for living, after all. And I have a renewed passion for living life to the fullest.

My first attempt at this was going for a long weekend to Portugal by myself, staying at a hotel. It was pleasant but didn't really put me out of my comfort zone.

Then, I had always heard about the Camino de Santiago, also known as The Way of St. James; a renowned pilgrimage of medieval origin that sees pilgrims journey to the Cathedral of Santiago de Compostela in Galicia in the northwest of Spain. It appealed to me, but it was not something that would ever have appealed to James, so this was not something we would ever have done together.

I pondered it for a while, unsure if I was strong enough physically or mentally to go alone, walking 150 km in five days on unknown terrain with people I had never met. I had heard about blisters, sore feet, aching limbs and an array of mishaps that could befall me.

In quiet preparation, I joined the Sperrin Hillwalkers Club in September 2021. We met every two weeks, and the walks were graded 1-3 depending on the length of walk, the steepness of the climb and the terrain. I started off slowly but very soon got hooked on hill climbing. Each time we had a new, steeper walk, I questioned if I was fit for it. I always was and preferred the steeper hills in the end.

During the first year, I climbed many of the mountains on my bucket list. Binevenagh, Benbradagh, Mount Errigal and Muckish. My favourites were Slemish and Croagh Patrick, amongst many more. I love putting on my boots, getting my backpack ready and setting off on my own on Sunday mornings. It has become a priority for me, and I did more hikes than most people in the group during that first year I joined the club.

Having trained, I decided I would give the Camino a go and planned to do it around my sixtieth birthday. It was something to aim for and a meaningful way to mark this milestone in my life that is denied to so many.

I booked it in January 2022 for the beginning of May 2022. I was on a hill walking weekend with the Sperrin Group in April 2022 when the full details of the Camino walk were emailed to me. My fears and doubts returned. The walks were six to seven hours long and the longest was 35 kilometres. Could I do this? Was I taking on too much? What if I failed?

I talked it over with Louise – she is the one to hear about all my insecurities – and she reassured me I was well fit for it. 'Hadn't I been in training for six months?'

My confidence grew and so did my excitement. I was looking forward to walking in the open countryside, along the rivers and vineyards and through the rolling hills without anyone to worry about.

It was one of the best holidays I ever had. Apart from the beautiful scenery, the sunny weather, the peaceful countryside, and the happy people I met, it was the sense of achievement that made it so distinct from any other holiday.

I now knew I could do things on my own and enjoy them. It was a refreshing and spiritual experience and as I walked, I thought about James, my family, Paul, Paddy, and Mammy and Daddy, but my thoughts were not sad; I was very grateful to have been given this opportunity. I appreciated how my body supported me along the way, with no blisters or sore feet and not even a headache for a full week. I was blessed.

Glen

It was 2006, the year after Mammy died, that James and I thought about buying a holiday home. It would be an investment for the future and somewhere relaxing where we could spend quality time together when we got older.

We found a new development in Glen, Carrigart, Co Donegal and James put a deposit on the house, which was only at the early stage of construction. It only had the footings and subfloor in.

On the day after Sean Kelly's wedding (Lizzie's son), which was in Stranorlar, Co Donegal, we took Sean and Geraldine to see our latest purchase. There wasn't much to see but it was the location and the area we wanted to share with them. Geraldine fell for it right away; she had also longed for a getaway from Sean's busy garage at home and the constant visitors and customers who arrived at all times of the day and night. When we were viewing our site, she walked to the site beside ours, which was at the same stage of construction. Then she exclaimed, 'Sean, you can see the beach from our house as well!'

She had set her sights on buying the house next door. After a bit of discussion, Sean agreed, and we had holiday homes side by side.

Sean and Geraldine used their house more frequently in the beginning and for longer periods than us. When I would say this to Geraldine she said, 'Oh, we are older, when you and James get older you will use it more.'

We did use it from time to time but never for more than two or three consecutive days. We thought we still had plenty of time in the future to enjoy it and James was still working at full speed. In fact, Louise and I probably used it more than James and I. However, I still had great memories of the times we did spend there. James really loved the quiet setting and the small house with the open fire, and he really did relax and unwind when we took the time to go there.

After James passed, I lost interest in the house. It was meant to be our retirement house and the thought of going there alone only made me sad. So, when we were sorting out all our financial business after James, I said I no longer wanted the house and we let it go.

It was in 2021 when Sean McKeever contacted Jonathan and told him the house was back on the market, asking whether we would consider buying it back again. Sean and Geraldine had looked nostalgically at the house over the past seven years and were sad that it no longer belonged to us. Jonathan approached me tentatively one day and told me the house was up for sale by auction and would I like to have it back. With the passage of time, the memories of the house no longer made me sad, and instead I looked back with fondness on those days. I agreed it would be lovely to have it back. I was sure it was something James would have liked, too.

I was boarding a flight to London to go to Jonathan's wedding when he rang to say the auction had started and he was the highest bidder so far for the house. When I touched down in London, I got a message from Jonathan announcing I was now the owner of the house for the second time.

During the summer of 2021, I spent much of my time getting it redecorated; a new kitchen went in, and Louise and I enjoyed shopping for furniture. I now love going to Glen all by myself. I feel James's presence there, and I feel very at peace, relaxed and never sad. I was meant to have it back. It is my place of refuge, and, like the Camino, it is a place to be alone but not feel lonely.

The Next Chapter

'Life is short and unpredictable. Eat the dessert first!'

Helen Keller

I have a very optimistic outlook on my life. I am full of anticipation for what is next. I want to see more of the world, enjoy new experiences and learn new skills.

At the minute, however, I am still very busy.

Seating Matters is going through a period of growth, and I am heavily involved in delivering the clinical training across the UK and Ireland. A third work trip to Australia is taking place in the next few weeks. However, with more clinical staff on board, I plan on reducing my input at the end of 2023.

I look after the property for Yenreit Investments, too, which entails looking after the tenants, maintenance of the property and ensuring all rent is paid on time. Some days this can be very busy. I am also currently the treasurer of St Finlough's Hall, and I am taking responsibility for getting it refurbished and modernised for the local community. I have organised many fundraising events in the past, but still need to raise about £30,000 to complete the work.

I am president of St Dismis, a group aligned to Saint Vincent de Paul who visit Magilligan prison every week to support prisoners. I lead the team, do the rotas and liaise with the prison staff.

Each week I try to keep Tuesday free to look after James, John, Rose, Maria, Anna, and Oliver. I do the school drop off and pick up. Sometimes work clashes with Tuesday, but where possible I try to keep it free. I also try to have one day for Sarah. And I love having the children for a sleepover at least once or twice a year. At the sleepover, they eat what they want, they do what they want, and they go to bed when they want. There are no rules at the sleepover as long as everyone is safe and happy.

Then, at weekends, I enjoy my hillwalking. I feel invigorated when I am out walking the hills, so I try to go as often as possible. I also like to get to Glen for a few weekends. It has been a perfect place to write this book. It is quiet and peaceful and when my eyes get tired, I head to the beach for a walk or sit quietly and people watch in The Downings as I eat my lunch. I need to do this more often.

I have now passed my sixtieth birthday, and another is approaching soon. I don't feel old. I don't feel like I should slow down. I still have lots of energy, but because of my experience with life and death I do want to have more time to do things for myself. I still feel that life is very fragile, and I have a sense of urgency about getting things done. I have no guarantee for how long I will live, no one has, but this does not scare me it just motivates me to get up and go.

I have no fear of death, but I do have a love for life. I am so proud and happy that I can say this now. When I contemplated life without James it seemed unbearable, but it is not. I have succeeded in making my life meaningful for myself and hopefully I have touched and improved other people's lives along the way, too.

I want my children and grandchildren to live their life to the full and not put things off until they 'have more time' or they 'have more money' or until they 'reach this particular goal'.

If you want to do something or go somewhere, just do it, NOW.

Lastly

I will leave the final message in this book to the Serenity Prayer…

God, grant me the serenity to accept the things I cannot change,

The courage to change the things I can change

And the wisdom to know the difference.